PARACHUTES, PATRIOTS AND PARTISANS

HEATHER WILLIAMS

Parachutes, Patriots and Partisans

The Special Operations Executive and Yugoslavia, 1941–1945

HURST & COMPANY, LONDON

First published in the United Kingdom by
C. Hurst & Co. (Publishers) Ltd,
38 King Street, London WC2E 8JZ
© Heather Williams, 2003
All rights reserved.
Printed in India

The right of Heather Williams to be identified as the author of this work
has been asserted by her in accordance with the Copyright, Designs
and Patents Act, 1988.

A Cataloguing-in-Publication Data record for this book is available
from the British Library.

ISBNs
1–85065–592–8 *casebound*

CONTENTS

v

MAPS

following page xiii

Yugoslavia within pre-1941 borders
Partition of Yugoslavia, 1941
Federal Yugoslavia, 1945–1991

ILLUSTRATIONS

between pages 60 and 61

King Peter taking the oath after the coup on 27 March 1941
Scenes of celebration in Belgrade after the coup
Citizens murdered by the Germans, April 1941
Italians interrogating a Yugoslav prisoner
General Draža Mihailović
Recruits being addressed by the General
Swearing an oath to King Peter and Mihailović in Serbia
Group of cavalry officers in Serbia
Members of the British mission being entertained in a village
Colonel A. B. Seitz of the OSS
Colonel Babić with some of his staff and Captain Earle of the
British mission
'Wanted' notice offering a reward for the capture of Josip Broz Tito
and Mihailović
Tito addressing a crowd in Belgrade
People in a Belgrade street on the same occasion.

vi

PREFACE

During the 1920s and 1930s most Britons regarded Yugoslavia as 'one of those faraway countries' of little or no importance to British interests. As war drew closer the British Foreign Office paid more attention to Yugoslav affairs, but largely in relation to neighbouring countries, especially Greece and Turkey. Throughout the war British interest waxed and waned, usually stimulated by military and political needs outside Yugoslavia and increasingly those related to the USSR. The story of the Second World War in Yugoslavia is a complex and tragic one: during that period the country was not only fragmented and occupied, but suffered a bitter civil war in which more Yugoslavs lost their lives to fellow Yugoslavs than to the Axis forces they opposed. It has also come to be very much a disputed history where British involvement with the wartime resistance movements is concerned.

Since the Special Operations Executive (SOE) was largely responsible for liaison between Yugoslav resistance and British policy makers, it is not surprising that the history of SOE and Yugoslavia has caused much debate and sometimes much upset over the years. An examination of SOE's role in wartime Yugoslavia provides an illustration of the varying degrees of interest, the lack of background knowledge prevailing in circles such as the British Foreign Office, and the influence of external pressures that counted for more than the country itself. It also brings into focus the rivalries, antagonisms and confusion which prevailed within and between various British bodies concerned with the running of the war. SOE's relationship with its American counterpart, the Office of Strategic Services (OSS), also provides some interesting insights into British attitudes to the transatlantic ally.

After the Axis invasion and occupation of Yugoslavia two main resistance movements emerged, and because they had very different agendas it was not long before they found themselves in conflict.

The British initially supported the resistance movement based on the remnants of the Yugoslav armed forces headed by Colonel— later General—Draža Mihailović. He was perceived to be the legit- imate representative of the Yugoslav government, Britain's ally during the war, and to be a bastion against 'communist chaos'. Later, the British changed horses and threw all their support behind Josip Broz—Tito—and the very communists they believed to be the authors of that chaos. At the time the change gave rise to a huge amount of controversy within SOE—what one of the protagonists described as the 'battle between the Children of Light and the Children of Darkness'. By the end of the war, when the commu- nists had control of the country, some of those who had helped to ensure this outcome, particularly Winston Churchill, decided that it was not quite what they had intended. British-Yugoslav relations rapidly cooled as Tito and the Yugoslav Communist Party estab- lished their one-party state, using their wartime victory to legiti- mize their seizure and retention of power. The Tito-Stalin split in 1948 came as a welcome surprise to the Western powers and appeared to vindicate the decision to support the Partisans. Tito and the Yugoslav communists extended their legitimacy by win- ning approval and financial support from the West for their own peculiar form of communism, established as part of the demonstra- tion of both their independence from and superiority to Stalin's Soviet communism. Those who had wholeheartedly upheld the decision to back the Yugoslav Partisans during the war could now point to this 'independent' communist state as a success-story and be proud of their own role in the affair. It was mainly the latter who began writing their memoirs: most famous of these must be Fitzroy Maclean's *Eastern Approaches*, perhaps followed by William Deakin's more measured *Embattled Mountain*.

A version of the history of wartime Yugoslav–British relations developed which extolled the virtues of the communist resistance and portrayed it as so superior militarily that it was the only possible choice for the Western Allies to back, regardless of its political colouring. It read backwards from the events which started in 1948, and created the myth that Tito had always *meant* to be independent of the Soviet Union and that the wartime assessment that he was more inclined to be a patriot than a Soviet-style communist was justified. Adding to the case was the underlying—if not openly expressed—implication that Mihailović and all his forces were tainted by collaboration with the Axis occupiers, thus justifying the transfer of Britain's support. This was generally accepted as the British story of SOE and Yugoslavia and became incorporated into mainstream historical studies; one contributory reason for this was the fact that records of SOE's activities in wartime Yugoslavia were not open to non-official historians until 1997. This interpretation largely continued to be dominant until the 1980s when, following the demise of Tito, the cracks in the Yugoslav path to socialism began to appear, exacerbated by the hiatus created by Tito's lack of forward planning for the state after his passing.

More critical assessments of Yugoslav communism and the British friendship for this hybrid began to gain an audience. One particular reappraisal that set the cat amongst the pigeons was Nora Beloff's *Tito's Flawed Legacy*, published in 1985: she was not only critical of British support for Tito's regime, but traced the roots of that support to a communist plot in SOE's Cairo office. Identifying one James Klugmann, who had served in SOE Cairo for a lengthy period and was an important figure in the British Communist Party, as a major player in that plot, Beloff claimed that Churchill had been 'hoodwinked' into switching support from Mihailović to Tito. An alternative interpretation of the war in Yugoslavia portrayed Mihailović as a tragic figure, betrayed and abandoned by his erstwhile allies. This was not a new thesis, but one that found a degree of support among some of the British liaison officers who had served with his forces, and who, on growing older and looking back over their own lives, became increasingly unhappy with what one, Mike Lees, dubbed 'the received wisdom'. They corresponded with each other and with academics interested in wartime Yugoslavia. Lees took to the Public Records Office and unearthed his own and other unweeded SOE signals, eventually producing *The Rape of Serbia* in 1990. Their interpretation was entirely different: they did not regard the forces with whom they were serving as collaborationist. They made an important distinction between collaboration and pragmatic accommodation, and admitted that the latter was a useful ploy they had used themselves on many occasions; they stated that those forces had been loyal allies, even good friends. These ex-officers felt the decision to abandon the forces with which they had served to be wrong, using words like 'dishonourable' and 'shameful'; there was a feeling that something not quite right had occurred—something in their own history which had been beyond their control and which they felt needed explanation. The battle between the Children of Light and the Children of Darkness resumed, with the debate over whether or not there had been a conspiracy in Cairo SOE—heightened by the fact that SOE's Yugoslav documents remained closed while it raged—fuelling the idea that the archives contained some 'great secret'.

In addition to the debate over whether switching from Mihailović to Tito was the result of a left-wing conspiracy, there are also questions over just *how much*—if any—influence SOE had over policy-making. I regard the central question as being whether SOE's involvement with the resistance forces made any appreciable contribution to the war against the Axis powers. By supporting first the royalist resistance and, when they proved unsatisfactory, switching to the communists, the British expected to gain military advantage from the increased level of guerrilla activity in Yugoslavia. Because this activity was designed to allay potential conflict with Britain's Soviet ally, rather than being of benefit to Yugoslavia itself, the long-term aims of the two opposing resistance movements were not fully taken into account. Rather than any significant military advantage being gained, SOE's interference in Yugoslavia merely exacerbated the civil war that was just beginning when its first mission arrived in the country. The decision to give all-out support to the communist Partisans coincided with the western Allies' ability to be more active in the region, and SOE, supplemented by large numbers of Commandos and other military personnel, became incorporated into more regular military operations, which led in turn to a dilution of what influence it had on policy making. Because my interest is mainly centred on the political aspects of the organization and my space is limited, I have given a general overview of the final year of the war in Yugoslavia. Many other books cover the British military operations with the Partisans in great detail, as the bibliography makes plain.

During its short life SOE was a controversial organization, and its role in wartime Yugoslavia can still generate heat. Sadly, many of

those old warriors who took up the cudgels once more in the
1980s, as Tito's Yugoslavia decayed and slid towards another tragedy, are no longer on the scene. I was fortunate enough to meet
many of them and am grateful for the time and hospitality those
men and women gave me so generously while I was researching
this book. Their oral testimony contributed greatly to my understanding of how it felt to be embroiled in such a conflict. I must
also thank Simon Trew and Keith Dear, who have both read the
manuscript and made constructive criticisms and helpful correc-
tions, while I owe much to Stevan Pavlowitch whose friendship
and encouragement have been invaluable and who has kindly
allowed me to use some of his collection of photographs to illus-
trate this volume. I fit into neither the Children of Light or the
Children of Darkness, but feel that history is more a twilight or
dawn—in which light we attempt to discern as much historical
truth as we can and do as much justice to the past and to the protagonists as possible.

Llanilar H. W.
November 2002

ABBREVIATIONS

AVNOJ	Anti-Fascist Council for the National Liberation of Yugoslavia: the 'parliament' established by the communist-led resistance
BAF	Balkan Air Force
BBC	British Broadcasting Corporation
BLO	British Liaison Officer
BSC	British Security Council (in USA)
C	Head of Secret Intelligence Service
CD	Executive Head of SOE
CIGS	Chief of the Imperial General Staff
C-in-C	Commander-in-Chief
COS	Chiefs of Staff
CPY	Communist Party of Yugoslavia
D	Section D of Secret Intelligence Service, forerunner of SOE
DMI	Director of Military Intelligence
DMO	Director of Military Operations
FO	Foreign Office
GHQ	General Headquarters
HSS	Croatian Peasant Party
ISLD	Inter Services Liaison Department: cover name for Secret Intelligence Service in Cairo
JIC	Joint Intelligence Committee
MEDC	Middle East Defence Committee
MEW	Ministry of Economic Warfare
MI	Military Intelligence
MOI	Ministry of Information
MO4	Special Operations Executive in Cairo
NDH	Independent State of Croatia: established April 1941, essentially a German satellite
NKVD	Soviet Intelligence Service

NLA	National Liberation Army: Yugoslav communist resistance
OSS	Office of Strategic Services: American equivalent of SOE & SIS
PM	Prime Minister
PWE	Political Warfare Executive: responsible for black propaganda
SAS	Special Air Service: an elite raiding force
SBS	Special Boat Service: another elite raiding force
SIS	Secret Intelligence Service
SOE	Special Operations Executive
SOM	Special Operations Mediterranean: established in southern Italy April 1944 to co-ordinate all special operations in the area
USAAF	United States Army Airforce
WO	War Office
W/T	Wireless Telegraphy
YGE	Yugoslav Government in Exile

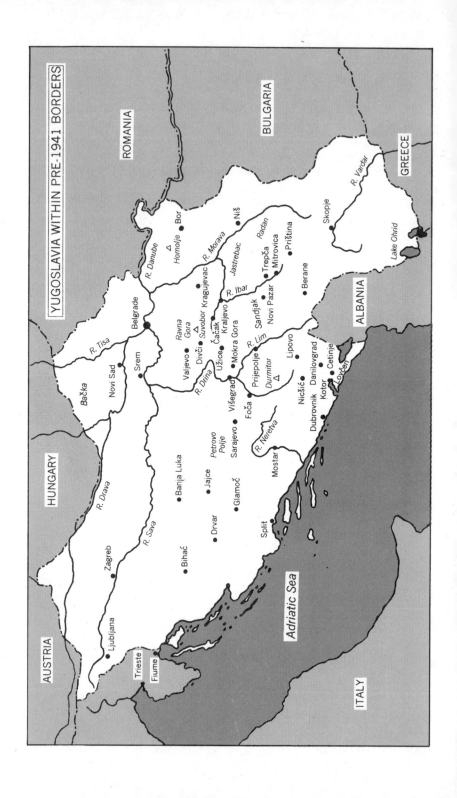

YUGOSLAVIA WITHIN PRE-1941 BORDERS

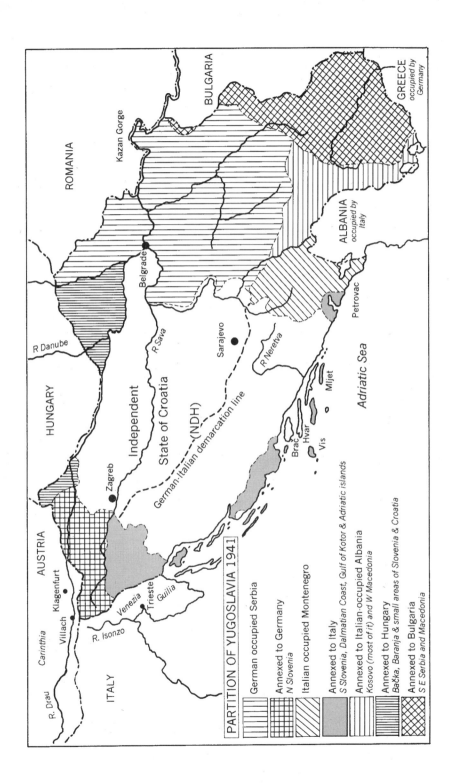

PARTITION OF YUGOSLAVIA 1941

German occupied Serbia

Annexed to Germany
N Slovenia

Italian occupied Montenegro

Annexed to Italy
S Slovenia, Dalmatian Coast, Gulf of Kotor & Adriatic islands

Annexed to Italian-occupied Albania
Kosovo (most of it) and W Macedonia

Annexed to Hungary
Bačka, Baranja & small areas of Slovenia & Croatia

Annexed to Bulgaria
S E Serbia and Macedonia

Independent State of Croatia (NDH)

German-Italian demarcation line

AUSTRIA

HUNGARY

ROMANIA

BULGARIA

GREECE
occupied by Germany

ALBANIA
occupied by Italy

ITALY

Adriatic Sea

Carinthia

R. Drau

R. Isonzo

Klagenfurt

Villach

Venezia

Trieste

Giulia

Zagreb

Belgrade

Sarajevo

Kazan Gorge

Petrovac

R Danube

R. Sava

R. Neretva

Mljet

Vis

Hvar

Brac

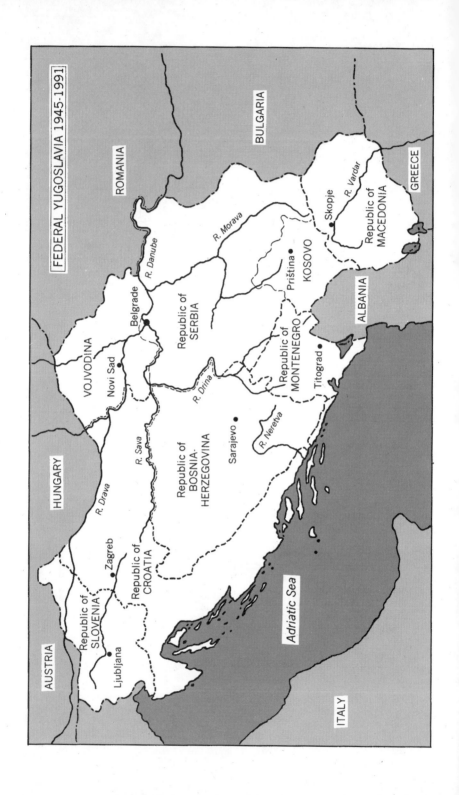

FEDERAL YUGOSLAVIA 1945-1991

1

SOE: SWASHBUCKLERS AND SECRET AGENTS

During the inter-war period the image of the secret agent which captured the popular imagination was one of glamour, danger and excitement. It was an image that had been fostered by the secret agents themselves: having failed in their appointed task of combating communism and fomenting counter-revolution in the Soviet Union, many turned their hands to writing memoirs and spy fiction. John Buchan was a classic example; having worked for British Intelligence, he based his character Richard Hannay upon himself and his colleagues. When more SOE files became available at the Public Records Office in 1998, they revealed plans for an assassination attempt on Hitler that directly corresponded with the plot of Geoffrey Household's *Rogue Male*, which was published on the eve of the Second World War, just as its author departed for Romania to work as an intelligence officer there. However, the fictional agents whose exploits excited readers and cinema audiences in the 1930s were a great deal more successful than their real-life counterparts. Probably the most accurate part of their image was that of the gentleman amateur: recruitment to the Secret Intelligence Service (SIS) was done on the 'old boy network' where having attended the right school and being a member of the right club was considered enough of a recommendation.

Throughout the 1930s SIS found great difficulty in obtaining intelligence from the Soviet Union. By contrast, Soviet Intelligence was considerably more successful during this period, recruiting some of Britain's most famous—or notorious—spies, of whom Kim Philby, Donald Maclean, Guy Burgess, Anthony Blunt and John Cairncross are the best known. The Soviets were also one jump ahead in recruiting at Britain's leading universities while SIS did not tap into this obvious resource until the brink of war, when they managed to recruit some of the self-same people. SIS found it diffi-cult to acquire either manpower or the necessary tools of the intel-ligence-gathering trade, due in part to the limited funds provided by the Foreign Office. A major source of income, and 'cover' for agents, was running the British passport offices in foreign capitals, but this became complicated as demand for visas and passports from Jews and anti-Nazis increased, eating into the time available for the unofficial occupation of these passport control officers. In late 1936 Admiral Hugh 'Quex' Sinclair, head of SIS, established a new intelligence-gathering body specifically to gain information on Nazi Germany, and to a certain extent on Fascist Italy. The 'Z' organization, headed by Claude Dansey was based on his network of business contacts, and was so secret that most members of SIS staff were unaware of its existence.[1]

In April 1938, shortly after the *Anschluss*, SIS set up Section 'D'—D for destruction—to lay plans for sabotage and subversion in case of war. Section D was headed by Major Lawrence Grand, by all accounts every inch the secret agent, he was tall and thin with a thick black moustache, always with a long cigarette holder in his mouth and a red carnation in his buttonhole. Grand was noted for the fertility of his imagination or, as Kim Philby put it, 'His mind ... ranged free and handsome over the whole field of his awesome responsibilities, never shrinking from an idea, however big or wild.'[2] When Kim Philby was recruited to D, Guy Burgess, who had been a fellow undergraduate at Cambridge, was one of the interviewers who appointed him. Unbeknown to SIS, both men were Soviet agents and operating an old boy network of their own. Philby was surprised at how easy it was to get into British Intelligence and noted that there was no such thing as 'positive vetting' in those days. While Grand had the big ideas and enthusiasm, not all members of his staff were quite so energetic and he was further handicapped by a lack of funds for his secret operations.

When Bickham Sweet-Escott, who had worked for the Z organ-ization, was recruited into Section D in spring 1940, his interviewer opened with the statement: 'For security reasons I can't tell you what sort of a job it would be. All I can say is that if you join us, you musn't be afraid of forgery and you musn't be afraid of murder.'[3] He did not have to commit cold-blooded murder as it happened, but this was typical of the cloak and dagger approach of some Section D agents, whom he assessed as likely to be John Buchan fans. Sweet-Escott had been recruited because of his background knowledge of the Balkans, gained while employed by the British Overseas bank. The Balkan section of D was controlled by George Taylor, described by Escott as 'a brilliant but ruthless Australian', and Belgrade was the centre of D's Balkan organization, where Julius Hanau—code named 'Caesar'—ran the organization assisted by Bill Bailey, a mining engineer from the Trepča mines in Mitrovica, Kosovo. Sweet-Escott, who was introduced to D by a friend, duly went on to recruit his own old chums to the organization; at one stage, he recruited his sister to provide secretarial backup after running out of candidates. Lutie Sweet-Escott, in those pre-shredder days, became an expert at burning sensitive papers as the Germans advanced, a task she was to perform in Belgrade, Athens and Cairo.

In March 1939, Military Intelligence also set up a body to operate behind enemy lines. Military Intelligence Research—MI(R)— was headed by Lieutenant-Colonel J.C.F. (Jo) Holland and had a special interest in guerrilla warfare and underground resistance movements. Colin Gubbins, who went on to play a leading role in SOE, was his right hand man and produced a number of manuals on secret armies and organizing resistance against occupying forces.

Even after the creation of the Z organization, hard and fast information on the strength of the Nazis was far from adequate as their threat became increasingly apparent from the mid 1930s. Assessments of the Luftwaffe were particularly tricky, but by the time of the Munich crisis in September 1938 Military Intelligence had a fairly accurate picture of the number of German army divisions. Both the move into the demilitarized Rhineland in March 1936 and *Anschluss* with Austria in March 1938 were foreseen, but their timing was not. In the run up to the Munich crisis, an analysis of the situation in Czechoslovakia underestimated the capabilities of the Czech military and, coupled with an overestimation of those of the German, lent weight to the argument for appeasement and the handing over of the Sudetenland. While the Nazi aggression against the rest of Czechoslovakia was not unexpected, its timing caught intelligence officers on the spot by surprise: two of them were on a skiing trip as the crisis went critical, and later complained that they had not been informed that German troops were massing on the borders.[4]

The lack of information was to a large degree attributable to the fact that during the 1930s the Government Code and Cypher School (GC & CS) was only able to break the codes of *some* low grade German signals, and those of high grade German signals not at all. Even when information was available it was not always effectively analysed or co-ordinated with other pieces of intelligence. The Joint Intelligence Committee (JIC) had been established in June 1936 for precisely this purpose, but the slowness of the various services' intelligence to co-ordinate amongst themselves, combined with the FO's lack of interest in the committee, meant that duplication and piecemeal treatment of information continued. It was not until July 1939 when the three service directors of intelligence and their deputies started to meet with a FO chairman that all military intelligence was simultaneously considered in conjunction with SIS's political intelligence.

Despite this improvement, the quality of intelligence gathering and assessment during the immediate pre-war period and during the 'phony war'—between 3 September 1939 and May 1940—remained patchy. The Nazi-Soviet pact in August 1939 caught Whitehall off guard, and the German invasion of Norway in April 1940 provided another nasty surprise: in both cases the information that was available had not been properly interpreted. To make matters worse, the Sicherheitsdienst (SD), the SS secret service headed by Reinhard Heydrich, had penetrated SIS in the Netherlands, and in November 1939 Heydrich used this to embarrass SIS and its Whitehall bosses by what has been called the 'Venlo incident'. This involved SD men posing as representatives of high-ranking dissidents in the German armed forces and claiming that they wanted to overthrow Hitler and make peace with Britain, and resulted in two highly placed SIS agents being lured into German captivity.

When war started the speed of the German *Blitzkrieg* caught SIS off balance: as one country after another fell, SIS lost almost the whole of its network with the exception of the Balkans. Perhaps the final straw for the service chiefs and the FO was the misreading of

French military strength and morale, which was compounded by the failure to anticipate the German attack though the Ardennes in May. The only intelligence success during the French campaign seems to be more attributable to good luck than good judgement, when documents from a captured German staff car were found to contain detailed information on the strength, organization and leadership of the German army. More immediately important was a document showing plans for troop movements which would have cut off the British Expeditionary Force from the Channel: without the fast pre-emptive move by General Lord Gort which this information prompted, the Dunkirk evacuation could not have taken place.[5]

Before the reader becomes too despondent at this catalogue of failures and confusion, it might be worth mentioning a major—perhaps *the* major—success of British intelligence in the Second World War that came just before the fall of France. This was the breaking of the German 'Enigma' machine cypher codes at Bletchley Park in Northamptonshire, the wartime base of GC & CS: the German air force code was cracked on 22 May 1940, the naval code in Spring 1941 and the army code in Spring 1942. 'Quex' Sinclair had had the foresight in 1937 to turn to the universities and earmark the brightest recruits for service in case of war, first picking language specialists and then mathematicians. This newly assembled team was based at Bletchley Park and built on the work of Polish and French code-crackers; all three countries had co-operated closely in the late 1930s, pooling information and ideas. Intelligence gleaned from intercepted enemy signals became known as 'Ultra'—short for ultra secret as its existence was only revealed to a very limited number of people, to ensure that the Axis powers were unaware that their wireless traffic was being used against them.

When 'Quex' Sinclair died in November 1939, he was succeeded by Sir Stewart Menzies as head of SIS with Dansey as his assistant chief. The following month Prime Minister Chamberlain commissioned Lord Hankey, the former cabinet secretary, to investigate complaints from the service ministries regarding the unreliability of SIS. While the FO initially did not share the opinion of the service chiefs, by May 1940 they acknowledged that an overhaul of SIS was needed. On 27 May the Chiefs of Staff discussed a paper entitled

'British strategy in a certain eventuality',[6] the eventuality, of course, being the fall of France. They decided that possible revolts in occupied territories would need direction and co-ordination with sabotage and other tactics, and to facilitate this a special organization was required whose creation was a matter of urgency.

As soon as he heard of this projected new organization, Hugh Dalton, recently appointed Minister of Economic Warfare, began lobbying for control of the subversive and propaganda side of Special Operations. Dr Dalton was an energetic and forceful character with a booming voice and very positive opinions in favour of an aggressive rather than defensive policy towards the Axis powers. As a member of the shadow cabinet he had played an important part in convincing the leadership of the Labour party and dissenting Conservative MPs that a National government could only be established under the leadership of someone other than Neville Chamberlain. While a number of factors contributed to Chamberlain's final decision to resign, the resolution of the rebel Conservatives that Labour had to join the government and Labour's determination not to serve under Chamberlain was the final push. Winston Churchill became Prime Minister on 10 May, and Dalton became a member of the Coalition government.

The Ministry of Economic Warfare (MEW) had been constituted on 3 September 1939; its original brief, to organize a blockade of the German economy, was expanded to include strategic bombing of enemy industry combined with sabotage and psychological warfare. Enthusiasm for the policy of blockade derived from the perception that the First World War had ended when German morale succumbed to the British blockade; during the 1930s this idea had been prominent in much of the forward planning for the possible eventuality of war with Germany. It was hoped that such methods might defeat Germany without the involvement of large land-forces, since no-one wanted a repetition of the 1914–18 trench warfare. The BEF evacuation from Dunkirk and the subsequent fall of France only served to strengthen this conviction.

Dalton envisaged Special Operations as a natural extension of the economic war, with secret agents continuing the destruction of those German resources beyond the reach of strategic bombing. After much lobbying of bodies and individuals who might influence the decision, Dalton was able to put his case at a meeting with Foreign Secretary Halifax and other ministers and officials on 1 July. He argued that subversive warfare should be entirely separate from regular military operations and, therefore, outside the control of the service departments, contending that the "war from within" would be far better conducted by civilians than soldiers:

> What we have in mind is not a military job at all. It concerns trade unionists, socialists etc., the making of chaos and revolution—no more suitable for soldiers than fouling at football...[7]

Neither Major-General Frederick Beaumont-Nesbit, Director of Military Intelligence, nor Sir Stewart Menzies, or 'C' as the head of SIS was known, was entirely happy about giving over his share of this activity, furthermore the making of chaos and revolution was not a concept familiar to the Foreign Office. In addition, Dalton's implementation of the policy of blockade had already brought him into conflict with the FO over the diplomatic complications this caused with neutral countries. However, 'Dr Dynamo'—the half mocking, half affectionate nickname coined by Gladwyn Jebb—continued to press his case for control of what was to become the Special Operations Executive, urging Clement Attlee to impress upon Winston Churchill that such an organization could only be led from the left.[8] Churchill was not wholly convinced that Dalton was the man for the job, but Sir Alexander Cadogan, Permanent Under-Secretary at the FO, supported his candidacy, and having secured the backing of his Labour Party allies, especially Attlee, Dalton's appointment was officially confirmed on 22 July. Whereupon Churchill uttered the phrase that will forever be associated with SOE—'And now set Europe ablaze'. The appointment of a Labour politician as head of SOE was an important factor in cementing the new coalition government, and also possibly for allaying some of Labour's long-standing mistrust of the secret services. However, Dalton was not made a member of the War Cabinet.

The Special Operations Executive was given its name by Neville Chamberlain, who remained a member of the War Cabinet after Churchill succeeded him, and it was he who drew up SOE's founding charter in July 1941. SOE brought together three existing organizations: Lawrence Grand's Section D and MI(R) were amalgamated with an organization dedicated to black propaganda based at Electra House on the Thames Embankment, and consequently known as 'EH', headed by Sir Campbell Stuart with Rex Leeper as his assistant. The organization was initially re-divided into three parts: Propaganda SO1, Subversion and Sabotage SO2, and Planning SO3. The latter was short-lived, as its plans, according to Bickham Sweet-Escott, 'were so global and far-reaching, and incidentally covered such an enormous acreage of paper ... [that] in a few months SO3 duly planned itself out of existence.'[9]

Gladwyn Jebb was invited by Dalton to become his 'chief lieutenant' and given the title Chief Executive Officer. He was an undoubted asset, both in helping to formulate the ideas behind SOE and in representing the organization's interests in Whitehall, facilitated by Jebb's special relationship with Alexander Cadogan, for whom he had worked before taking up Dalton's invitation. Although not entirely convinced of SOE's effectiveness, Cadogan was always prepared to consult with Jebb and to intervene at the FO to ensure that SOE was allowed some leeway. He also took a more relaxed view of some of SOE's rather shadier schemes than did Lord Halifax the foreign secretary. Sir Frank Nelson, a former Conservative MP who had combined business interests with work for the 'Z' organization in Basle, was appointed executive head of SOE—known as 'CD'—and was responsible for the day to day running of SO2. Nelson had been nominated by 'C' 'in hope of keeping these amateurs under control' and soon made it apparent that a fresh start was to be made, including the establishment of a country section or 'desk' for each operational area.[10]

Some old Section D hands remained in London but Dalton, determined to make a success of his fledgling organization, soon introduced a vast array of new faces and removed those that did not fit. Most notable among the latter was Lawrence Grand who was not happy at being demoted to second in command and was making life difficult for Jebb. This was compounded by his extravagant 'cloak and dagger' style, which was inconsistent with the new professional image of SOE: romanticism was out, dynamism was in. Kim Philby was retained but did not stay long in SOE, preferring to transfer to SIS where he felt his talents could be put to better use. Guy Burgess was not kept on as Jebb, rather perceptively, felt he was unsuited to confidential work. George Taylor remained from Section D, becoming chief of staff to Nelson, with responsibility for organizing the new country sections and general operations, assisted by Bickham Sweet-Escott. Philip Broad joined Jebb from the FO, and Robin Brook left the City to become Jebb's own private secretary. Dalton was keen to keep Brigadier Colin Gubbins from MI(R) as director of training and operations, and Jebb later described him as 'the real motive force in the machine'.[11] There followed a rapid expansion which, because of the secrecy of SOE, was made by continuing Section D's practice of using the 'old boy network', resulting in the recruitment of large numbers of merchant bankers, stockbrokers, industrialists and lawyers. So far the makers of chaos and revolution were bastions of respectable society and ex-public schoolboys. An agent recruited in Romania by two SOE agents described it thus: 'It was, they said, a kind of club: you were invited to join.'[12] SOE soon outgrew its existing premises and eventually found a permanent home in Baker Street which was to become synonymous with the organization itself, while the FO—not surprisingly—dubbed its members 'Baker Street Irregulars' after Sherlock Holmes's gang of street urchins.

The Balkan contingent of Section D transferred more or less intact into SOE. Agents there included a number of journalists, whose profession gave them good cover for being in the region while they fed pro-British propaganda to the indigenous press through the 'Britanova' press agency, and engineers who were useful for their sabotage potential. The Trepča mines, owned by Chester Beatty who was a friend of Lawrence Grand, proved a particularly good source for the latter. Others were businessmen, British Council officials, and a variety of other 'old boys' who seemed potentially useful. The agents had been active in the Balkans since 1938, and after September 1939 the area became vital to the economic war, especially with regard to denying Romanian oil and grain to the Third Reich. Following the German successes in May and June 1940, which severed virtually all Section D's links in western and northern Europe, the Cairo office became responsible for supplying and liaising with the Balkan organization as well as organizing operations in the Middle East. This office was controlled by George Pollock who was sent to Cairo when SOE was created. The Istanbul office was also to be an important contact point with the Balkans. In addition, SOE missions were established in other neutral areas, such as Lisbon, Stockholm and Berne to facilitate communications with, and infiltration into, occupied territories. The Massingham mission was set up in Algiers for work in France and Italy.

SOE took over Section D's relationship with the Jewish Agency for Palestine, which had expanded its role as war approached to oppose and undermine the Nazis and later established the Rescue Committee for European Jews. SOE and the Jewish Agency had a reciprocal agreement: agents of the latter were often natives of occupied countries whose knowledge of both language and terrain were obviously useful to SOE, while their infiltration into occupied areas by SOE allowed the Jewish Agency to find out what was happening to the Jewish population there.

'Setting Europe ablaze' was easier said than done, and one major problem was a lack of people with sufficient experience to conduct operations. These had to be recruited in competition with the armed forces, checked for suitability and reliability, and then taught the practicalities of irregular warfare such as demolitions, silent killing, parachuting, using a wireless transmitter (W/T) and simply surviving in enemy territory. SOE schools had to be established and the training of agents for occupied territories balanced with the demands of setting up an underground resistance movement at home in case of invasion. Eventually there were about sixty SOE establishments in Britain, mainly based in country houses, which were used as training schools, holding centres where agents waited away from the public gaze for transport into the field, and research centres where SOE 'toys' were developed. SOE had a parachute school at Ringway, Manchester. Training schools were established in Palestine, Australia, Algiers, Ceylon and India as well as Camp X on the Canadian border with the USA. In addition to physical training a wide range of skills had to be imparted such as forgery, lock-picking and other useful nefarious techniques. This led to the recruitment of many disparate experts, including Jasper Maskeleyne who was a popular magician in the music halls of the 1930s, astonishing his audiences with his special effects. One SOE agent bound for Yugoslavia was amazed, after a cloak and dagger trip through night-time Cairo, to find the door of a house in a dingy back alley opened by none other than the famous magician himself.[13] Maskeleyne, as well as being an expert on camouflage, supplied handy gadgets for officers going into the field, such as trouser button compasses, and also ran an escape school. Leonard Appelbee the artist provided some useful 'toys' for SOE, including boxes of matches with microfilmed coded material inside each match and exploding models of Buddha to be surreptitiously placed in Japanese military messes. A minute telescope, disguised as a nicotine-stained cigarette holder, was devised by Charles Fraser-Smith who also modified dominoes and hairbrushes to hold maps and other essential items. Explosive devices—including exploding camel dung for use in the Western Desert—and miniature cameras were dreamed up and produced by SOE's scientific team.

In 1941 Colin Gubbins conducted a survey of SOE assets and personnel in order to prepare a detailed programme for future action and concluded that major operations on any telling scale would not be feasible until the winter of 1942–3. This was based mainly on the assessments of military personnel which contrasted with those produced by civilians, but in the event turned out to be a pretty accurate forecast. The time lag between SOE's initial interest in Yugoslavia and its ability to deploy agents in any numbers there was to be an important factor in the Yugoslav situation.

Another major flaw in the 'setting Europe ablaze' concept was the plan for the establishment of 'secret armies' within occupied Europe, with SOE acting as the 'detonator' which would supply, organize and set in motion these armies as and when required. This was simply expecting too much of the people in occupied Europe at that stage of the war. Most of them were still in a state of shock following the speed of the collapse of their own forces and the arrival of the occupiers, while many members of the French and Belgian armed forces were prisoners of war following defeat. Probably the only exception was Poland, occupied by both the Germans and Soviets it seemed that national survival depended on active resistance, and a movement emerged which eventually became the Polish Home Army.

In addition to the limitations imposed by the practicalities of establishing the new organization, there were those imposed by the more established—and more powerful—bodies upon which SOE had to rely. George Taylor, writing a potted history of SOE in October 1945, noted that the advantage of the new set-up in July 1941 was the 'consolidation and clarification of purposes under a single minister of cabinet rank', but at the same time there was 'still no organic relation to the Foreign Office or to the Chiefs of Staff'.[14] In other words, SOE did not have a clearly defined position which could give it clout when it was needed, and Dalton was not in the War Cabinet. On his appointment Dalton had been instructed to keep the Chiefs of Staff (COS) abreast of SOE operations, but although their charter stated that irregular activities should be co-ordinated with general strategic planning, SOE was not represented on the COS Committee, having to rely on the Joint Planning Staff meetings for liaison with the COS. The Chiefs of Staff were adamant that SOE was not to be a fourth, independent service but must remain operationally dependent upon the other services—a factor which was to have far-reaching consequences when the question of aircraft and supplies for SOE missions arose. Neither were the regular military minds entirely convinced by SOE's irregular and 'amateur' approach or even, in some cases, of the potential usefulness of resistance movements.

SIS was not inclined to be well disposed to SOE which was viewed as amateurish and was resented for swallowing up Section D, and SIS regarded SOE as posing a potential danger to its own intelligence network. In many respects the two organizations had opposite objectives. Intelligence gathering had to be invisible, while, as Gladwyn Jebb put it 'our whole raison d'être was to stir things up'. Sir Stewart Menzies of SIS had direct access to Churchill, a privilege not enjoyed by SOE's Sir Frank Nelson. For the first two years of its existence SOE was dependent upon SIS for its communications. By an agreement of September 1940, all SOE wireless traffic was handled by SIS who had a right to accept or reject it, an arrangement that also meant that SIS had access to all SOE information, but did not return the favour. Nor was SIS over generous with wireless transmitters that were so essential for keeping in touch with agents in occupied territory. SOE for its part resented the fact that when the Axis forces overran the Balkans in spring 1941 they were left without any radio contact with the area. Eventually SOE brought in its own boffins and John 'Radio' Brown and Jerry Parker developed more efficient radios for SOE which, from the middle of 1942, enabled SOE to run its own communications, independently of SIS. This alleviated the situation somewhat, but the rivalry continued. In 1944 Churchill noted 'the warfare between SOE and SIS [...] is a lamentable but perhaps inevitable feature of our affairs.'[15] Members of SIS popularly referred to SOE as 'the Thugs',[16] and an SIS man being sent into Greece was warned to steer clear of SOE and its political dabbling.

SOE's relationship with the FO could also be a difficult one, as they often had different agendas and throughout the war each was inclined to regard the other as incapable of grasping the complexities of balancing political and military requirements. Many members of the Foreign Office harboured deep suspicions of SOE and its activities which, by their very nature, were bound to have political implications. Dalton was continually exasperated by what he regarded as FO obstruction, particularly in relation to his organization's plans to disrupt Romanian oil supplies to Germany. The FO, in return, appears to have been constantly vigilant for signs of SOE usurping the role of regular diplomats and reacted tartly when an eminent Yugoslav politician conveyed his congratulations on Anthony Eden's appointment as foreign secretary in December 1940 through SOE rather than Ronald Campbell, the British minister in Belgrade.[17] The FO was anxious not to have SOE agents perceived as official representatives of HMG policy; although this, perhaps inevitably, did happen as some agents used employment at British legations as cover for their more subversive activities. While they were unaware of the existence of SOE *per se*, many Yugoslav politicians who looked to the democracies as their natural allies, were aware or suspected that its members were some sort of intelligence agents, and possibly saw them as a useful unofficial channel for communication with the British government.

While there were conflicts and rivalries with the other services and the FO, SOE was also plagued by internal disputes and jealousies, especially over the question of propaganda. Sir Robert Vansittart, Dalton's Chief Diplomatic Adviser, persuaded Dalton to appoint Rex Leeper head of SO1. As Leeper headed the Political Intelligence Department of the FO this would appear to make sense, but this leaves out of count the influence of personalities. Dalton and

Leeper soon came to loathe each other, but it was Leeper's relationship with Jebb that created insurmountable problems. He was
twelve years older than Jebb, had been senior to him at the FO, and
quite simply did not accept that he was answerable to Jebb, who as
Chief Executive Officer was in charge of co-ordinating the work
of SO1 and SO2, and bypassed him, acting as though he was
accountable only to Dalton.[18] The frictions between the two created bad feeling and wasted time in disputes which spilled over into
the two sections. The growing distance was not helped by the
physical separation of SO1 moving to Woburn Abbey—'the Country' as it was known. In Jebb's opinion 'SO1 tended to regard their
colleagues as rather bungling amateur assassins, SO2 began to think
of SO1 as half-baked theorists who were not to be trusted for reasons of security.'[19] The rivalries and petty hierarchies did not bode
well for Dalton's concept of one united subversive organization.

The matter was eventually settled by the creation of the Political
Warfare Executive (PWE). The birth of PWE was a classic example
of the 'Whitehall War', which raged so furiously at times that one is
tempted to wonder who was actually regarded as the principal
enemy—not always the Axis powers, it seemed. There were many
heated demarcation disputes between the Ministry of Information
(MOI) and SO1. Dalton and Jebb both felt that subversion and
black propaganda had to be co-ordinated: if SOE was to 'set Europe
ablaze', how were they supposed to do it without stoking the fires
of discontent among the occupied peoples? However, the MOI was
not keen to relinquish responsibility for overt propaganda and
argued that it made sense for all propaganda to come within its
sphere of influence. Eventually Duff Cooper, worn down by these
disputes, resigned as Minister of Information in July 1941. If Dalton
took this as a sign that he had won the battle for control of propaganda he was much mistaken. Cooper's successor was Brendan
Bracken, whose combination of political friends and his own
aggression meant that he was to have the final victory. Bracken
managed to outmanoeuvre Dalton at a meeting between the two
ministers and Eden on 8 August 1941, convened to discuss the
establishment of the Political Warfare Executive, of which Robert
Bruce Lockhart was to be director-general. It took Dalton a while
to realize that Bracken's plan was that PWE should swallow SO1 at

Woburn Abbey, but Dr Dynamo fought back by attempting to interfere with the BBC—much to the chagrin of BBC officials—and, in the last resort decided to ignore the existence of PWE altogether by telling SO1 staff to carry on as normal and retain control of covert propaganda. Relations between Dalton and Bracken, never more than coldly polite, now degenerated into open warfare with shouting matches becoming a regular feature of meetings between the two. Bracken, however, had the advantage of his friendship with Churchill and the fact that Eden liked him but did not like Dalton.

This personal war of attrition was only resolved when, in the wake of the fall of Singapore, a government reshuffle on 19 February 1942 moved Dalton from MEW to become President of the Board of Trade. While it was perceived as a victory for Bracken, the new post was in fact a promotion for Dalton, although it reflected Churchill's need to keep things on an even keel in the coalition government more than a desire to upgrade Dalton. For while Dalton admired Churchill, the feeling was not reciprocated. Lord Wolmer, later Earl of Selborne, succeeded Dalton at the MEW and as head of SOE, and SO1 became fully integrated into PWE, under the MOI and FO. Gladwyn Jebb did not transfer his allegiance to Selborne and soon left. Frank Nelson left because of ill-health and was replaced by the banker Sir Charles Hambro as 'CD'. Later, in September 1943, Colin Gubbins became CD when Selborne decided that SOE needed a professional soldier as its executive head.

As the war progressed so SOE developed and expanded; inevitably, as its numbers grew the 'old boys network' method of recruiting became obsolete. SOE took in greater numbers of staff from military sources, and so it had to become more formal, organized, and subject to military discipline. Peter Wilkinson, a member of SOE from the start, on returning to Baker Street after a long absence, lamented the changes he found there: 'I had grown to look on SOE as a culture rather than an organization and I did not find this militarism altogether congenial.'[20] Given the number of SOE's detractors, not all of them unjustified in their criticism, its existence was sometimes precarious. Throughout the war SOE was constantly at risk of being taken over by the regular military authorities, a fate it narrowly averted on several occasions. One of the main trouble spots was the Cairo office, where there seemed to be an annual scandal, followed by a shake-up and change of personnel. Despite this, the Cairo office continually attempted to break free of the control of Baker Street and at times followed its own policy, regardless of London's instructions. The word 'racket' was often bandied about when military people or diplomats referred to Cairo SOE. Hugh Seton-Watson, rather irreverently, took up this idea with enthusiasm and designed an unofficial logo for SOE, consisting of a tasteful arrangement of tennis rackets and balls. SOE did make it to the end of the war intact, but while Wilkinson and Gubbins were laying plans for the future of SOE as hostilities ceased the powers-that-be decided that it had run its course and wound the show up.

2

EXPERIMENTS IN SUBVERSION
AND SABOTAGE: DOING SOMETHING
IN THE BALKANS

The Kingdom of the Serbs, Croats and Slovenes—or Yugoslavia—came into being on 1 December 1918. The end of the First World War and the demise of the Habsburg Empire suddenly made possible the long-cherished dream of Serbian and Croatian intellectuals: unification of the South Slavs in one state. This was expressed in the Corfu Declaration of July 1917, issued by the Serbian government in exile on that island, and the Yugoslav Committee made up of South Slavs from Austria-Hungary, in exile in London. Intent became reality when the provisional government of the Habsburg South Slavs, the National Council in Zagreb, declared for unification in November 1918. The newly formed state was to be a constitutional democracy under the Karadjordjević dynasty of Serbia.

However, the *idea* of Yugoslavia was one thing, the *reality* was quite another. To balance the political and regional differences of people who, despite their common origins and many similarities, had diverse experiences and expectations was a difficult task. The new state was made up of Serbia and Montenegro, both independent kingdoms that had already voted to unite and which had gained territory from the Turks during the Balkan wars of 1912–13, and included Kosovo and part of Macedonia. From the dissolution of Austria-Hungary came Croatia-Slavonia, Slovenia, Bosnia-Herzegovina, Dalmatia and the Vojvodina: these areas had been administered in a variety of ways and Croatia had enjoyed home-rule. During Yugoslavia's first ten years of parliamentary democracy the balance of power constantly shifted as the various parties formed into unstable coalitions, in attempts to reach agreement on constitutional

issues. When the leader of the Croatian Peasant Party was shot and
fatally wounded in parliament in 1928, King Alexander, tired of
the failure to stabilize domestic questions, dissolved parliament and
appointed a new government under his personal rule the following
year. At the same time he changed the name of his state to the Kingdom of Yugoslavia in an attempt to stimulate a common 'Yugoslav'
identity to replace Serb, Croat or other regional consciousness.

In 1931 a new constitution set the seal on King Alexander's personal powers. While the king regarded this, along with the promotion of a Yugoslav identity, as the solution to disunity and division, it
had almost the opposite effect: many Serbians perceived it as an
abrogation of their democratic parliamentary experience and Cro-
atians largely regarded it as an attempt to impose centralist domination from Belgrade. The latter idea stimulated separatist feeling in
Croatia, especially amongst members of the extreme right-wing
nationalist Ustashas who increasingly looked towards Italian fascism
and the emerging Nazi party in Germany. Macedonia also posed
problems, for there IMRO, the right-wing terrorist organization
had split into two murderous opposing factions; one wanted the
absorption of both Greek and Yugoslav Macedonia into a greater
Bulgaria, while the other favoured a separate Macedonia in a Balkan federation. The Communist Party of Yugoslavia (CPY) had
been outlawed at the end of 1920 and the advent of King Alexander's personal rule meant ruthless persecution for the party. In the
short-term this was bad news for the CPY, but by the end of the
1930s it had restructured itself into a tightly knit Bolshevik-style
party under the leadership of Josip Broz—'Tito'. Although it was
not large, the degree of its organization and the fact that it was not
aligned to any one national group, meant that the CPY was able to
exert a fair degree of influence, particularly with the young.

Foreign policy was rather more successful than domestic, and
during the 1920s the Little Entente between Yugoslavia, Czechoslovakia and Romania was established to safeguard against any restoration of the Habsburg dynasty. In 1933 the Entente established a
permanent council and secretariat to further economic co-operation
and liaison regarding military matters and the following year King
Alexander formed the Balkan Entente consisting of Yugoslavia,
Greece, Turkey and Romania as a means of countering Italian

influence in the region. He also hoped to strengthen ties with France, a traditional friend, as a counterweight to Italy. It was in pursuit of the latter policy that in October 1934 he made a state visit to France, where he was assassinated by an IMRO agent in the pay of the Ustashas. His son King Peter II was still a child, but King Alexander's system of 'personal rule' was continued by a regency, headed by his cousin Prince Paul.

Politically and diplomatically Yugoslavia was oriented towards the western democracies and supported the League of Nations, but economically found itself increasingly tied to Italy, Austria and Germany. The Yugoslav economy was badly affected by supporting the League of Nations sanctions against Italy, following Mussolini's invasion of Abyssinia in 1936, and as a result Yugoslavia became ever more dependent upon Germany as its main trading partner. While this brought short-term economic benefits, it held many long-term political dangers; the German stranglehold on Yugoslavia's economy was used by the Nazi regime to put pressure on the Yugoslav government, for example constantly urging it to leave the League of Nations as a 'gesture of friendship'. When international tensions increased during the later 1930s the Yugoslav government became ever more aware of these potential dangers and appealed to France and Britain to try to redress the balance. Britain did make up some of the lost trade, but as the Balkan countries were not traditional trading partners of the British there was limited scope for Yugoslav imports. In addition the British tended to stick to their *laissez-faire* attitude to trade and were reluctant to inter-relate economics and politics. An SOE agent in Romania later lamented the fact that during the 1930s Britain was unwilling to engage in political trading, keeping relations on a purely economic basis.[1] Only after the declaration of war in 1939, and the establishment of the Ministry of Economic Warfare, was any serious attempt made to counter German economic domination of the Balkans: one notable success was the Goeland Transport and Trading Company, established and financed by MEW, the efforts of which resulted in Romanian oil exports to Britain between December 1939 and April 1940 far exceeding those to Germany.[2]

Traditionally Britain had only taken cognisance of the Balkans in relation to *other* Powers, especially Russia and France in the nineteenth century. Following the First World War the British were anxious not to see either Germany or the Soviet Union dominate the region, and their central aim was to maintain stability in the eastern Mediterranean in order to safeguard access to, and trade with, imperial interests to the east; neutrality in the Balkans and Eastern Europe best suited these. The Foreign Office was very much aware of the potential value to Germany of the food and mineral wealth of the region in the event of war and a British blockade of German ports. The countries in the region were not strong enough individually to withstand Germany or the Soviets, but in concert they could do so. Turkey was perceived to be the key to a united and neutral Balkans: not least because it was the only state without a border dispute with Bulgaria left over from the Balkan wars. Accordingly, the main diplomatic and economic input into the area was directed at the Turks as they were important to British imperial interests and because of their strategic position. In 1936, following Hitler's reoccupation of the Rhineland and Mussolini's adventure in Abyssinia, a joint War Office and Admiralty memorandum to the British government recommended the wisdom of concluding an alliance with Turkey as a matter of urgency. Although the strategic considerations were recognized, an Anglo-Turkish alliance at that time was rejected by the Foreign Office who were fearful not only of arousing the suspicions of other Powers, but of making Britain appear weak. Characteristically of the FO, the conclusion was that it would not do 'to run after the Turks'.[3] Diplomacy was complicated by the fact that France and, more particularly, Germany were also trying to win over the Turks who were apparently happy to exploit the competition without feeling entirely obliged to any party. An additional complication was traditional Turkish wariness of the Soviet Union's long-term territorial ambitions.

Germany's occupation of Prague and annexation of Bohemia and Moravia in March 1939 and Italy's invasion of Albania three weeks later stimulated the creation of a 'Peace Front', initially comprising Poland, Romania, Turkey and Greece, to deter Nazi Germany from acts of aggression against those countries. In April 1939 Britain gave Greece and, under pressure from France, Romania a similar guarantee to that issued to Poland.[4] The guarantee to Greece was, to a large extent, to encourage Turkey to support the Western Allies. An Anglo-Turkish pact in June 1939 was succeeded by an Anglo-Franco-Turkish one in October, by which the Turks pledged assistance in case of war in the Mediterranean while stipulating neutrality in any conflict with the Soviet Union. Yugoslavia did not want such a guarantee, nor to align itself with the Peace Front for fear of undermining its own neutrality. The Yugoslavs were also rather chary of being seen to be veering too much towards Britain and France, and felt it necessary to register disapproval of the Turkish pact as a threat to Balkan neutrality.[5] In fact, following the outbreak of war in September 1939, the Turks declared themselves to be 'non-belligerent' rather than neutral—a status which conferred a much greater degree of flexibility and allowed them to exploit the ambiguities of their situation until February 1945, when they finally declared war on Germany. It also allowed wartime Istanbul to become a hotbed of spies and conspiracies, with secret agents of all nationalities rubbing shoulders, and 'enemies' often drinking in the same hotels and being entertained by the same young women. Charles Richardson, an SOE officer in Cairo, visited Istanbul in late 1941 and, after being treated to an exhibition of the British Embassy's impressive store of weapons and explosives, was informed that 'Istanbul contained at least four secret British organizations, and not one of them would tell the others what it was up to.'[6]

Germany's action in Czechoslovakia created a shock wave in Yugoslavia and this was exacerbated by the Italian invasion of Albania. Count Ciano, Italian Minister of Foreign Affairs, had earlier suggested to Prince Paul that Italy and Yugoslavia should partition Albania between them: this was refused, not least because it would give the Italians a foothold in the Balkans. They now had that foothold. Meanwhile, as Ciano noted in his diary on 7 April, 'international reaction was almost non-existent. The memorandum Lord Perth [British ambassador to Italy 1933–9] left with me in the course of a cordial visit might have been composed in our offices.'[7] In the light of this lack of international protest regarding Albania, it is hardly surprising that the Yugoslavs wanted to keep a low profile and, in the case of war, to remain neutral. Ronald Campbell, British minister at Belgrade, described it as a desire to be 'allowed to pursue

in its own way its aim of placating the Dictatorships without sever-
ing its ties with the Democracies'. The French ambassador in Belgrade described it as '*laissez-nous faire*'.[8]

The fact that the Italians were intriguing with Ante Pavelić,
leader of the Croatian Ustashas, and using their position in Albania
to stir up separatist feelings among the Muslim population in Kosovo,
was hardly comforting to the Yugoslav government. There was also
the question of the large German minority in the Vojvodina where
the National Socialists had gained ascendency in cultural and
economic organizations.[9] Pressures from the deteriorating international situation, coupled with its own internal political complexities, confirmed to the Yugoslavs that the policy of neutrality was
their best hope of survival. In August 1939 Prince Paul's government attempted to resolve the long-term internal Serb-Croat problems by making Croatia a self-governing province—or *banovina*—
headed by Vladko Maček, leader of the Croat Peasant Party. It was
hoped that this would counter Pavelić's agitation for Croatian
secession from Yugoslavia. In the event it turned out to be only a
limited measure, as it made the Serbs discontented, and Pavelić continued to scheme with the Italians and Germans for their help in
the 'liberation' of Croatia.

The Nazi-Soviet pact of 23 August 1939 created unease in Yugoslavia, where it was interpreted as a sign that the chances of war were
greatly increased: the Yugoslavs were also disappointed that France
and Britain had failed to reach an agreement with the Soviets. Hitler's invasion of Poland on 1 September 1939—which brought Britain and France into a state of war with Germany two days later—
was followed by the Soviet invasion of Poland on 17 September.
The Soviet action produced mixed feelings in Yugoslavia, where it
was initially interpreted as a means of barring the way of the Germans to the Black Sea, the Slav countries and the Balkans. But the
Yugoslavs were soon disabused of this idea by refugees fleeing the
Russian occupation of Poland and by news of the Soviet treatment
of the Baltic States. In addition, the swift collapse of Poland was
depressing: while appreciating that Poland was a long way from
Britain and France, the Yugoslavs had expected the guarantors of
Polish neutrality to do more to help. It highlighted the fact that the
Balkans were also a long way away. The fall of France in June 1940
was a further severe psychological blow.

Section D had been active in the Balkans since 1938 and in 1939–40, as the area became increasingly important to the economic war, large numbers of agents were active there. Following the German victories of May and June 1940, Section D lost touch with its network in western and northern Europe, leaving the Balkan section as the only really operative part of the organization. Belgrade became an important centre for subversion in the region, with activity in Italian-occupied Albania being directed from there, while subversive operations in Austria and Germany were based in Slovenia, where the 'Society of Yugoslavs in Italy' had been very helpful to D since 1939. The active force in the society was Dr Ivan Chok, a Slovene lawyer who held a nominal post in the Yugoslav Ministry of the Interior.[10] Section D's irregular and subversive operations did not go unnoticed by the British diplomatic representatives in the region, and while Balkan neutrality was being promoted there were many aspects of the organization's exploits which, they felt, were not compatible with their own interests. Governments in the Balkans were nervous enough about Axis—and Soviet—intentions without a bunch of dangerous freebooters upsetting them further. Propaganda was one thing, but bringing in caches of explosives and engaging in political skulduggery was quite another.

Section D activity had not escaped the notice of the German intelligence service either. In April 1940 Julius Hanau, 'Caesar', the then head of the Balkan section in Belgrade, had been expelled from Yugoslavia after his plans to block the Danube to interrupt the supply of Romanian oil to Germany had been uncovered, causing protests from the German minister and a good deal of political embarrassment. Caesar was replaced by his deputy, Bill Bailey, and shortly thereafter Section D became SOE. In August 1940 Prince Paul told the British minister, Roland Campbell, that the Germans were asking to install Gestapo posts in Yugoslavia, on the grounds that 'British Secret Service were making bombs in conjunction with Jugoslavs' and that the Yugoslav government was allowing terrorist activity on its soil. Apparently one of the Yugoslav agents employed by SOE was also in the pay of the Germans and, in addition, following the capture of the French archives the Germans constantly hinted at the dark secrets to be found within them. Prince Paul begged Campbell to put an end to SOE's activity lest it gave the Germans an excuse to take over the country.[11]

Baker Street did not react very sympathetically to the plight of either the Prince Regent or the British minister: the latter was assessed as too timid and 'We should be doing more, not less, in Jugoslavia.'[12] Gladwyn Jebb pointed out that the Germans did not need an excuse; if they wanted to exert force on Yugoslavia they would do so anyway and he felt that this was no reason to curtail SOE activity. Campbell was also concerned about subsidies paid by SOE to the Serb Peasant Party which were tied in with the possibility of a coup, something which definitely infringed the rules of diplomatic relations. This was also viewed differently by London SOE. In July 1940 Yugoslav politicians who did not support Prince Paul's handling of the international situation were discussing with SOE plans for two coups d'état. One in Yugoslavia would overthrow Prince Paul's government but maintain the dynasty, while another in Bulgaria would depose King Boris as the first step towards a Yugoslav-Bulgarian federation. Campbell thought the whole plan was rather dubious as, if it failed, it would divide the country and make it easy prey for the Germans. He had, therefore, told his legation staff to discourage it. The FO agreed with Campbell, but also entertained the idea that while the plan was premature 'later it might be of first class importance to HMG'.[13]

Poor Campbell was not having a good time: the 'wilder elements' of SOE were creating diplomatic difficulties all round. In mid August 1940 he had a sharp communication from George Rendel, HM Minister in Sofia, complaining about the activities of Julian Amery in the Bulgarian capital. This young man was the son of L.S. ('Leo') Amery, Secretary of State for India, and while working for Section D/SOE, he was using a post at the Belgrade legation as his cover—thus making him Campbell's responsibility as far as Rendel was concerned. It seems that Julian Amery had been in Sofia intriguing with the Bulgarian opposition, making 'unfortunate statements' regarding the overthrow of the 'Russo' Bulgarian dynasty and encouraging the idea of Bulgarian-Yugoslav union. This appeared to have been entirely on his own authority, but Baker Street was not as ruffled about his actions as the unfortunate diplomats. While the FO felt that the best way to promote Balkan neutrality was to support King Boris and encourage him to resist Axis pressure, the Balkan SOE contingent had different ideas about

Bulgaria. A major reason for this was that Milan Gavrilović, leader of the Serb Peasant Party, and his deputy, Miloš Tupanjanin, were probably the most important of SOE's Yugoslav contacts, and both these individuals, and their allies in military and intellectual circles, had close links with the Bulgarian Left Agrarians who supported Bulgarian-Yugoslav union. These links included Kosta Todorov and Alexander Obov—who had taken political refuge in Belgrade in the 1920s and 1930s—and Dr Georgije M. Dimitrov: SOE simply took over the long-standing Yugoslav relationship with them. SOE also adopted the idea of Bulgarian-Yugoslav federation which seemed the best solution to the Macedonian question. The FO, meanwhile, feared that such a federation would open the Aegean to the USSR, a long cherished aim of the Russians and one much feared by the British.

Just to add to the diplomats' case against Amery, he had also been rather 'indiscreet' in handling affairs in Albania, by making payments to the adherents of King Zog—who was not, at the time, officially supported by Britain—on the premises of the British Legation. Baker Street, in an attempt to soothe Campbell, decided that the best policy might be to withdraw the young and over-enthusiastic Amery, who was in any case due to be called up by the RAF.[14] Eventually Amery had a reprieve when his mother intervened with Hugh Dalton who, after a personal interview with Julian, decided to retain his services for SOE. Caesar meanwhile, although now back in London, continued to dabble in Yugoslav affairs in conjunction with Leo Amery, much to the chagrin of Sir Frank Nelson.[15] There was also the question of storing explosives in the legation cellars—another undiplomatic activity as far as Campbell was concerned, although he did not go as far as the British minister in Budapest who apparently had SOE's stockpile of explosives thrown into the Danube.[16] While Baker Street understood Campbell's concerns that the discovery of these might allow German pressure on the Yugoslavs to break diplomatic relations with Britain, the build-up of such stores was perceived as essential for carrying out SOE plans in the region. The stores in the Belgrade Legation were in fact destined for use in Austria, not Yugoslavia. When Bill Bailey, now head of SOE Balkan section, went off to Istanbul, he left SOE business in the hands of Sandy Glen and

Robert Lethbridge, respectively naval attaché and passport control officer, with the result that their extra duties interfered with the normal running of the legation. Adding insult to injury, Bailey had instructed junior members of SOE to communicate with Lethbridge behind the back of Glen as the latter was too close to Campbell. No wonder the minister felt that co-operation with SOE 'would try the tolerant patience of Abe Lincoln himself'.[17]

The problems between Campbell and SOE were discussed at a high level FO-SOE meeting in London, at which it was decided that 'a person of some standing' would be sent to take charge of the whole operation in Belgrade, with the proviso that he should enjoy full diplomatic status and be directly responsible to Bailey. Eventually the person was located in the form of Tom Masterson who was well known and respected in the Balkans: he had been awarded the DSO in the First World War for his part in blowing up the Romanian oil wells before the German invasion in 1916. Masterson was about sixty years old and a much more respectable figure than some of the 'wilder elements'; after his arrival in November 1940 SOE's relationship with Campbell was far less tense.[18]

The Italian invasion of Greece in October 1940 radically changed the Balkan situation, and made it necessary for Britain to honour its pledge of military assistance to the Greeks. Initial Greek successes against the Italian forces were heartening, but it was obvious that it could only be a matter of time before Hitler would be impelled to come to the aid of his Axis ally: the route this aid would take must lie through either Bulgaria or Yugoslavia. British diplomatic efforts were, accordingly, concentrated on attempting to establish a Balkan front with Yugoslavia and Turkey acting in concert to support Bulgaria—regarded as the most likely route for German forces bound for Greece. The British did not want Yugoslavia to come into the war on the Greek side on its own: this risked a German invasion and swift movement along the Yugoslav railways into Greece. The only possible use of Yugoslavia joining the war would be if Turkey and Bulgaria came in on the same side.[19] By the end of 1940 hopes of a neutral bloc in central south-eastern Europe were looking rather improbable. The 'Pact of Steel', between Italy and Germany of May 1939, had expanded into the Tripartite Pact when Japan joined in September 1940. The German Foreign Ministry then persuaded

Hungary, Slovakia and Romania to adhere to the Pact in November 1940. Once Bulgaria gave in to German pressure and also signed the Tripartite Pact on 1 March 1941, the heat was turned on Yugoslavia. Germany was more concerned to ensure that the Yugoslavs did not join the Greeks and push out the Italians than about allowing German troops transition to Greece.

Prince Paul was in a cleft stick. Although personally pro-British he was all too well aware of Yugoslavia's precarious position. His advisers had given the pessimistic forecast that, in the event of an attack following a refusal to acquiesce to German demands, Yugoslav military forces would only be able to hold out for approximately one week. In November Orme Sargent had noted that it seemed from Campbell's reports that the Yugoslav General Staff were in greater need of their resolve being stiffened than Prince Paul. While he felt that the subsidy being paid to the Serb Peasant Party was 'no doubt doing us good' he continued 'but could we not spend at least some of the money on the General Staff? Rumour has it that several Yugoslav Generals have built themselves villas with money supplied by the Germans. Perhaps we could help them to add wings?'[20] In reply to this suggestion it was pointed out that SOE subsidies to the Serb Peasant Party and other political and patriotic organizations was not out and out bribery, but meant to fund resistance to the Axis if the British were forced out of the Balkans. Hoping to avoid that eventuality, funds were also provided to establish an alternative government or nucleus of men who would resist Axis demands.

In January 1941 George Taylor, Nelson's chief of staff, was dispatched to Belgrade to aid Masterson. Dalton and Nelson briefed him over dinner at Claridge's, emphasising that 'this has got to be a success'. Taylor was to have everything he needed in order to ensure that it *was* a success—ample funds and backing, not to mention the ability to ignore any opposition he might encounter since Dalton had the prime minister's support.[21] Taylor's instructions were to co-ordinate all the political contacts SOE had been cultivating so assiduously, to see if they could dissuade Prince Paul and his government from signing the Tripartite pact and, if not, whether a coup to overthrow Paul's government could be fomented. Taylor was also to complete the plans for sabotage which would deny German access to Romanian oil, and to Yugoslav lines of communication and raw materials, in the event of invasion. Perhaps the most delicate part of his allotted task was to organize post-occupational planning and make preparations for guerrilla resistance if—or when—the Balkan peninsula was overrun. The latter, in its presupposition of defeat for the Yugoslav and Greek armed forces, was hardly an encouraging aspect for the people in those countries; it also highlighted the fact that Britain had little to offer in the way of material support, relying instead on assurances that the United States would join the fray and that the Western Allies would win in the end, so this was the side on which to be.

On his arrival Taylor assessed pro-British Serb public opinion as SOE's best hope of influencing the Yugoslav government's policy: from mid-February until around mid-March it was still thought possible to press the prince regent into maintaining neutrality. SOE hoped to counteract German threats by convincing Prince Paul that submission to these would not be tolerated by the Serb people and would result in the overthrow of his government, and possibly the end of the Karadjordjević dynasty (a pretty accurate prediction in the event although Taylor was not to know how this would eventually come about).

The Serb Peasant Party was the most useful of SOE's political allies since it was actually part of the government, having made a tactical alliance with Paul. Its line on foreign policy was anti-German while its pro-Allied propaganda had been subsidised by SOE since July 1940, and SOE had complete confidence in Miloš Tupanjanin, who was deputising for party leader Milan Gavrilović, since the latter had been sent by Prince Paul as Yugoslav minister in Moscow. (The Yugoslav government had recognized the Soviet Union in June 1940 and diplomatic relations were established between the two states for the first time, with legations in Belgrade and Moscow.) Gavrilović himself was a great friend of the British, and was very warmly regarded by them in return. SOE's political contacts also included the opposition parties—Radicals, Democrats and the Yugoslav National Party—which had many influential members who held sway over Serb public opinion. The long-standing antagonism of these parties to their government meant that HM diplomatic representatives could not engage in overt dealings with them, whereas SOE was in almost daily contact. Taylor regarded SOE's influence with the party leaders as 'undoubtedly effective in preventing this good material being led astray',[22] but it was not always easy to get them all to act in concert. One of SOE's closest friends, Ilija Trifunović Birčanin was chairman of *Narodna Odbrana*, one of the patriotic associations of veterans of Serbia's resistance during the First World War. These associations were particularly influential with the Serbian public and they submitted many petitions to Prince Paul, setting out Serb objections to giving way to German threats, while SOE published a large volume of pamphlets on the same theme, designed to arouse public opinion. In short, all possible means of bringing pressure on Prince Paul not to sign the Tripartite Pact were utilized by SOE.

However, this pressure was not strong enough to dissuade Prince Paul: he secretly visited Hitler in Berlin on 4 March, when the latter pressed him to sign the Pact. Two days later the Regency Council voted unanimously to tie Yugoslavia into a *limited* form of the pact which stipulated that neither Axis soldiers nor war materiel should traverse Yugoslav territory. Germany agreed to the Yugoslav terms in mid-March, but insisted that the modifications regarding the military clauses be kept secret. There has been some suggestion that the Yugoslavs were in fact procrastinating by negotiating a limited form of the Pact in the hope that it would buy time until Hitler turned his attention to the Soviet Union. Apparently the Yugoslavs had heard of the invasion plans from Berlin, where they had an excellent intelligence source. Their military attaché there was having affairs simultaneously with three society ladies who moved in high-ranking circles of industrialists and officers. These hapless women unwittingly repeated the latest gossip from their social gatherings to their lover, who pieced together all the snippets of information thus gleaned to produce accurate and detailed analyses.[23]

Evidence of the lack of enthusiasm for the Pact in the Yugoslav government is given by their handing over to the British the pro-Axis ex-premier Milan Stojadinović, as a precautionary measure to preclude his possible reinstatement under Axis pressure, and in November 1940 General Milan Nedić had been replaced as Minister of War by General Petar Pešić who had an anti-German reputation.[24] While not wanting to move irrevocably towards the Axis,

Prince Paul and his ministers were in no position to respond to British urgings not to sign the Pact, and when the United States minister joined the debate the Regent replied: 'You big nations are hard, you talk of our honour but you are far away.'[25] Prince Paul was not amenable to meeting Anthony Eden, so the Foreign Secretary dispatched Terence Shone from the Cairo embassy to attempt some last-ditch diplomacy in Belgrade, in an attempt to persuade the Yugoslavs to throw in their lot with the British and Greeks and reject the Axis. The problem was that the British had little to offer in terms of practical aid—arms, aircraft, shipping and manpower were all in desperately short supply. The best the British seemed able to suggest was that the Yugoslav armed forces could capture all the arms they needed by fighting the Italians in Albania, for which Campbell thought the Yugoslavs had already laid some plans. Since the turn of the year SOE's Lieut.-Colonel Oakley-Hill had been organizing guerrilla bands throughout Albania and hoped to co-ordinate these with Yugoslav action in that country.[26]

Shone did his best but made no headway and, after hearing of the German agreement to the Yugoslav terms, felt that the situation was hopeless. George Taylor had reached the same conclusion by 18 March and SOE's objective changed from that of endeavouring to influence Prince Paul's government to that of endeavouring to bring it down—preferably before the Pact was signed. This was the subject of discussion at a meeting of SOE, intelligence and diplomatic representatives at the British Legation on 19 March. When Tupanjanin persuaded three Serb ministers to resign in protest at the draft pact this prompted the Yugoslav cabinet to continue its deliberations behind closed doors to counter opposition. It was apparent that they were going ahead with the Pact, leaving *a coup d'état* as SOE's only option...

Deciding to foment a coup was one thing; actually bringing it off was quite another. SOE's contacts, excellent though they might be for influencing public opinion, were not necessarily the stuff from which coups are made. SOE assessed that although the army was against the Pact its leaders were wary of provoking war with Germany, while the air force, a small but united body, who might be less reluctant, did not possess the political capacity to carry through after the initial overthrow. SOE was faced with the problem of co-ordinating all the necessary elements while time was fast running out: 'The work of SO2 during these days therefore was essentially that of urging the necessity of action for a coup d'état upon all our friends and everyone with whom we had contact', as Taylor put it, while hoping that once the first step had been taken everything else would fall into line.

When Dragisa Cvetković, the prime minister, and Aleksander Cincar-Marković, the foreign minister, departed for Vienna on 24 March to sign the Tripartite Pact on the following day, SOE was still doubtful if and how the coup was to be made. Alexander Cadogan in London received the news of the Yugoslav ministers' departure with some gloom, noting in his diary that all the Balkan news was bad—Yugoslavia was collapsing and it was becoming apparent that Turkey was not going to join the fray on the British side: 'Can only ask G.J. [Gladwyn Jebb] to blow up the Jug train! But he probably can't do that.'[27] The suggestion that SOE should blow up the train on which Cvetković and Cincar-Marković were returning from Vienna was in fact conveyed to Taylor in Belgrade, but according to Taylor himself, Ilija Trifunović Birčanin had informed SOE on Monday 24 March that the coup was 99 per cent certain and preparations were making good progress. To take such drastic action at this juncture would mean the introduction of martial law which would upset the plans.

When the coup actually came about, it took SOE by surprise: Trifunović Birčanin had said that he did not expect any action for 48 hours, and that he would give SOE twelve hours notice for them to inform the British government. In the event, the coup was brought forward by twenty-four hours when the planners heard of Prince Paul's departure from Belgrade. Alarmed that he had got wind of their plans and was making for Germany with King Peter, they were reassured to hear he was only on his way to his hunting lodge in Slovenia, so had decided to take advantage of his absence. By 2 a.m. on Thursday 27 March everything was ready. However, this had not given Trifunović Birčanin time to contact SOE, who initially feared that the military activity in Belgrade was a counter-coup by Paul; it was not till 8 o'clock in the morning that they heard all was well.

The leaders of the coup were General Dušan Simović, commander of the air force, his second-in-command Brigadier-General

Bora Mirković, Major Živan Knežević of the King's Guard (in Taylor's opinion the brains behind the operation) and a number of military officers and retired officers. The Briton who claimed to be closest to the makers of the coup, and most in the know, was not a member of SOE, but Tom Mapplebeck, an honorary air attaché. Mapplebeck had lived in Belgrade since shortly after the First World War, in which he had served as an aviator, and had many contacts in the Yugoslav air force. He was a great friend of Mirković who supplied him with copies of the Yugoslav General Staff's weekly intelligence summaries: these Mapplebeck translated and passed on to Campbell and the service attachés.[28]

However much encouragement and help on the propaganda side the coup had received from SOE and various other British agencies in Belgrade, it was a totally home-grown affair and a predominantly Serbian one at that. Signing the Tripartite Pact had provided the trigger. The majority of Serbs found it unthinkable to throw in their lot with the people they had fought against at such great cost in the previous war. News of the coup, and King Peter's assumption of the royal prerogative six months before his official coming of age, sparked off scenes of wild rejoicing in the streets of Belgrade— although these were not echoed in Zagreb. It produced a frisson of optimism in Britain where, for a short time, it gave a fleeting glimpse of early victory, coming as it did at the time of British successes in North Africa and signs of Italy weakening. This, in the event, turned out to be the triumph of hope over reality. It also cast SOE fleetingly (and, to a large degree, spuriously) in the role of an effective, well organized and useful extra arm of diplomatic and military policy. Hugh Dalton gladly—if a trifle dishonestly—accepted congratulations on 'my Jug achievement'.[29] In retrospect one can hardly blame him, as it must have made a pleasant change to hear the organization he was inclined to regard as his brainchild praised instead of blamed—at best as an expensive waste of time, at worst as a positive danger to more established representatives of HMG.

What the British, including SOE, failed to understand was that the coup was not simply a reaction to the Pact, but was the result of long-standing grievances against Prince Paul's government and a desire to address the internal problems of Yugoslavia. Not least of these was the unease felt in Serbia—and even more particularly among Serbs in Croatia—at the creation of the autonomous *bano-vina* of Croatia in August 1939. The misreading of the longer-term causes of the coup caused perplexity in British diplomatic and government circles; Cadogan noted: 'Somewhat puzzling and rather discouraging news from Belgrade. Government seems to have put out a statement that their foreign policy isn't changed!'[30] If the coup had taken place before the Pact had been signed, as SOE had hoped, the new government, which was a coalition of all parties and included both Serbs and Croats, as well as Slovenes and Muslims, might have been more ready to stand up against the Axis, but to tear up the Pact once it had been signed seemed too much like direct provocation.

The new government was no more enthusiastic than its predecessor about entertaining the British Foreign Secretary in Belgrade. So Eden had to kick his heels in Athens while General Sir John Dill—*very* secretly—tried to negotiate in Belgrade. Dill, Pierson Dixon of the FO and Brigadier A.W.S. Mallaby for the War Office attempted to persuade General Simović to join Britain and Greece. Simović was not keen to commit himself, hoping to avoid war with Germany, while all too aware of its possibility; he estimated that if the blow did fall it would be within twelve to fifteen days, whereas more pessimistic Yugoslav opinion thought they had only about five days.[31] The attitude of the new Yugoslav government, especially with regard to military preparedness and tactical deployment, was thought highly unsatisfactory by British ministers, and caused great anxiety as to whether Britain would be able to gain full benefit from the coup. It put SOE back into virtually the same situation as in the pre-coup days, attempting to put pressure on the government through its various friends and contacts. SOE had not been too pleased at Simović heading the new government, but he was the only possible figurehead on whom all parties could agree. SOE's closest associates, especially Tupanjanin and Trifunović Birčanin, were equally disappointed and within a few days, according to Taylor, were discussing the possibility of another coup.

SOE's schemes for sabotage did not benefit greatly from the coup either. Plans to block the Danube, disrupting oil and grain supplies to Germany, had been made as early as autumn 1939. These included the Kazan scheme, which involved laying charges in readiness to blow a large quantity of rock into the narrow Kazan gorge,[32] and the sinking of cement-laden barges to block the Greben narrows, and in the Sip canal to block that waterway. The success of these proposed actions depended upon the consent of the Yugoslav government: the Kazan scheme had been partially completed by Section D agents by December 1939 but was halted by the Yugoslav government for fear of provoking the Germans.[33] In the autumn of 1940 SOE had an interview with the Yugoslav minister of war and the chief of general staff, with the object of interesting them in restarting the Kazan operation, and as both appeared amenable SOE handed over the plans in December and put them in touch with their contractors. However, Taylor discovered that no further progress had been made by January 1941, and it was impossible for SOE to continue the work themselves undetected, since all the surrounding tree cover had been removed; the area was virtually under military control and in full view of German patrols on the Romanian side of the river. In early February Campbell had discussed the scheme with Prince Paul who *said* he was anxious to see it completed, but this must be done without the Germans getting wind of it. SOE felt that the only remaining chance of proceeding would be to bring the strongest possible pressure to bear on the prince regent and his government by their Serbian friends and by the British government via their minister in Belgrade. Campbell's view was rather more cautious. He agreed that strong action was called for if anything effective was to be done about blocking the Danube, 'but SO2's suggestions obviously raise much wider questions of policy'. A minister in the Yugoslav government had recently told Campbell that attempts to press either the government or individual members were counterproductive, particularly with regard to British interests. Campbell told the FO however, that he would make another attempt in respect of the Kazan scheme if the FO could provide him with a lever to use in his negotiations.[34]

The lever provided was a personal message from Churchill to Prince Paul, urging him to complete the Kazan scheme for use as a trump card in case of a threatened invasion: 'You would merely have to tell them that, if a single German soldier crossed the frontier, the German oil supplies from Romania would immediately be halved.'[35] The portrayal of the scheme as a valuable means of defence was a nice piece of SOE thinking: no mention was made of the benefits Britain would derive from the denial of Romanian oil supplies to the Nazi war effort. The accompanying telegram from the FO to Campbell concludes: 'I am afraid we are not in a position to make any promises of military help or war material, but if you think that an offer of financial assistance would help please let me know what form it should take.' The leverage initially appeared to work when an agreement was reached, but little practical progress was made. SOE was able to utilize its direct contacts and 'other means of influence', so that by 4 April Taylor knew that 12 barges had been loaded at Novi Sad: between the end of February and 18 March SOE had, through its agent, purchased and transported about ten thousand pounds worth of cement and iron. Meanwhile the Yugoslav government's only progress was to send out tenders on 10 March.

The coup, if anything, had increased SOE frustration on the sabotage front, as all the ground had to be gone over once more with the new minister of war and chief of staff. The only overt action open to them was 'nagging the General Staff', as Taylor put it. Dalton cabled him on 3 April: 'Minister and all high authorities know you realize fully that a successful blocking of Danube before it is too late would be the decisive factor in this war for England....'[36] No doubt Dalton was aware that it could be a decisive factor for SOE too.

SOE did not have the monopoly on sabotage plans in Yugoslavia. In addition to SOE's long-standing plans to destroy lines of communication, it seems that the Czech secret service had sufficient 'staff' in place in February 1941 to carry out demolitions along the whole length of the Belgrade-Salonika railway. It was a massive job involving scores of bridges and tunnels. Dalton's associate, Philip Noel-Baker, had already secretly contacted Eduard Beneš, head of the Czech government in exile, regarding the scheme, and recommended to Eden that it was worth spending half a million pounds on dynamite and bribery to ensure the line would be out of action if the Yugoslavs did not fight. Timing of course was vital, as the plan had to safeguard *against* demolition before it was certain that the Yugoslavs had surrendered.[37] Meanwhile, the 'Jupiter' organization—the German secret demolition teams—also had their own ideas for 'avalanches' in case Yugoslavia *would* fight, meaning to block roads and rails to delay Yugoslav mobilization.[38] SOE sabotage plans did not actually involve carrying out demolitions of bridges, mines etc, but only the supervision of operations. The country had been divided into five sectors, and one SOE representative was meant to be in each to observe sabotage activity. This all presupposed Yugoslav resistance holding out long enough for the operations to be carried out.

Unfortunately there was no time. Incensed by what he regarded as open defiance, Hitler ordered 'Operation Punishment': Yugoslavia was to be destroyed. On 6 April, without a declaration of war, Belgrade was attacked by German bombers. The total disarray caused by the bombing of Belgrade and other sensitive military centres, followed by the rapid advance of German motorized forces, for which the Yugoslav 'oxcart' army was no match, and the lack of information, particularly as to precisely where the front was, meant that SOE representatives were unable to give accurate reports of sabotage. Only later did it emerge that Dr Chok's organization did some useful demolitions in Slovenia when the Germans invaded.

In the ensuing chaos some SOE agents made their way to Istanbul or the Middle East, others followed the fleeing Yugoslav government in the convoy of legation staff, service attachés, pressmen *et al*. The Yugoslav government and King Peter left by air for Athens and the Middle East on 15 April, while most of the remainder of the convoy eventually finished up at the bay of Kotor. Taylor met one of SOE's agents en route who informed him that four cement-laden barges had been sunk in the Danube, but he disappeared before Taylor could get the full story. If the plan to block the Danube had worked, the river should have been closed for six months, almost until ice would slow down traffic anyway, but its partial implementation meant the river was blocked for only a short time.

Back in London, Dalton was anxiously awaiting news on the Danube; information was slow to emerge and initially sounded disappointing, but on 30 April he received a telegram from SOE, estimating that the river would be blocked for a minimum of three months. Dalton immediately passed on the good news to Churchill and 'other eminences'; but at a meeting of the Defence Committee on 16 June, Dalton had to report that the Danube was free again. Churchill consoled him: 'Never mind, you blocked it for two months. That was good.'[39] This was actually looking on the bright side, as the river was impassable for between three and five weeks only, and did not have a major impact upon Romanian oil supplies to Germany.

At least sabotage was a *limited* success, post-occupational planning appears to have been a complete failure. SOE and the service attachés in Belgrade had discussed resistance with various patriotic groups, but had made no arrangements for its own stay-behind mission. On the chaotic flight from the German invasion Sandy Glen wondered 'Should we stay, seek concealment in the hills?', but concluded that this would serve no purpose since no preparations had been made and they had no radio.[40] Mapplebeck was the only person in the convoy with a working transmitter. Of the seven W/T sets that SOE had managed to prise out of SIS, only one ever came on air. SOE's Belgrade station, secreted in the French Embassy, remained silent.[41] Oakley-Hill attempted to start a revolution in Albania, but preparations were incomplete and he found himself without arms or communications and eventually became a prisoner of war.

Once at Kotor, Campbell despatched Mapplebeck to Nicšić airfield to assist in the airborne evacuation of the remnants of the Royal Yugoslav airforce and General Bora Mirković to Greece. Mapplebeck had earlier arranged a flight for Terence Shone and Mapplebeck's Serbian wife—accompanied by her fox terrier in spite of Shone's protestations that dogs were not meant to fly—with four boxes of Yugoslav gold. In Piraeus harbour Mapplebeck sought passage for his airforce evacuees on the cargo ship *The Port Halifax*, but the captain of this vessel initially refused on the grounds that he did not have sanitary facilities for passengers. Mapplebeck regarded this as a minor matter—the Mediterranean was wide enough to deal with the sewage problem. Thus about 500 Yugoslav airforce personnel were sent to the Middle East, while Mapplbeck met up with his wife, the Yugoslav gold and the fox terrier, and proceeded there himself.

Meanwhile, at the bay of Kotor, two Sunderlands had been sent in to retrieve Yugoslavs who were too important to fall into Axis hands, and the Z organization's six agents.[42] Campbell remained behind and claimed everyone, including George Taylor and all other

SOE agents, to be diplomats, thus entitling them to immunity. The Italians treated them well and they were eventually repatriated, possibly as a result of negotiations regarding the German Consul General in Addis Ababa who, inexplicably, had remained in the Abyssinian capital after the British occupation.[43] It was not until June 1941 that George Taylor returned to London to give his report, by then the war had moved on and the short lived flurry of interest and excitement created by the Yugoslav coup d'état was almost forgotten. Section D and SOE's long laid plans for 'doing something in the Balkans' appeared to have borne little fruit.

3

RETURN TO OCCUPIED YUGOSLAVIA

The Yugoslav campaign had lasted barely ten days. There was little chance of repelling the Axis onslaught; even if they had been fully mobilized, the Yugoslav armed forces had neither the manpower nor the modern equipment to match the invaders. Hitler, in a hurry to bail out the Italians in Greece so that he could return to his plan to invade the USSR, ensured that the strength of the attack on Yugoslavia was one that could not long be withstood. He also recalled the Serbian army of the First World War, and overestimated the resistance that Axis forces would meet in Yugoslavia, as did the British.

Faced with military collapse, the Yugoslav government fled into exile with the young king, despite Churchill's rather unrealistic urging that King Peter and his ministers take to some mountain fastness to organize guerrilla activity. Before his departure on 15 April, General Simović passed on his responsibility as Chief of Staff to the Supreme Command to General Kalafatović, leaving him to conclude an armistice with the Axis. This action was later to cause bitter resentment and political problems for Simović as prime minister of the Yugoslav government in exile.

The capitulation was signed in Belgrade on 17 April, and Yugoslavia ceased to exist. The Independent State of Croatia (the NDH), which took in Bosnia-Herzegovina, was formed under the leadership of the self-styled *Poglavnik* Ante Pavelić, backed by his brutal fascist Ustasha forces. The NDH joined the Tripartite Pact on 10 April: ostensibly independent, it was in effect a German satellite and was split into areas of German and Italian influence. Slovenia was partitioned between Germany and Italy. The Italians annexed a strip of the Dalmatian coast and some of the Adriatic islands, and occupied Montenegro where they made an abortive attempt to

establish a client monarchy. Serbia suffered the greatest dismem-
berment. All the territorial claims of its neighbours were granted: in
the south most of Macedonia was annexed by Bulgaria, the western
part of Macedonia and Kossovo was claimed by Italian-occupied
Albania, and in the north the Vojvodina was annexed by Hungary.
The Germans occupied the remainder of Serbia and the northern
part of Kosovo where the Trepča and Mitrovica mines are situated,
eventually establishing a puppet government under General Milan
Nedić, a former Yugoslav minister of war, in August 1941.

The news which emerged from Yugoslavia, usually brought out
by refugees, painted a grim picture of cruelty and deprivation in the
dismembered country. There were dreadful stories of the mistreat-
ment and malnourishment endured by captured Yugoslav military
personnel—and their families—as they were marched away to prison
camps. Even worse were the stories of Ustasha persecution and
massacres of the Serbs living in the NDH. Pavelić's policy decreed
that of the 2 million Serbs in the NDH, one third were to be forc-
ibly converted from Eastern Orthodox Christianity to Roman
Catholicism, one third were to be expelled to Serbia, and the remaining third were to be killed. The latter task was undertaken by
the Ustashas with a ferocity that horrified the German and Italian
authorities, and many NDH Serbs fled to the Italian zone for protection. Others, not waiting for expulsion, fled to Serbia where
their stories exacerbated the fear and unrest already generated by
the German occupation. The Ustashas declared the Muslims to be
Croats, in the same way that the Nazis had decreed the Slav Croats
to be honorary Germans, but followed the Nazi example in their
treatment of Jews and Gypsies. By the end of the war over 90 per
cent of Yugoslav Jews had perished.[1]

After leaving Yugoslavia King Peter and his ministers had made
their way from Athens to the Middle East, and from there to London in June 1941, where they were welcomed as heroes because they
had, apparently, defied the Axis. Sir George Rendel was appointed
British minister to the Yugoslav government in exile (YGE). When
news of the massacres reached the YGE, it added to existing problems which there had been no time to resolve between the coup
and invasion, created divisions between Serb and Croat members,
and produced a cabinet crisis. Serb ministers wanted to publish

reports of the atrocities and have the whole Croatian nation denounced. Croat ministers argued that, if the reports were true, responsibility lay with a few hirelings of Pavelić, and that real Croatian feelings were represented by Vladko Maček, leader of the Croatian Peasant Party, who steadfastly refused to co-operate with either the Germans or Italians.[2] Maček had stayed in Yugoslavia after the invasion and his deputy Juraj Krnjević was a member of the YGE.

There was a feeling among the Serbs that the military debâcle had, in part, been due to betrayal by Croatian members of the armed forces, and the wholesale murder of the Serb population of the NDH appeared to be proof of this betrayal. Simović even went so far as to ask the British to bomb Zagreb. This suggestion did not go down well at the Foreign Office, and did little to enhance Simović's standing. At the time of the coup, SOE had expressed doubts about Simović's leadership, but noted there was little alternative. Since his arrival in London there had been growing doubts at the FO about his capacity to maintain unity in his cabinet. George Rendel, newly appointed British minister to the YGE, noted that the Yugoslav view in London was that Simović had achieved the almost impossible task of uniting the cabinet—against himself; while his handing-over of control to Kalafatović and swift departure was regarded by some Serb émigrés in the Middle East as a dereliction of duty.[3] Douglas Howard, head of the FO Southern Department, noted that the proposed bombing of Zagreb was 'typical of the muddled thinking for which General Simovitch is becoming famous',[4] and, even if it were possible, such action would merely serve to alienate the pro-Allied Croats. However, the FO concluded that there was really no-one to replace Simović and, as he had been portrayed in the British press as the symbol of Yugoslav unity, the British government had no option but to continue its support of him.[5] Throughout the war, the British regarded the eventual reconstruction of Yugoslavia as essential—a factor which was to be a very strong influence in their subsequent policy.

The FO was not entirely convinced about the scale of the reported massacres, and Orme Sargent, deputy under-secretary at the FO, warned that the sources were entirely Serb, and it would be unwise to accept their veracity without further confirmation.[6]

Hugh Seton-Watson, in the Istanbul SOE office, wrote that in his dealings with Serb émigrés he had detected a definite drive against Slovenes and Croats, and the exploitation of every item regarding Ustasha atrocities to prejudice the British government against the Croats.[7] Seton-Watson was later accused of being pro-Croat, an accusation he vigorously denied, claiming that this idea had been fostered by lies and intrigues against him in Cairo.[8] Sandy Glen however, recalled that in the atmosphere of tension which prevailed in Yugoslavia immediately before the war, it had become very easy to take sides: he had taken the side of the Serbs, which led him into disputes with Seton-Watson and Stephen Clissold of SIS. From evidence in the SOE files it is clear that Seton-Watson did want to play down Ustasha atrocities but was very keen to maximize coverage of German war crimes against the Serbian population.

As well as stories of atrocities, news of widespread revolts against the occupying forces had been filtering out of Yugoslavia during the summer of 1941, which was much more welcome news. The British were heartened to hear of large-scale uprisings (as distinct from the underground resistance in France, or the civil disobedience in the Netherlands for example) in Hitler's 'Fortress Europe'. What they failed to understand at this point was that the Yugoslav resistance was not a co-ordinated continuation of the April campaign, but a series of localized and independent actions in response to particular hardships and persecutions. The only common denominator was the predominantly Serbian nature of the revolts, since it was the Serbs who suffered the greatest hardships and the greatest losses.[9]

The Yugoslav collapse had been so swift that the invaders had not been able to round up all members of the armed forces and many evaded capture and took to the mountains and woods. There they formed groups of military chetniks, based on the chetniks of the First World War in Serbia who carried out sabotage behind enemy lines. One of the leaders of these groups was Colonel Dragoljub (Draža) Mihailović, who planned to lie low until his forces could make a major contribution against the Axis in concert with the Allies. There were also the patriotic organizations or civilian chetniks, grouped around local *vojvodas* (leaders) who played an important part in local politics and social organization in the inter-war years.

Head of the Chetnik Association in Serbia was *Vojvoda* Kosta
Pećanac, a right-wing veteran of the first war whose own chetnik
band became openly collaborationist with the Axis occupiers.
There were in addition a vast number of groups who called themselves chetniks as a cover for being out and out bandits. In autumn
1941 General Nedić created his own 'legal chetniks' to restore civil
order and make the German occupation of Serbia easier. These
were a mixed bag, officially collaborationist there were some who
were just biding their time to fight against the occupiers but in the
interim were not averse to drawing a regular wage to feed their
families and guarantee them a reasonable degree of security. Once
Mihailović raised his standard many felt that their long term loyalties and interests lay with him, albeit secretly for the moment.

Not surprisingly, the first uprising occurred in the NDH in self-
defence against Ustasha persecution. The Croat exiles in London
were right in their assertion that the Ustashas were a minority;
because there were too few of them to carry out the elimination of
the Orthodox Serb population efficiently they enlisted local
Muslims to help and added an extra layer of internecine hatred.
These Ustasha auxiliaries were also a minority and were denounced
by Muslim leaders and intellectuals, but terror was met by counter-
terror and retaliatory massacres by the Serbs in Bosnia-Herzegovina.

In their portion of Slovenia the Germans immediately implemented a policy of germanization with mass deportations to Serbia
and Croatia of Slovenes not assessed as suitable citizens of the Third
Reich. It was this that sparked off opposition in Slovenia.

Serbia itself was in a state of chaos: the occupation was brutal,
food was short, and the horrific tales of refugees from the NDH
added to the general feeling of desperation. The German invasion
of the USSR on 22 June 1941 produced a spontaneous uprising,
encouraged by the fact that many frontline German divisions had
been withdrawn to the east, leaving less effective troops to man the
occupation. The Yugoslav Communist Party, which had at first agi-
tated against war and then kept a low profile, also joined the risings.
The attack on the USSR had inspired similar revolts against the
Axis throughout Europe: as in Yugoslavia, communists joined the
fight partly to aid the USSR, and partly in the expectation of early
assistance from the Soviets. The military chetniks and Mihailović,

who had been establishing their organization and carrying out sabotage until this point, had no choice but to join in the summer
uprising once it had started in order to defend the civilian population from the brutal reprisals used by the Germans as a cost-effective
way of fighting the insurgency.

Initially Montenegro was quiet as the Italian regime promoted a
friendly and civilized occupation, ensuring food supplies and security for the population. The Italians also attempted to protect Serbs
from Ustasha atrocities in their areas of influence. But on 12 July the
Italians proclaimed the Independent State of Montenegro at the
capital Cetinje, and an uprising started the following day. Resentment of the Italian attempt to create a separate Montenegro when
the people had emotional ties to the idea of being part of Serbia was
compounded by the experiences of refugees from the NDH, and
the Orthodox Serbs who had fled into Montenegro to escape persecution by the Albanian population of Kosovo. The uprising was
orchestrated by chetnik bands, many led by regular military officers,
and it took the Italians a month to restore order. After this the Italians withdrew into garrison towns and the chetniks mainly took to
the countryside. It was at this point that the communists decided
that the time was ripe for revolution. The Montenegrin communists pursued this with such vigour, destroying all symbols and records
of the old regime and murdering anyone who was a 'class enemy',
or just opposed to the communist excesses, that eventually the
Montenegrin chetniks fought against them to defend the civilians.
It did not take the Italian military governor long to realize that arming the chetniks meant he did not have to fight either the communist or nationalist opposition, a risky policy but one that was likely
to cause less problems for his limited occupying forces than the
German attrition in Serbia.

Members of the exiled Yugoslav government regarded news of
the revolts with rather mixed feelings. On the one hand it enhanced
their standing as allies; on the other, accompanying reports of reprisals for any anti-Axis action alarmed the Serb ministers, while the
emphasis on the predominantly Serbian nature of resistance made
the Croat ministers even more uncomfortable. This discomfort was
to increase once the myth of Draža Mihailović was set in motion.

Much was made of the revolts in newspapers and BBC broadcasts
to Yugoslavia itself—something which was not wholly welcome to

the Yugoslavs in London, or to those within Yugoslavia. The US secretary at the Belgrade legation, who left Yugoslavia on 12 July 1941, brought a message from a representative of the Serbian resistance begging the BBC and other elements of the propaganda machinery to cease all reference to the Serbian guerrillas in the hills of south Serbia, since this provoked the Germans to react with punitive expeditions. The US diplomat said he had been informed that the guerrilla bands were quite numerous, but their leaders had no intention of attacking the Germans until the latter's grip began to weaken. The Serbs had also requested more publicity for Ustasha atrocities, although they emphasized that it was to be made clear that these were committed by a minority led by Pavelić, not the Croats as a whole.[10]

Broadcasting stories about the resistance not only conflicted with Yugoslav interests, but also with the prevailing SOE policy; this, ostensibly, was still one of encouraging the formation of secret armies in occupied countries, which, when the British returned to Europe, would provide local assistance by diversionary operations. PWE's 'black' propaganda radio station, Radio Šumadija (established in August 1941), urged restraint upon the insurgents, backing up General Simović's broadcasts to Yugoslavia in which he condemned premature risings for the reprisals these brought upon the civilian population. On 4 September Pierson Dixon of the FO Southern Department, having discussed the matter with the YGE, advised Ivone Kirkpatrick at the BBC that he should 'avoid as far as possible reproducing matter which would have the appearance of being designed to incite the population to continued resistance'.[11]

During August and September, the BBC played down the rising, but by October PWE could no longer resist the propaganda value of Mihailović. That summer he had sent messengers out of the country requesting help for his movement, and had also managed to make direct communication when his radio signals were picked up by the British naval monitoring station in Malta in August 1941. Since then, stirring stories of how he had refused to accept the capitulation, and taken to the woods to continue the struggle with likeminded members of the Yugoslav armed forces, had been appearing in the free world's press. Romantic articles were published, extolling the virtues and exaggerating the prowess of Mihailović as a resistance leader: these stirring stories had, apparently, originated with Raymond Brock, an American journalist in Istanbul.[12] PWE was keen to capitalize on this heroic image of Mihailović; in the early days of the war there was little to offer occupied peoples *except* propaganda. By the spring of 1942 Mihailović had been built up into the hero of European resistance, and was portrayed as a shining example to the rest of Europe. This image was also played back to Yugoslavia— regardless of the detrimental effect this might have on the position of the colonel and his forces. In November 1941 London SOE decided, when broadcasting a message of loyalty to King Peter, to use only Mihailović's name, despite the fact that he was the first of six signatories.[13]

Despite the general philosophy of encouraging secret armies still enshrined in official SOE policy, and the apparent support for the YGE's desire to keep things quiet, policy regarding Yugoslavia was already shifting under the influence of events within the country and the British response to them. Churchill and Eden were both keen to encourage the revolts in Yugoslavia. In autumn 1941 the attitude to Yugoslav resistance was markedly different to that in other occupied countries: a factor which was to continue throughout the war, and possibly influence the eventual outcome of events in that country. Jebb, writing to Douglas Howard at the FO Southern Department on 2 December 1941 on the subject of sabotage and reprisals, refuted Simović's opinion that communist sabotage injured the Serbs without hurting the Germans. All sabotage, he wrote, disturbed the Axis, and reprisals were a double-edged sword: the more savage they were, the more recruits came to the resistance movement, 'the more they rouse the people and make them ready to accept any sacrifice'. (This, in a nutshell, was the policy of the communist resistance too.) However, Jebb went on to say:

This principle does not apply to countries where we are endeavouring to form subversive organisations on a large scale and where there has been no revolt up to now: but it certainly does apply to a country where operations versus the occupiers [have begun] ... only by hotting up the whole nation to murder Germans and Italians ... that revolt has any prospect of maintaining itself at all.[14]

The need to establish large scale secret armies had diminished since the entry of the USSR into the war as a British ally, and once the

United States was brought into the war by Japan's attack on Pearl Harbor in December 1941, the whole concept was entirely dead. Dalton and Jebb seem to have favoured the idea for a little longer, while the Yugoslav government and Mihailović adhered to it until almost the end of the war. The idea was in any case a flawed one since the 'detonator' policy of arming on a massive scale large underground organizations which would lie dormant until the British call to arms, had not really taken into account the practicalities of organizing and providing arms for these secret armies; neither did it recognize the diversity of opinions and aims of the many occupied peoples, or the fact that *their* long-term objectives might differ from those of the British.

SOE officers in the Middle East and Istanbul also welcomed news of the summer uprisings and were keen to capitalize on them. Having left no stay-behind team, and not having heard from any of its agents, SOE had to rely on refugees and messengers coming out of Yugoslavia with information on what was happening there in terms of resistance—both actual and potential. Before he left for London Simović, and also representatives of Greek and Bulgarian exiles, had agreed to authorize SOE to work with underground movements in the Balkans.[15] There was little opportunity for action, however, until hard and fast news was received in Istanbul in June–July 1941. A variety of names of leaders of local guerrilla bands emerged and Bailey, in charge of the SOE Balkan section in the Middle East, suggested that SOE should build up centres of resistance in the Balkans and influence their character by the supply of arms, money and political guidance. Jovan Djonović arrived in Istanbul in June to establish an intelligence centre on behalf of the YGE: he had been an SOE contact in Belgrade and continued to work closely with the organization in Istanbul. Djonović and SOE concurred on the urgency of infiltrating someone into occupied Yugoslavia.

Two notable sources of information for SOE were Stanislav Rapotec, a Slovene reserve infantry lieutenant, and Dragomir Rakić, a Serb industrialist. Both made their way separately to Istanbul, where they contacted Djonović. Rapotec arrived in Istanbul at the end of June 1941, having left Split two weeks earlier with instructions from an underground organization being formed there to contact the government in exile and ask its members to provide direction for the opposition to the occupiers. En route Rapotec had visited Ljubljana, Zagreb and Belgrade, contacting many other potential resisters, including a variety of politicians and disaffected members of the NDH army. In Belgrade he had heard from a friend that Colonel Mihailović had not surrendered, but instead had formed a resistance movement in Serbia. Rapotec had also been instructed to contact the British with a plan to deliver by British submarine the means of establishing a radio link with Split.[16]

Rakić arrived in Istanbul at the end of July, bringing news of two resistance groups operating in Serbia. One was led by Colonel Mihailović and a number of other officers, who were creating a military organization in western Serbia, with their headquarters on the Suvobor plateau. The other was led by communists, and their anti-Axis activity was resulting in reprisals of one hundred Serbian lives for each German one. Colonel Popović, the director of Yugoslav military intelligence in Cairo, had, apparently, also heard of the two movements in Serbia from two Polish officers who had come to the Middle East via Yugoslavia. Mihailović appealed, through Rakić , for funds with which to keep his organization afloat, as he was paying local peasants for supplies for his men. As a result of this appeal, Djonović asked SOE for a loan.[17]

Djonović suggested enlisting Soviet help to get back into Yugoslavia as he already had some useful Russian contacts. Bailey endorsed this plan, as he felt it essential to involve the Soviets at an early stage, while they were still fighting for their lives, rather than later when, if the tide turned in their favour, they might be more difficult to work with. London SOE agreed on this policy, and plans for missions to Yugoslavia were put in train. John Bennett, who was responsible for SOE Yugoslav operations in the Middle East, left Jerusalem and met Djonović in Istanbul on 4 August 1941 to discuss the plans: the latter arranged a meeting with a Soviet agent named Nikolaev. Djonović already had two people earmarked for the mission—Dušan Radović and Vasilije Trbić . Radović was a retired air force colonel and Trbić was a former commander of Serbian irregulars in the wars with Turkey in Macedonia, who later became a politician—first as a Radical representative and then as a member of the Yugoslav National Party in opposition to Stojadinović's pro-German government.

It appears that at this juncture Djonović and his organization were following their own inclinations and formulating their own plans, without necessarily referring to the YGE. Rapotec was surprised at how critical Djonović was of Simović's leadership, and at Trbić's antagonism towards both the political and military leaders, whom he blamed for the April debacle. Djonović's negotiations with Nikolaev seem to have been underway for some time before the YGE representatives in Cairo, or Simović in London, were made aware of them; although Djonović later claimed to have appraised the Yugoslav vice-premier, Slobodan Jovanović, of his intentions at an early stage. While the plans were being formulated, Simović met Taylor and Masterson in London to discuss Mihailović's secret base at Subovor, and a few days later Bailey reported that a courier was being despatched to ascertain the location of the landing ground there and was expected to return to Istanbul in about ten days.[18] Although keen to utilize Soviet help to get back into Yugoslavia, London SOE instructed Bailey not to deal directly with the Soviets in Istanbul for fear of upsetting the neutral Turks; the matter was to be handled by the SOE mission in Moscow. While waiting to hear the outcome of the Moscow negotiations Bailey wrote a report on 31 August assessing that the best option was to send a mission by air and/or submarine from Cairo. On 5 September, Julian Amery now in Cairo SOE, asked for Radović and Trbić to go to Cairo right away, to be sent in 'next week'. On the very next day, Nikolaev came up with the offer of an immediately available 'plane, capable of taking eight. At a meeting between Nikolaev, Djonović, Bailey and Bennett on 6 September, it was decided that Radović should go to Moscow and from there fly to Suvobor. He was to be accompanied by a British officer, a wireless operator and four Yugoslav airforce personnel from Amman and to contact resistance bands in Montenegro, Macedonia and the Sandjak. Meanwhile Trbić was to proceed to Cairo and, accompanied by a British officer and a wireless operator, go into Yugoslavia from the other direction. Thus two missions would be en route simultaneously. On 7 September Bailey commended this plan to Baker Street: he and the Yugoslavs in Istanbul were very enthusiastic about sending a mission via the USSR.[19] They thought it would be a useful demonstration of Anglo-Russian co-operation, but at the same time limit possible Russian intentions.

While Djonović and the SOE agents in Istanbul had been beavering away at organizing these missions, there were other events afoot on the British and Yugoslav political front. In the summer of 1941 there was a major shake-up in progress in Cairo SOE: the first of many as it turned out. In late May, Eden had shown Dalton a private wire from General Wavell to General Dill, saying SOE Middle East was 'a racket'. There were allegations of corruption and inefficiency, conflicts with other services and internal feuds between SO1 and SO2. The problems between SO1 and SO2 stemmed from rivalry over who should control black propaganda; in January 1941 Dalton had instructed Pollock to take charge of both branches and unite them into one organization. He had failed to do this, leaving the way open for turf wars between them. Oliver Lyttelton, minister of state in the Middle East was highly critical of the lack of security, waste and ineffectiveness of SOE Cairo, and had even threatened court martial for some of its members.[20] GHQ Middle East pressed Dalton ever more urgently to address the problem and eventually Dalton sent Sir Frank Nelson himself to investigate.

After two false starts Terence Maxwell, a peacetime banker, was chosen to take over command of SOE Cairo from George Pollock: Dalton commented on his appointment that he had heard Maxwell was "good at Augean stables".[21] At the end of July, Maxwell, accompanied by Sir Frank Nelson and Bickham Sweet-Escott, left for Cairo. On their arrival Sir Frank Nelson was presented with a file purportedly containing incontestable proof of the allegations against SOE. According to Sweet-Escott the contents of the file was actually mere gossip and hearsay, combined with copies of reports and telegrams filched from SOE files. The latter, he concluded, had been the work of two SOE people who were working for GHQ: 'it looked very much as if a spy had been deliberately planted on us by the soldiers', an act which he described as symptomatic of the poisonous atmosphere existing in the secret and semi-secret departments of Cairo in the summer of 1941, and which continued during the following two years.[22]

The 'spy' was in fact the Countess of Ranfurly, aided by Bill Stirling, brother of David Stirling who founded the SAS. Lady Ranfurly had gone to the Middle East to be near her husband, who was with the Sherwood Foresters in the desert, and the only way that she could stay in Cairo was to find some useful employment. In November 1940 the chairman of Shell Oil had recommended her to SOE where her secretarial skills were very useful. Initially pleased to be able to remain in Cairo and have a well-paid job, she soon found that working for the organization raised all sorts of doubts as to the validity of its actions and the probity of her fellows there. In March 1941 she warned Eden—while he was in Cairo attempting to influence events in Yugoslavia—that there was something fishy at the SOE offices. By early May she was certain that the whole show was rotten and confided her fears to General Wavell, C-in-C Middle East, whose house-guest she happened to be at the time. As SOE did not come under the War Office, he could take no direct action, but shared her doubts about the organization's security and asked her to copy any suspicious documents. This she managed by secreting papers in her bra before leaving the office each evening and typing copies before returning the originals on the following morning. Bill Stirling passed the copies to Wavell's chief of staff. It was Lady Ranfurly's file of copied papers on which Lyttelton based his case against Cairo SOE.[23]

Sweet-Escott felt that most of the problem stemmed from SOE's critics failure to fully understand its functions. Artemis Cooper, in her fascinating portrait of wartime Cairo, attributes Lady Ranfurly's suspicions to anxiety over her husband, who had been taken a prisoner of war, and to comparisons of his plight with the 'good-time Charlies' in Cairo SOE.[24] In fact, SOE did not have a monopoly on 'good-time Charlies', and life in wartime Cairo at times seems to have been one long party if one moved in the right circles and had adequate funds. The BBC's Richard Dimbleby got into hot water for wanting to broadcast a radio article critical of the hedonistic lifestyle of staff officers at Command HQ. They spent their days playing polo and their nights at parties: their cult of foppish dressing, with uniforms tailored from the finest cloth, had given Dimbleby his theme of 'the gaberdine swine'. At about the same time an army film unit, charged with producing a documentary about British military life in Cairo, had to *stage* a crowd scene as no-one worked regular hours—they simply drifted into their GHQ offices (known as 'Grey Pillars') at any time between eight and noon. A favourite haunt of both SOE and regular officers was the bar of Shepheard's

Hotel. It was here that Captain Mike Lees, in search of excitement, later heard of SOE's existence from an inebriated SOE officer (known to the military as 'the cloth cap boys') and, after getting instructions on how to find its offices from the barman, found his way there and wangled himself into the organization.[25] If the barman had not known the location, then most Cairo taxi drivers could have driven him to the 'secret offices', while outside a street vendor called his wares—'Newspapers, cigarettes, OBEs'.[26]

Despite Sweet-Escott's opinion that the allegations were predominantly baseless gossip, Nelson assessed, after discussions with Lyttelton and General Auchinleck (who had succeeded General Wavell as C-in-C), that the services no longer had confidence in SOE, and that a major reorganization was needed to repair the damage. Accordingly the heads of SO1 and SO2, and a number of their subordinates were immediately posted back to Britain, leaving Maxwell in charge of both branches. His position was complicated by the fact that he was new to SOE and had neither of his predecessors on hand to brief him on the current situation. It was at this point that SOE moved into Rustem Buildings, which was immediately dubbed 'Red Pillars'. The local taxi drivers soon got used to this new location.

Sweet-Escott stayed on temporarily to help Maxwell on the propaganda side, and at this point G(R)—SOE's military counterpart in the Middle East—was amalgamated with SOE Cairo, and Colonel Terence Airey became Maxwell's chief of staff. Tom Masterson was sent from Britain to organize political action. Policy-making was still the domain of the Minister of Economic Warfare, but actual operations were to be approved by the C-in-C Middle East, while the newly-formed Middle East Defence Committee (MEDC) presided over by Lyttelton the minister of state, was, in principle, a safeguard against activities which could have undesirable political implications. When Nelson returned to London, Dalton was very pleased with his reorganization, and the fact that he had won Lyttelton over. However, Sweet-Escott noted that while the principle of the new structure *sounded* fine, in practise it was not such an easy matter to co-ordinate the demands of the military and political bodies: 'Perhaps it would have solved the problem if there had been anyone in Cairo or London who was in a position to balance short-term military advantage against long-term political disadvantage'.[27] This was a defect which was to complicate matters in future SOE dealings with Yugoslavia.

Before the dust had settled on the SOE shake-up in Cairo, Julian Amery arrived to try to organize the mission to Yugoslavia. Maxwell still had his hands full with administrative matters and was not fully cognisant of the situation in Yugoslavia, and Masterson, who was to be Bailey's successor, had not yet arrived. As Amery tells it, he wrote to his father Leo Amery—Secretary of State for India—emphasizing the importance of immediate action to avoid the risings petering out for lack of external support, and that it was thanks to his father's intercession that a submarine was made available for the mission.[28] Probably Amery is claiming rather more credit here than can actually be ascribed to his influence. (Another SOE officer recalls the raised eyebrows caused by him, then twenty-two years old, emerging from a meeting at Rustem Buildings and announcing that he was off to contact the cabinet.[29]) In addition, according to Amery's own memoirs, he was doing a fairly passable imitation of a Cairo 'good-time Charlie' himself.

Simović, after receiving Rapotec's preliminary report from Istanbul, approached Churchill on 14 August and again on 22 August, asking for a British submarine to go to Split to establish communications with the people Rapotec represented there.[30] Churchill asked Dalton what could be done to help the Yugoslav guerrillas, and two days later, was informed that plans were underway, and £20,000 in gold—presumably the loan requested by Djonović—was being sent to Mihailović by courier from Istanbul. In the meantime, Bailey's report of 31 August from Istanbul recommending the air and submarine route via Cairo also probably played a part in getting things moving.

One way or another, Amery and Bennett, who had returned from Istanbul, now had a submarine at their disposal, and a codename for the mission—'Bullseye'—but no men. Trbić, on arriving in Cairo and discovering that the means of transportation was submarine—rather than aeroplane—and the destination was Montenegro, flatly refused to go. Finding a British officer for the mission was no problem: D.T. 'Bill' Hudson had already volunteered to go with Trbić and Radović from Istanbul. When nothing appeared to come of this, Hudson, fed up of hanging about doing nothing in Istanbul, had worked his way back to Egypt, arriving in Cairo in early September. He had been there a few days when he was called on for the Bullseye mission at literally 24 hours notice. Hudson had been a mining engineer in Yugoslavia, spoke passable Serbo-Croatian, was a long-standing member of Section D/SOE, and had carried out some useful sabotage before leaving the country in a hurry in February 1941, after blowing up an Italian ship in Split harbour.[31]

Amery and Bennett went to see Colonel Popović in Cairo, who—with the aid of Generals Ilić and Mirković—supplied the three Yugoslav members of Bullseye: Majors Lalatović and Ostojić and Sergeant Dragićević as the W/T operator, all Serbs from Montenegro.[32] When Amery left with the team by air for Malta to join the submarine, he was under the impression that Radović's joint Yugoslav, British and Soviet mission was also on the way.

This was not the case. It appears that the projected mission in co-operation with the Soviets came to naught, in part due to the personal antagonism of Simović towards Dušan Radović. A pre-war falling out between the two men seems to have been compounded by Radović's criticism of the other's conduct of the Yugoslav campaign, and of the failure of Simović and Ilić, Yugoslav minister of war in Cairo, to make use of the Yugoslav military personnel who had escaped to the Middle East. The plan was fairly well advanced when Simović began to cast doubts on Radović's reliability and loyalty. The first hint of trouble came at a meeting on 8 September between SOE London and Radoje Knežević, minister for the king's household and brother of Živan, to discuss the two planned missions and obtain authorization for Yugoslav personnel to accompany Radović. Knežević mentioned some personal dissentions between Radović and Simović, and a few days later suggested that SOE might get around the problem by not mentioning Radović by name, but simply to ask Simović to authorize Djonović to use his own discretion. This did not come off, as on the same day Ilić wrote to Simović complaining about 'English' interference and complicity with Radović and his friends in the Bosnian Peasant Party.[33]

The Yugoslavs in the Middle East were becoming irritated by constant requests from various British secret organizations for personnel to send on missions, and Ilić suggested that liaison should be through *one* officer—his choice being Bailey. More importantly, he wanted the 'English' to give an undertaking not to do anything within Yugoslavia without first consulting the YGE, since precipitate action ran the risk of reprisals which might undermine the long-term potential of Yugoslav resistance. SOE was not at all inclined to consult the YGE on their operations in Yugoslavia, preferring to have a free hand there. After some discussion it was decided that the best policy was to carry out projects discretely so that Ilić would not know of them. However, the cat was already out of the bag regarding this project, and as Simović had clearly demonstrated that his differences with Radović were irreconcilable, he had even suggested that the latter was in the pay of the enemy, SOE did not want to upset the YGE by appearing to encourage Djonović and Radović to act independently of their own government.[34]

In spite of this decision Radović, with the connivance of Bailey, had travelled to the USSR in the second half of September in preparation for his return to Yugoslavia. On instructions from Baker Street SOE Moscow had called a halt to the flight, but this left Radović cooling his heels in Moscow, becoming ever more restless and suspicious, while SOE debated what to do with him. One thing was certain—that he should under no circumstances be allowed to return to Turkey, presumably for fear of his intriguing with Djonović, and Ilić would allow him to go to Cairo only if he was to be employed by the British. Radović did not favour this himself but contemplated joining the Soviet airforce: SOE did not trust the 'Russians', believing they might return him to Turkey or send him into Yugoslavia. Peter Boughey, an old Belgrade hand now SOE's liaison officer with the YGE, felt that sending him into Yugoslavia was probably the best solution as he was friendly with Mihailović and could be useful, and anyway Simović would not count for much by the war's end. There was in fact a rumour in Moscow diplomatic circles that Simović was about to be replaced by Milan Gavrilović, and Radović had asserted that he would be willing to co-operate with the latter if this was the case. Jimmy Pearson, head of the Balkan and Middle East desk at Baker Street, did not care for this particular sort of political skulduggery but suggested some of his own: one solution he proposed was to double cross Radović by sending a reassuring message purporting to come from Ilić and allowing *him* to deal with Radović when he turned up in Cairo.[35] With all these machinations, it is hardly surprising that the Soviets went cold on the idea of the joint mission, and a subsequent offer of replacement personnel from Ilić was rejected when London and Moscow SOE attempted to revive the idea.

The episode seems to have provided further ammunition to use against Simović. King Peter, trying to persuade George Rendel, British minister to the YGE, that Slobodan Jovanović should replace Simović as premier, accused the latter of having muddled everything. As an example he quoted 'a recent case in which a scheme to drop two agents into Yugoslavia from the air had been indefinitely held up and eventually allowed to miscarry'.[36]

Even so, with or without the participation of Radović, it is possibly questionable whether the YGE shared Djonović and SOE's enthusiasm for the joint venture. In view of the news of a communist resistance developing within Yugoslavia, the YGE might have been naturally cautious about Soviet participation.

Hudson's brief was to discover what was happening in Yugoslavia and to co-ordinate all forces of resistance he encountered there. Amery implies that the whole purpose of the Bullseye mission was to make contact with Mihailović.[37] In fact, as well as being instructed to gather information on the situation in Yugoslavia, Hudson was also told to contact various people known to SOE before the invasion. These included Colonel Radonić, whom Hudson discovered to be in prison, and Dule Dimitrijević, a veteran of the *Narodna Odbrana*; Hudson reported that the latter would make a popular leader in Bosnia and other regions.[38] Amery also asked Hudson to contact some Albanians with whom he had been involved in pre-war Belgrade when trying to organize a revolt against the Italian occupation in Albania. If Mihailović's name was mentioned to Hudson before he left Cairo, it was one among many: it was not until he had been in the country for some time that he was told to contact Colonel Mihailović and his COS Colonel Pavlović; they were transmitting uncoded messages, and Hudson was to go to Suvobor and provide them with secure codes.[39] Because Amery, on setting out for the Montenegrin coast, was still under the impression that the mission via the USSR was also en route—specifically bound for Mihailović's HQ at Suvobor—it would have been a pointless duplication to send Hudson there too. It was only when the latter mission fell through that Hudson received the message to proceed to Suvubor. As Yugoslavia had been divided into so many parts—often along ethnic-religious lines—and the Axis occupiers were using the differences within the population to further their own ends, the success of Bailey's plan to influence the nature of Yugoslav resistance through practical support depended upon contacting *all* groups within the country; therefore Hudson was to contact all resistance, regardless of national, religious or political belief.

The Yugoslavs in the Bullseye team *were* apparently specifically instructed to go to Mihailović, and there has been much speculation on what other orders they were given. While travelling to Montenegro Amery tried to discover what private instructions Popović had given them: 'They did not give much away: but it was clear that the communist danger was very much in their minds'.[40] Popović later said that Ilić instructed him to explain the situation in Yugoslavia, and he included the information he had received from the Polish officers (namely the existence of a communist resistance), and 'exhorted the two officers to heed Serb interests'. Apparently Lalatović was told by Ilić 'to locate and assassinate a colonel and ensure the country welcomed back the exiled government'.[41] It seems that the colonel was Radović, so Ilić was also under the impression that the joint Soviet mission was going ahead and that Radović would soon be back in the country and, he thought, intriguing against Simović's government.

The speculation on the instructions to the Yugoslav members of Bullseye is reflected in some of the FO attitudes, where there was a certain degree of suspicion that the YGE was not telling the British all it knew about the situation within Yugoslavia (which it probably was not). The British were inclined to the opinion that they were the senior members of the Yugoslav-British relationship and therefore could call the shots. This was apparent in Amery's attempts to ascertain private aspects of the Yugoslav briefing, later the insistence that Mihailović, by then a minister in the Yugoslav government, should only communicate with his government via SOE, and eventually the British pressing Tito upon King Peter. The British desire to be in the driving seat meant that the autonomy of the YGE was in many respects constantly assailed.

From the outset SOE was concerned with fulfilling its *own* conception of how resistance in occupied countries should be managed, often, it seems, with little or no reference to the exiled governments in whose countries it was operating. Dalton's opinion was that exiled governments:

.... may be found not to have too much following when the storm breaks in their home lands. New men who have stayed and faced out the German occupation, and have bolder and more revolutionary ideas, may be preferred to those who have lived, not very dangerously, abroad.[42]

Nevertheless, the Bullseye mission was a joint co-operative venture with neither Hudson in command of the Yugoslavs or vice-versa. After his arrival, Hudson did his best to co-ordinate—and mediate between—the various strands of resistance, but this was easier said than done.

Despite the importance SOE attached to getting back into Yugoslavia, the first mission seems to have been a fairly ad hoc affair, and in many respects set the tone for subsequent missions. When the submarine *Triumph* reached the coast of Montenegro on 20 September 1941, Amery discovered that 'some staff officers in Cairo had unaccountably forgotten some essentials'; these ranged from field glasses for Hudson (the captain of the *Triumph* kindly donated his own), through harnessing to carry the heavy wireless set, to spare shirts and sticking plaster. The list of essentials supplied from the submarine's stores should possibly be born in mind when reading too much conspiracy into later missions receiving drops of left boots or snake-serum.

4

BACKING MIHAILOVIĆ: ONE SOE OFFICER AND NO SUPPLIES

After landing at Petrovac on the coast of Montenegro, the Bullseye mission first encountered the communist-led resistance. Among its members was an orthodox priest Hudson had known before the war in his days as a mining engineer. One of the priest's specialities had been blessing newly-constructed mine buildings—an essential service since the locals refused to use unblessed edifices. This had been quite a lucrative sideline for the priest who now greeted Hudson like a long-lost brother and assumed that he had come to join the Partisans. Hudson did spend some time with them, attempting to arrange a supply drop, and following up on the people Amery had asked him to contact. Majors Lalatović and Ostojić went, as soon as they could, to Mihailović's headquarters, and Hudson eventually followed them there after Cairo's instructions to take secure codes. On the way he stopped at the town of Užice, which was at the centre of territory 'liberated' by the communist resistance to meet their leader—Josip Broz, alias Tito.[1]

Following the uprisings in summer 1941 the communist and non-communist forces had been co-operating in joint actions against the Axis, and a large area in western Serbia had been 'liberated' in a series of attacks by one or both resistance movements. Hudson's arrival coincided with the start of the breakdown in co-operation between the two, which had always been a fairly fragile arrangement in any case. As the relationship deteriorated, minor clashes and disputes over liberated areas and chains of command turned into outright antagonism and open hostility.

Quite simply, the objectives of Tito and the communists on the one hand, and Mihailović and other Yugoslav officers on the other, were totally incompatible. The latter mistrusted the political commissars who were attached to every communist fighting unit, and objected to the propaganda they disseminated wherever they went. Even more of an anathema was the Partisan tactic of destroying land records and eliminating local notables in an attempt to sweep away the old order to make way for a new communist order. Tito was keen to use the experience of the trained soldiers of the old Yugoslav army, but wanted them to act under his direction to further his revolutionary aims rather than fight for the reinstatement of the king and exiled politicians. There was also the question of reprisals: the Germans, hard pressed and undermanned at the beginning of the revolts, had implemented a policy of executing 100 civilians for each German soldier killed and fifty civilians for each one wounded. The communist leadership was not swayed by this: people escaping from such fearful retribution made useful recruits, and the breakdown of normal society and its regular pattern is one of the keystones of revolution. The reaction of the mainly Serb Yugoslav officers and Mihailović was entirely the opposite: German reprisals, coupled with the loss of Serb lives in Pavelić's NDH, aroused fears of ethnic extinction. It was regarded as too high a price to pay for short term gains in actions that were hard to sustain, before positive aid from the Allies could be looked for to drive out the occupiers completely. Their whole philosophy was geared towards the preservation of the traditions and lives of the Serbian people. Soon after his arrival, Hudson assessed Mihailović's policy as one of becoming increasingly a shield for the populace. When Tito and Mihailović met on 19 September 1941, Mihailović proposed that the uprising should be brought to an end: he also demanded that the partisan forces come under his command as he was the legitimate leader of the remnants of the Yugoslav army. Tito refused, but wanted the two forces to act together and continue the uprising.[2]

In response to the guerrilla activity, in autumn 1941 the Germans launched an all-out attack on both resistance movements in Serbia, in an effort to crush opposition once and for all. Reinforcements were brought in, and towns and villages in the 'liberated' areas were soon retaken, followed by appalling reprisals against their civilian populations. In October the Germans shot 1,755 people in Kraljevo

Above King Peter taking the oath after the *coup d'état*, 27 March 1941. In the group behind Peter, General Dušan Simović, head of the new government, stands on the far right and Slobodan Jovanović next to him. *Below* Scenes of celebration in Belgrade after the coup—a portrait of Peter is attached to the car radiator.

LE NOUVEL ORDRE DANS LES BALKANS.

Contrasting scenes of the Axis occupation. *Above* Citizens murdered by the Germans as an example immediately following the invasion, April 1941. *Below* Italians interrogating a Yugoslav prisoner, September 1941.

General Draza Mihailović.

Above Eager recruits addressed by the General. *Below* Swearing an oath of allegiance to King Peter and Mihailović in Serbia.

Above Group of cavalry officers in Serbia. *Below* Members of the British mission being entertained in a village.

Above Colonel A. B. Seitz of the OSS, part of the US mission to Mihailović's headquarters. *Below* Colonel Babić (second from *left*) with some of his staff and Captain J. A. Earle of the British military mission.

Axis "Wanted" notice offering a reward of 100,000 gold reichsmarks for the capture of both Tito and Mihailović reproduced in *Novo Vreme*, the paper published in Belgrade by the collaborationist Nedić government, 27 July 1943.

Above Josip Broz Tito speaking from the balcony of the National Theatre, Belgrade.
Below People in a Belgrade street on the same occasion.

and 2,778 males—many of them mere boys taken from their school-rooms—in Kragujevac.[3] Hudson witnessed the aftermath of the massacre and recalled: 'Morning and night was the most desolating atmosphere because the women were out in the fields and every sunrise and sunset you would hear the wails…lamentations for their dead. This had a very strong effect on Mihailović.'[4] The reprisals further exacerbated the differences between Mihailović's and Tito's policies, which were so apparent when they met for the second time on 26 October.

Hudson did his best to mediate between the two, apparently only arousing the antagonism of both sides, while the situation slipped into a state of civil war. In an attempt to bring this to a halt, or at least to not make matters worse, Hudson stopped the meagre flow of supplies from SOE.[5] Unfortunately he did not tell Mihailović and his followers that he had done so until they had waited for the whole of one night for a sortie to arrive, while the Germans approached from three sides and the Partisans attempted to close off the fourth side to prevent his escape. Mihailović and his people did manage to get away, but it was a close run thing and he was so furious with Hudson that, without Lalatović's intervention, he might have been tempted to shoot him.[6] Relations were already strained because of a dispute over radio codes; Hudson had given Mihailović the one as instructed by Cairo but had refused to hand over the code he used himself.

News of the developing civil war was greeted with dismay in London, and messages flew back and forth on the necessity for the two sides to settle their differences and concentrate on fighting the common enemy. In mid November 1941 the SOE analysis, based on Hudson's reports, was that the Partisan guerrillas were not actually communists themselves, but mostly comprised of local peasants who had rallied to them when they led the revolt in Montenegro. The chetnik bands, on the other hand, contained remnants of the regular Yugoslav army, and Mihailović had been recognized by the YGE as the leader of all forces in Yugoslavia. To support the Partisans would be tantamount to a repudiation of the exiled government, and in any case it was essential that the revolt should be seen as a fight for Yugoslavia by all Yugoslavs—rather than one engineered from Moscow and led by communists fighting for the Soviet

Union. It was also felt that Mihailović was the better standard-bearer of Yugoslav unity. If he was recognized by the British as well as by his own government, and supported by arms and money, he stood a far better chance of establishing undisputed authority than did the partisans. While acknowledging that there were problems, the SOE view was that British policy should be to back Mihailović. To reinforce this, it was also regarded as essential that Moscow should see this policy as being in the best interests of the USSR, and in their radio broadcasts encourage the partisans to rally to Mihailović's banner.[7]

On 22 November Mihailović sent his government a message in which he claimed: 'I have done everything and succeed in stopping this fratricidal war declared by the other side'.[8] Dalton was pleased that he had 'composed his quarrel' with the communists and now the civil war was over—or so the British thought—the question of getting supplies to Mihailović was treated as a matter of urgency. SOE was to provide all possible aid to Mihailović, not only to continue the fight against the occupiers, but to demonstrate to the partisans that he was receiving the support of the British, Yugoslav and Soviet governments. Rather ironically, in view of his deteriorating relationship with Mihailović, and the fact that the quarrel was far from composed, Hudson was given some of the credit for the two sides having reached an agreement. This probably reflected Dalton's desire to show the FO and other critics how useful SOE really could be, thereby justifying its existence. For something of the same reason, SOE was anxious for the revolt against the Axis to continue; while the British military regarded it as premature, they felt that since it had begun, it should be supported. Dalton pressed Eden to use his influence with the air ministry, as the aircraft SOE had available in Malta did not have the range to deliver supplies to Yugoslavia: bombers were needed to deliver them by parachute. With its usual efficiency, SOE had the supplies in Malta and the parachute containers in Britain. Eventually it was agreed to divert a Whitley at the expense of SOE operations in other countries, when a further plea from Mihailović to the YGE told of the desperate shortage of everything and the possibility that his followers would be forced to capitulate if supplies did not come soon.[9]

In the light of his desperate situation, and his perception of the communists as the greater threat because of the chaos they were intent on creating in the short-term, and their long-term political ambitions, Mihailović decided to parley with the Germans. The meeting was at Divci, on 11 November, with Lieut.-Colonel Kogard, head of German Military Intelligence in Belgrade, and Captain Dr Matl on the one side and Mihailović and three of his officers on the other. Mihailović emphasized that he was not offering to collaborate, but was simply asking for arms to fight the communists. Kogard demanded his unconditional surrender and the German police were about to arrest him when Matl intervened and insisted the German side should stick to their promise of safe conduct for the Yugoslav officers.[10]

Less than a month later, Mihailović and his closest associates narrowly escaped capture in a German attack, went to earth in the Serbian mountains, and disappeared from the airwaves for a month.[11] Some of his followers camouflaged themselves as members of Nedić's own forces. Other members of his forces returned quietly to their homes to await the next opportune moment to take action against the Axis. Winter, in any case, is not the season for guerrillas.

This was not an option open to Tito and his movement, which consisted of a large proportion of people who had lost their homes in the Ustasha persecutions in the NDH, and people from urban areas rather than from peasant communities. Tito's forces were also organized differently, retained as a large band in revolutionary manner so it was impossible to disguise them as ordinary local peasants. After the Germans had retaken Užice on 27 November he gathered his forces and left for the more remote and inaccessible mountainous area of the Sandjak, later moving on to south-eastern Bosnia. It was to take the Partisans three years to return to Serbia in any strength, and then only with a great deal of help from the Allies: first from the west and then from the advancing Red Army from the east.

Hudson was still attempting to reconcile the two resistance leaders, going to and fro between Tito and Mihailović's headquarters. He had gone to Užice, partly in the hope of finding power to operate his failing W/T set, and was with Tito when he decided to leave Serbia. Hudson, who went as far as the Sandjak with the Partisans, seems to have regarded the departure for Italian-held territory as running away, and announced that he would return to the Mihailović

camp to see what was happening there. The Bullseye W/T operator, Sergeant Dragićević, did not return with him, opting instead to
stay with the partisans: Hudson felt this was no loss since he suspected
him of sabotaging his set because of his pro-Partisan sympathies.[12]

Hudson's return coincided with the German attack on Mihailović's
HQ on Ravna Gora on 7–8 December, and when he caught up
with Mihailović on the Cemerno mountain he found that he was
persona non grata: his attempts at mediation, contacts with the partisans and cancellation of supply drops without warning, combined
with the desperate military situation led Mihailović to withdraw his
permission for Hudson's presence. Mihailović seemed to miss the
point that Hudson's return at this time was, in fact, an indication of
Hudson's confidence in him as opposed to Tito. For the next few
months Hudson had to fend for himself, living in a little village a
few miles from Mihailović's HQ, relying on local peasants for his
survival and with no means of contacting SOE Cairo, having buried
his radio on parting from Tito. Hudson heard that Mihailović refused
to see him because he had stopped British aid. When Mihailović
had informed his government and the British on 22 November
that he had ended the civil strife, a congratulatory message from the
British government was accompanied by a promise of supplies and
support, with the proviso that these were dependent upon maintenance of a united front under his leadership.[13] Knowing as he did
that the hard-core communists would *never* come under his leadership, and that the 'quarrel' had no hope of being composed, he
obviously did not want Hudson to relay this to SOE. Although
when Hudson's radio was found and dug up, it was returned to him
in early May 1942. Hudson was eventually readmitted to Mihailović's
company in June 1942, when he was promoted to major and
awarded the DSO, but the rift was more patched up than healed,
and the relationship between the two men was never warm. Hudson's time in the wilderness also left him disillusioned with SOE
and mistrustful of it.

Hudson's last broadcast had been on 19 October and once he had
gone off the air, SOE had lost its only link to an agent in Yugoslavia.
An attempt to infiltrate two Yugoslav teams by submarine in
November had been aborted just as the first team was about to dis-
embark on the Montenegrin coast where Hudson himself had

landed.[14] This was a great setback, as by the time the teams returned to the Middle East, Mihailović had also gone off the air for security reasons. During November, Ilić and Lyttelton had discussed the possibility of establishing a permanent link by air, as Simović was keen to use the Yugoslav air force pilots in the Middle East. They also discussed the feasibility of a Yugoslav-manned submarine operating on the Montenegrin coast, which Hudson's early reports had indicated was controlled by insurgents. Mihailović's last broadcast was on 6 December, leaving SOE with no idea of what had happened to the resistance or Mihailović and Hudson after the concerted Axis attack.

While the FO pressed the Admiralty to provide another submarine, Masterson asked Ilić to prepare teams to go in by air. The latter felt this was too risky a proposition, given the onset of winter and preferred to send them in by submarine.[15] By late December a compromise was agreed whereby two teams should go by air and two by submarine; British officers were to be attached to three of the teams, at the behest of Pierson Dixon at the FO.

On 17 January 1942 the submarine *Thorn* left Alexandria with missions 'Hydra' and 'Henna' aboard. Henna, which consisted of Rapotec and his W/T operator Sergeant Stevan Sinko, was landed on the island of Mljet in the early hours of 26 January, with the aim of reporting on Slovene patriotic organizations. Hydra, after a delay due to the full moon, disembarked on the Montenegrin coast near Petrovac on 4 February: the mission consisted of Major Terence Atherton, a journalist and Section D agent in pre-war Belgrade, Lieutenant Radoje Nedeljković of the Yugoslav air force, and W/T operator Sergeant Patrick O'Donovan. Their task was to report on the situation in Montenegro.[16] On the same day, 'Disclaim', the first airborne mission, parachuted into Bosnia near Sokolac: the mission was headed by Major Cavan Elliot, accompanied by Second Lieutenant Pavle Crnjanski, Sergeant Petar Miljković and Sergeant William Chapman (W/T). This team was almost immediately picked up by Domobrans—the local home guard—and handed over to the Germans in Sarajevo. The other airborne mission, led by Major Head was not sent, but on 28–29 April two Yugoslav sergeants— Milisav Bakić and Milisav Semiz—who had been placed at Masterson's disposal by Ilić and Popović, landed between Berane and Novi

Pazar on the borders of Montenegro and Bosnia, only to be arrested by the local quisling militia and given to the Germans.

The missions had been briefed by Ilić and John Bennett, head of SOE's Yugoslav desk in Cairo. They were told to contact resistance forces in the areas assigned to them, ascertain the situation of these forces, and provide what information they could on the strength and positions of the occupiers. They were also told to try to contact specific individuals, including important Yugoslav political figures and people known to SOE. It seems they were all instructed to contact Mihailović, though not necessarily to join him.

After a few days the Hydra team met the Jovan Tomasević partisan battalion and was taken to the headquarters of the Lovćen unit. There they were greeted with some suspicion, partly because of Hudson's departure from Tito's camp to return to Mihailović, and partly because the Partisans believed that the British and the Yugoslav government had sent orders to the chetniks in Montenegro *not* to co-operate with them, thereby causing them problems there. Nor were their suspicions lessened when Atherton named some of the people SOE had told him to contact. The commander of the Lovćen unit was instructed by the Partisans' Montenegrin High Command at Danilovgrad to isolate the mission from both partisans and peasants, and not to allow them to use their radio. They were taken to Danilovgrad and when they arrived there on 12 February the commander, Ivan Milutinović, was tempted to liquidate them as agents of the émigré government. But he contacted Supreme Command on 25 February and Tito ordered that they should be sent immediately to him, ensuring no contact was made with the chetniks in the meantime: 'Behave correctly—liquidation would indeed have had political complications. We have already informed [Comintern] and asked for explanation.'[17]

Milutinović also knew of Rapotec's and Sinko's landing on the Adriatic coast, and had ordered the Croat command to apprehend them. Meanwhile, Tito had heard of the arrest of the Disclaim mission. Having just managed to re-establish direct contact with the Comintern, Tito initially thought these missions might be a response to his request for help from the USSR, only to be disappointed to discover that the Comintern knew nothing of them. Tito suspected that the missions he had heard of were only the tip of the iceberg, and that as many as ten might have arrived in Yugoslavia. He thought they were responsible for encouraging chetniks to attack the Partisans, but this was not actually the case, it was a coincidence that the missions arrived at a time when the chetnik bands were more numerous and better organized than the Partisans, *and* attacking them when and wherever they could. A meeting of the Central Committee of the CPY on 4 April concluded that the 'English' were using their agents in Yugoslavia to foment discord between the Partisans and others. Their supposed aim was to create confusion and compromise the people's liberation struggle so that at a favourable moment, when the movement collapsed, the 'English' would land and appear as the saviours of Yugoslavia.

Despite these suspicions, and instructions to Partisan commands to find and isolate any such missions, Tito was very much aware of the political realities. The alliance of Britain, the United States and the USSR was always emphasized in all partisan dealing with the public;[18] while Tito would have preferred to receive Soviet missions, he would do his best to make the most of what he had. The missions, if possible, were to be convinced that it was the Partisans who were fighting the occupiers while the chetniks and Mihailović forces were collaborators.

Atherton, it seems, was given the full treatment on the latter points. He was taken on a tour of inspection by Moša Pijade of the partisan organization in Zabljak, Montenegro, and on the evening of his arrival at Tito's headquarters in Foča on 19 March, was shown what was claimed to be documentary proof of Mihailović's collaboration. Vladimir Dedijer, who kept the Partisan war diary, tells us these were documents captured on 14 March 1942 which showed that Mihailović's men were also Nedić men—an arrangement he claims to have been agreed secretly by the YGE. In early April Atherton was taken to inspect the front near Rogatica, to demonstrate that only the Partisan army was fighting. He was, in fact, exposed to the same sort of information and demonstrations that were to so impress F.W.D. (Bill) Deakin when the 'Typical' mission arrived just over a year later. Albeit that the latter landed in the middle of the Axis encirclement of the Partisans on Mount Durmitor when the Partisans, fighting for their lives, put up such a tremendous struggle against their enemies.

We shall never know if Atherton was as impressed as Deakin, or whether his reports to SOE would have echoed Deakin's enthusiasm for the Partisans, as Atherton never actually managed to get any messages out because his radio was not working. Tito told the Comintern on 24 March: 'The English mission is convinced that *all* chetniks are collaborating, directly or indirectly. Since it has no links with its own centre, has asked us to pass on information on the real situation.'[19] However, Tito did not allow Atherton and his companions access to his own radio links, probably because he did not want them to know he was in communication with the Comintern. It seems likely that Atherton *was* impressed by the partisans: the increasing quarrels between him and Nedeljković, the Yugoslav member of Hydra, seem to point to this. Nedeljković had been told to go to Mihailović, and part of his brief was to ascertain the level of support for the YGE in Serbia. On finally reaching Mihailović's headquarters he claimed that Atherton was promising support to the Partisans, which he regarded as an incitement to civil war.

Whether or not Atherton was totally convinced by all the partisan evidence, he told Tito that, having seen his forces in action, he now had to go and see the others who were fighting. Tito replied: 'That will be difficult, because there is no such thing.'[20] In spite of being 'advised' not to go to the chetniks, the mission secretly left Foča on the night of 15–16 April, with the aid of General Novaković (a regular officer who had become a local chetnik leader, and was also a 'guest' of the Partisans), and set out to find Mihailović and Hudson. As soon as the Partisan supreme command heard of the mission's departure they sent out units to search for them. On 22 April Atherton sent a letter to Mihailović, asking him to let Masterson know he was alive and would soon send more detailed information.[21] This was never forthcoming, as Atherton and O'Donovan were murdered shortly after this letter was written. Subsequent investigations (by Hudson, Mihailović, Bailey and the partisans) concluded that the culprit was Dakić, a local chetnik who had helped the party get away from the partisans. Dakić's motive was given as gain; SOE issued all officers going into Yugoslavia with 200 gold sovereigns and a variety of currencies, and this was why he had, apparently, murdered the two Britons. Later Dakić claimed that he shot them because he was afraid that Atherton, among a group of twenty-five hiding in a cave and impatiently wanting to make a break, would give the whole party away.[22]

When Nedeljković, who had separated from the others, reached the Pljevlja area commanded by Major Ostojić on 10 May, he reported that Atherton was a friend of the partisans. Major Ostojić, in a letter to Mihailović commented that this English officer was worse than Marko (Hudson's *nom de guerre*): that he had instructions to force a struggle against the occupation whatever the cost to the people, and seemed prepared to make a graveyard of the country on behalf of the 'English'. Ostojić also thought that there were possibly other missions in Yugoslavia without the knowledge of Mihailović and his forces and in his opinion the 'English' 'should be told we do not sell ourselves, and are not ready to die for other people's interests'.[23] Nedeljković said that Atherton had every intention of returning to the Partisans in Bosnia–Herzegovina and Montenegro, which was the area assigned to him by SOE, probably on the basis of Hudson's earlier reports of patriotic forces operating there. However, Atherton's secret departure had confirmed Tito's worst suspicions, and he said he wanted no more such missions. The Atherton affair coloured the attitude of Tito and the Partisans to the British who, they were convinced, held them responsible for his murder.

So far the attempts by SOE to aid the Yugoslav resistance had managed to alienate a number of potential allies, had achieved nothing in terms of opposing the Axis, and had thrown very little light on the situation in the country.

Most accounts of the early SOE missions, acknowledging their failure, tend to forget Rapotec's mission. In fact, although Rapotec was not an SOE agent, his mission was a joint SOE-Yugoslav venture and in terms of fulfilling his briefing was undoubtedly successful. Initially, he too had failed to make radio contact with Cairo, having lost his set in the perilous days following his arrival in the country, and having to leave his W/T operator Sinko on Mljet because he was sick. However, Rapotec managed to elude capture and travelled widely in Yugoslavia, establishing contacts with a variety of organizations and leaders opposed to both the occupiers and the Pavelić regime. He emerged in Turkey on 2 July 1942 with an enormous quantity of information, including details of Croatian and Slovenian resistance, and intimations that many members of the

NDH armed forces were not necessarily committed to Pavelić. Rapotec also carried a vast array of impressions and interpretations of the complexities and paradoxes prevailing in occupied Yugoslavia, particularly in the western regions. In addition, he brought with him codes from Mihailović and Trifunović-Birčanin, now in command of the Dalmatia and Herzegovina regions, for the YGE to communicate privately with them, if only an independent radio link could be set up. Ilić had stressed the importance of establishing links with Mihailović that bypassed the British when Rapotec set out.[24]

In Istanbul Rapotec had a short meeting with Basil Davidson, but did not tell him very much, regarding the information and messages he carried as primarily for the Yugoslav intelligence service and government. His return from Yugoslavia coincided with the 'great flap' in Cairo, when Rommel seemed poised to take Egypt; SOE papers were hurriedly being burned, and SOE Middle East was divided between Cairo and Jerusalem. On 11 July Cairo asked for Rapotec to be sent to the Jerusalem office as soon as possible. There is no record of his time in Jerusalem, but from there he went on to Cairo where he told SOE a little more, though still not all. Despite Rapotec's reserve, SOE produced two fairly lengthy reports, one penned by Davidson in Istanbul and the other in Cairo. These reports included information he had not supplied, indicating that members of the Yugoslav military intelligence—Major Perić in Istanbul, and Popović and Gligorijević in Cairo—had been more forthcoming with their SOE contacts.[25] SIS attempted to elicit more information by suggesting he leave his papers in their hands when he was en route to Cairo, but he did not fall for that, and later in Cairo James Millar of ISLD moved into the same lodgings as Rapotec—hardly a coincidence.

The Cairo SOE report, dated 30 July 1942, stated that the only organized resistance consisted of Mihailović's chetniks, Partisans, and Serbian refugees, although local bands also carried out sporadic acts of sabotage. It assessed that Mihailović's organization was the most important, numerous and widespread force, numbering about 70,000, in bands of one to two thousand men, although only about 8,000 were actually mobilized at that time. Mihailović himself kept a small mobile headquarters—then located in the Durmitor area—

with regional headquarters at Mostar, Split, Zagreb, Ljubljana and Belgrade: current activity was limited to Dalmatia, Herzegovina, southern Bosnia and the Sandjak.

While the partisans had been the most active anti-Axis force after the collapse of Yugoslavia, their following had fallen off considerably after they left Serbia. They were, however, still strong in Slovenia and north-west Croatia, where the situation was described as akin to that in Serbia the previous year; in some areas—notably around Fiume, on the Istrian border, and Kozara Planina—the whole countryside was under their control. Davidson's Istanbul report of 11 July stated that the Partisans in Slovenia used Mihailović's name to dupe their rank and file into loyalty. Neither report mentioned Tito, although the Istanbul report named Moša Pijade as the leader of the partisans in Montenegro.

It also gave details of Rapotec's meeting in Split with Ilja Trifunović Birčanin, known to SOE as 'Daddy' from their pre-war relationship with him; he had under his command about 12,000 men, and they were responsible for cutting the Split-Zagreb railway line. It was planned that 'Daddy' would soon have his own transmitting equipment to keep in touch with Belgrade. Dr Feller—'Felix'—who had been put in charge of the secret W/T station in Zagreb by Masterson before the Axis invasion, was also in the Split area and part of Trifunović Birčanin's organization. Trifunović Birčanin was also in touch with an SIS W/T in Yugoslavia.[26] In Zagreb Rapotec had met the Yugoslav Revolutionary Organization, which operated the most efficient of Mihailović's W/T stations with which it contacted Belgrade; the organization also ran a courier system to and from Ljubljana and Belgrade. Ljubljana itself was the centre of a close-knit Slovenian organization, also in touch with Belgrade by radio. Rapotec had no knowledge of any Mihailović organization in southern Serbia.

Davidson's Istanbul report denied any contact with the Germans or Italians by Mihailović. While the Cairo report stated that chetniks had assisted the Italians in subduing the Partisans; and also that Mihailović had decided to avoid all serious clashes with the Germans and Italians until there was a general Allied offensive on the continent. Davidson's report was sent to London: in passing it to Colonel Taylor, Major Pearson commented that Mihailović's position seemed to be much better than that stated by Hudson and that the partisans seemed to be on the decline.[27]

Rapotec was not allowed to go to London to report directly to the YGE as he wished, and there seems to be some doubt over whether members of the Yugoslav government there actually saw his full report: SOE fed them contradictory information on the position of Rapotec, giving rise to the suspicion in the YGE that he was a British agent. Possibly Djonović and his SOE friends—especially when they heard of Trifunović-Birčanin's active involvement—wanted to keep the information to themselves, to establish a link with him and pursue their own policies without reference to the YGE. Rapotec re-emerged at an unfortunate time when the Yugoslav military in the Middle East were in open mutiny against the Yugoslav government in London. Members of SOE, and the mutineers whose side they took, might well have felt that they had the more legitimate claim to any intelligence available.

While Mihailović was incommunicado, anti-Simović feeling had finally come to a head. In January 1942 all the ministers resigned from the Yugoslav government, saying they could no longer work with him, and Slobodan Jovanović replaced him as prime minister. At the same time Mihailović was appointed minister of war, replacing Ilić who was deemed to be too closely allied to Simović. At this point Mihalović adopted the term Yugoslav Home Army to connect his forces with the regular military and dropped the term chetnik to distinguish his forces from irregular bands, and shortly afterwards, he was promoted to general. Far from solving problems the new line-up of the YGE gave rise to a six month crisis in the Yugoslav military in the Middle East, widening the divisions in the exiled Yugoslav community and exasperating their British hosts in London.[28]

At first refusing to go, Ilić eventually retired on 'health grounds', but handed over to Bora Mirković instead of the officer appointed to take command of the Yugoslav forces in the Middle East. Despite FO support in London for the exiled government's position, the British military in Cairo backed Mirković and his 'dissidents' as the British called them, or 'mutineers' from the Yugoslav viewpoint. Both SOE and ISLD (SIS) in Cairo also backed Mirković: a fact of which the Jovanović government was well aware, although the FO was not prepared to acknowledge it. When Momčilo Ninčić, minister of foreign affairs, and Milanović, first under secretary, told Orme Sargent that they felt a great deal of the trouble was due to the fact that British intelligence agents in Cairo sympathized with, and encouraged, the insubordinate Yugoslav officers, Sargent declined to accept the allegation, although admitting it privately in the FO minutes on the crisis.[29] Sir Ronald Campbell, now in Washington, had heard that SOE was encouraging the dissidents *and* influencing the British military authorities in the Middle East. Having had experience of SOE in Belgrade he felt this all had a 'familiar ring', but he was at a loss to understand why the FO were unable to enforce their view on the British Command in the Middle East. Cadogan agreed that the whole affair had been bungled by the British military in Cairo, but denied SOE responsibility.[30] It was not until the mutiny had more or less been settled that SOE London conceded that their people in Cairo had supported the pro-Mirković Yugoslavs. The only member of SOE to turn against the Mirković party at the time was Masterson; Lord Glenconner, in Cairo at the time, supported the dissidents but on his return to London concluded that his people in Cairo SOE had been wrong.[31]

The new Yugoslav government took over just as Ilić and Masterson were finalizing the preparations for the Hydra, Henna and Disclaim missions. Jovanović tried to stop these going ahead, fearing some conspiracy between Ilić and Masterson, who at the time was still backing the dissidents. Živan Knezević, head of the military office, suspected Ilić of acquiescing in SOE's plans simply to gain British support for his defiance of the government, in spite of the danger to the people parachuting into Yugoslavia in wintertime.[32] Ilić informed the YGE on 23 January 1942 that it was too late, the missions had already been sent: in fact the submarine missions had gone, but not Disclaim, which was dropped in on 4 February. Earlier, on 26 January the government had sent an urgent request for information on where the teams had been sent, accompanied by instructions that if any of the Yugoslav members had taken part in the mutiny, they were to be recalled immediately. Ilić did not reply to this until 11 February, two weeks later.[33]

It is quite interesting that it was Ilić—who had been dismissed from his post—who was receiving the YGE's messages. At this time a number of packages of correspondence from the YGE to the Yugoslav Supreme Command in Cairo found their way into the hands of the dissidents, rather than those for whom they were meant. Jovanović protested to George Rendel that confidential letters sent by air ministry bag, with a special request that they be handed personally to Lozić, acting C-in-C Yugoslav forces Middle East, had in fact been delivered to the mutineers. Rendel explained this as a simple mix-up—the request had not been translated.[34] Given that the YGE knew all the British organizations in Cairo were pro-dissident, this probably did not sound very convincing. The exiles, divided amongst themselves, did not appreciate the divisions within the various British bodies, nor that inefficiency and muddle might also prevail in British affairs, with the result that the Yugoslavs were often inclined to read hidden motives and meanings into confusing signals. This sensitivity, which was not always unjustified, led the YGE into sometimes misjudged attempts to assert its independence, a factor which, combined with the crises constantly afflicting the Yugoslav government, did little to enhance its standing in British eyes and eventually resulted in the British disregarding it altogether.

Possibly included in the 'misdirected' packages was a letter that Simović wrote to Jovanović on 26 February, which was subsequently published in *Novo Vreme*, a German-controlled Belgrade newspaper, and also in the German and Bulgarian press. Jovanović told Rendel that this letter had come into German hands by the mutineers giving it to Semiz and Bakić, the members of the ill-fated airborne mission, 'whom the British GHQ at Cairo, without the knowledge and agreement of the Yugoslav government, sent by air to General Mihailović and who were captured'.[35] Jovanović added that he had already discussed with Eden the undesirability of sending mutiny sympathizers into Yugoslavia. Semiz and Bakić had been selected in February on the advice of Colonel Popović who was still in charge of liaising with SOE, despite Jovanović's growing suspicions of his attitude to Nedić and the Serbian fascist Ljotić. Replying to Jovanović's complaint, Rendel pointed out that if Popović's recommendations turned out to be unacceptable it was most unfortunate, but not the responsibility of the British. In a more conciliatory vein, it was suggested that SOE would ensure in future that no Yugoslav would be infiltrated 'until the Yugoslav military authorities have had an opportunity of expressing their approval of the men selected'. In fact, at the very moment of Rendel giving this assurance, SOE was engaged on recruiting and training expatriate Yugoslavs in Canada who would be dropped into Yugoslavia without the knowledge, never mind approval, of the YGE.

SOE was adamant that *they*, not the YGE, should direct and control all operations. A memorandum from Jovanović, delivered by Major Živan Knežević on 30 January, which suggested that the Yugoslavs should take over the whole show themselves—directing operations and controlling wireless traffic—was greeted with horror in both Baker Street and Cairo. The latter stated that the Yugoslavs were not competent enough to organize the complex details: this might seem rather ironic coming from Cairo SOE given the number of muddles and intrigues they had already been embroiled in, not to mention those to come. What was more, Cairo pointed out, to agree would leave SOE with all the donkey-work while the Yugoslavs did all the exciting bits. More importantly, Cairo SOE had its own political agenda: not only did they not support the YGE but, it was argued, there was no evidence to suggest that resistance forces within Yugoslavia accepted their exiled government in London. The policy of the YGE might well be to restore the pre-war status quo: this meant that they would possibly be against supporting certain resistance elements, such as the Partisans. George Taylor felt that the best way to kill the scheme was to get Orme Sargent to counter Jovanović's proposals: thus, with the FO as 'executioner' SOE could stay in the background.[36]

The appointment of Mihailović as minister of war was more a political gesture than a practical move, since this was the time when he was being given maximum exposure as the most important leader of resistance in occupied Europe: by his inclusion in the government it was hoped that some of his success would rub off on the exiles. The impracticality of the gesture was highlighted by the fact that the YGE did not have direct communications with its minister of war. All communications were channelled through the British, namely SOE and SIS (who were still in charge of SOE's wireless traffic until summer 1942). Any message from Mihailović would be picked up by SIS, passed on to SOE, who passed it on to the FO, who passed it on to Rendel, who finally handed it to the YGE, provided all the above agreed that the Yugoslavs should receive it. Messages from the YGE to its minister of war took the same path in reverse, and were subject to the same conditions.

When the Yugoslav military crisis in the Middle East was at its peak, the British used their control over communications to try to keep the details of the affair from Mihailović until the matter was settled. There had been some suggestion that Mihailović should be consulted and give his opinion on the situation, and Rendel was convinced that he would come out in favour of the king and his government, but the FO did not want to take the risk.[37] While the crisis continued there was a great deal of concern about the effect it might have on Mihailović and his followers, and a constant fear that if the extent of the divide was known within Yugoslavia it would so dishearten the members of the resistance that they would give up altogether. The Directorate of Military Intelligence (DMI), hoping that the coming of spring would bring a renewed offensive, thus taking some of the heat off the Soviet Union, was afraid that the FO, wrapped up in the political machinations, did not appreciate the importance of Mihailović.[38] This was not the case: as FO impatience and irritation with the YGE and its 'petty quarrels' increased, so did the idea that Mihailović and his movement were the only important elements in the Yugoslav equation.

The question of independent communications was a continually vexed one, and it had been a contributory factor in the deterioration of the relationship between Mihailović and Hudson. One of the most important points Rapotec had made, first in 1941, and again on his return from Yugoslavia, was the urgent need for the YGE to communicate directly with its homeland, not only with Mihailović, but also with the various other groups Rapotec had contacted so that they could give positive direction. When the Yugoslav prime minister's military office wanted to confirm with Mihailović that Rapotec was in possession of codes, SOE refused to transmit the message: the YGE's protests were met with prevarication and obfuscation which eventually cast doubt on Rapotec's status and the secrecy of the ciphers he had brought out—a ploy probably designed to prevent direct communications.[39] The British wished to ensure control of all communications, not least because they suspected the YGE of instructing the resistance *not* to take any precipitate action which would provoke reprisals for little gain. The British military having warmed to the idea of revolt in Yugoslavia by spring 1942, no longer viewed it as premature, but as a useful diversion of Axis troops from the Russian front.

Representations by the Yugoslavs to the FO to the effect that SOE—the 'sabotage service', as they knew it—delayed and mislaid telegrams and issued orders of which the YGE had no knowledge, and requests for W/T transmissions to be entrusted to them, fell on deaf ears. By October 1943 the delayed and mislaid telegrams from Mihailović to the YGE—codename 'Villa Resta'—had reached enormous proportions. Whether by accident or design, Cairo SOE had accumulated a backlog of about 100 messages, one of which was ten months old. While admitting this was unacceptable, SOE decided it was best brushed under the carpet: 'To hand over ancient messages to the Jug government would certainly provoke a scream. If enquiries are made, I will produce an answer.'[40]

There was quite a stir at the FO when Rendel revealed, in July 1942, that the YGE did have independent communications, using agents from Istanbul.[41] In the light of this, the British were anxious that SOE should gain access to messages which were not transmitted by their own channels. Diplomatic bags were frequently opened, and packages of letters translated and read before being sent on their way.[42] Later, in September 1942, a secret Yugoslav radio link with Mihailović was established from Cairo, after air force captain Nedeljko Plećaš was parachuted into Yugoslavia, taking with him radio sets for Mihailović and Trifunović-Birčanin. There was a temporary break in this link after the Italian capitulation in September 1943, but it was restored at the end of that year when the secret transmitter was transferred from Cairo to Istanbul to evade the British. The Yugoslavs, constantly aware that they had to be one step ahead of the British, were afraid the latter would put pressure on the Turks to close down the link. Eventually, with help from the Free French, and despite FO attempts to put a stop to the project, Djonović was able to establish a communications centre in Algiers. This became fully operational in May 1944—just at the time when the British broke their Cairo link with Mihailović.[43]

The military crisis finally stuttered to a 'solution' in July, when the dissident elements in the Yugoslav forces were given the option of joining the British forces. Even so, problems persisted for months afterwards, along with YGE suspicions that the British were attempting to establish a 'Free Yugoslav Force', independent of the politicians in London.

Having adopted Mihailović as their protégé, SOE was able to do little in practical terms to help him. Shortage of aircraft, and the distance from North Africa to Yugoslavia—when Malta was no longer viable because of enemy action—meant that during 1942 very little in the way of matériel could be delivered to Mihailović. Eden, after a joint FO-SOE policy review, recommended to the Defence Committee in a memorandum of 28 February 1942, that SOE should have its own squadrons of long range aircraft.[44] However, the Air Ministry decided that only two Liberators could be made available to SOE, as Bomber Command needed all its long-range bombers. In March 'most secret sources' indicated that the Germans were preparing a major offensive against the USSR: after the heavy Allied losses incurred in the fall of Singapore, there was no possibility of opening the second front in Europe which the Soviet government was urging upon its Western allies. In view of this, Churchill advised Stalin on 9 March that the RAF was resuming its heavy air offensive on Germany, a decision specifically designed to be of substantial benefit to the USSR.[45]

The pressing—and conflicting—needs of all participants during this period of the war were difficult to reconcile. On 15 March a DMI report observed that since SOE had recommended that British backing for Mihailović would ensure that his forces, rather than the communists, would play the prominent role in Yugoslav resistance, he had received no substantial aid. It was now apparent that not only were the chetniks and communists fighting each other again, but also that the communists were playing a leading role in fighting the occupiers. While the Partisans' successes against the Axis were just as valuable, the situation presented two major problems: first, the inter-resistance conflict dissipated the energies of both sides and benefited only the Axis, and secondly partisan ascendancy contained the inherent risk of Russian domination in Yugoslavia. The report went on to say that the two long range aircraft assigned to SOE to aid Mihailović, were woefully short of the number needed to provide any really effective help, adding that the thirty Axis divisions in Yugoslavia, although they were second grade, were twice the number in Libya.[46]

Any effect this argument, and SOE's desperate pleas for additional aircraft, might have had, was overtaken by the German and Italian attack on Malta. While all concerned recognized that it was vital Mihailović received the maximum possible aid, military resources were under tremendous pressure. Rommel's advance in North Africa, Japanese advances in Burma, and the defence of Malta meant that no extra aircraft were available for SOE operations in Yugoslavia. The DMI, while setting out the political disadvantages of failing to supply Mihailović, concluded: 'It would not mean however that resistance to the enemy would cease.'[47] Unable to provide anything more concrete, the DMI could only hope that SOE could persuade Moscow to influence the partisans to cooperate with Mihailović.

During most of 1942, SOE had at its disposal only four Liberators for all its Balkan operations. Lack of precise information on the situation on the ground during the first half of the year, meant that the accuracy of the few sorties destined for Mihailović was rather hit or miss, with supplies often going astray or being stolen. By May 1942 a total of nine sorties had been flown and SOE had no idea if even this modest amount of material had actually come into Mihailović's hands.[48]

In spite of the desperate shortage of aircraft, negotiations between King Peter and the Americans for them to supply long range aircraft by which the Yugoslavs themselves could deliver arms to the resistance movement, was not looked on with favour at the FO. Intelligence from Peter Boughey, SOE's liaison officer with the YGE, that the US was set to supply four Flying Fortresses to the Yugoslav air force was far from welcome, and Glenconner and the Air Ministry set about nipping the plan in the bud. Rendel, however, drew the line at SOE New York approaching William Donovan, who at the time was establishing the Office of Strategic Services (OSS), the US equivalent of SOE, preferring that the FO should handle the matter in Washington. SOE also maintained that the US authorities in the Middle East, in attempting to intervene in the Yugoslav military crisis, were likely to make the situation even worse.[49]

The relationship between SOE and the newly-formed OSS was often friendly and co-operative on the personal level, particularly in the United States. Donovan and Sir Charles Hambro, who succeeded Nelson as executive head of SOE in May, signed the 'London Agreement' in June 1942, which established the basis for co-ordination and co-operation between the two organizations and set out geographical zones of interest for each of them.[50] SOE Cairo was less enthusiastic, harbouring doubts about the security of some of the Americans in the Middle East and viewing OSS—rather ironically in view of its own image—as blundering amateurs who did not have the experience fully to comprehend the situation. Yugoslavia might well have been a sideshow—at least for the greater part of the war—but SOE saw it as *their* sideshow. For their part, OSS officers found the divisions and quarrels within the British secret agencies an unedifying spectacle: both American intelligence and secret operations came under OSS. In the event, little came of the American promises of help, partly due to the same factors which prevented the British supplying extra aircraft, and partly because the United States regarded the Yugoslavs as a British responsibility. Unfortunately, the US authorities did not make the latter point entirely clear to the YGE, who, although they probably realized that it antagonized their British hosts, continued to look for American aid which would allow them a greater degree of autonomy.

SOE also had long-term British economic interests to take into consideration, not least of SOE concerns was the danger of the Americans planning post-war hegemony of big business in Yugoslavia, or even the whole of the Balkans. When Čubrilović, the Yugoslav minister of agriculture, visited the United States in February, SOE speculated that if the Yugoslavs became too fed up with the British then they might consider turning to the Americans for agricultural machinery—a valuable market. Bailey noted that the Yugoslav Legation in Washington had held discussions with an American agriculture adviser on the post-war restructuring of Yugoslavia.[51]

While only a limited amount of material aid was possible, propaganda was not in short supply, and the Mihailović myth-making continued apace in broadcasts and publications. This was not only of little use to Mihailović, but was actually counterproductive: the last thing a secret army needs is a world-wide advertising campaign. Protests and requests to play this down, from both the YGE and Mihailović, seem to have been taken rather too literally by PWE, and were followed by further protests that he was now being totally ignored and the Partisans being given attention instead, which was just as harmful.[52] PWE was attempting a difficult balancing act on Yugoslavia, not least because they were not sure themselves of precisely what was going on. While the policy was to support Mihailović, there was also a desire to make as much as possible of any news of action against the Axis. It was decided that vagueness was the best solution. Since the term 'Partisans' was not in keeping with backing Mihailović, Ralph Murray, PWE Balkan regional director, issued a directive forbidding its use: 'patriots' or 'fighting forces' covered all eventualities.[53]

In mid July 1942 Hudson wired SOE that it was essential for Mihailović's reputation, as a show of good faith *and* to stimulate resistance, that 'an impressive amount' of arms be sent to his area immediately. Hudson would be on the spot with anything up to one thousand men if sufficient arms were sent. London's reply thanked him for the information, told him to keep up the good work and supplies would be sent as soon as possible, although they feared this might be some time. The message concluded 'Good luck and keep going'.[54] A whole year after first news of the Yugoslav revolts had caused such excitement and hopes for positive action within SOE, the organization had only one officer with the Yugoslav resistance, and were doubtful about the security of his communications. The plan to influence the nature of resistance had come to virtually nothing due to the problems of supplying the arms and money which had been an essential element of the scheme. The deep-seated political divisions between the two resistance movements had been imperfectly understood by SOE and other British bodies concerned with Yugoslavia: attempts to bring together these irreconcilable factions had merely served to arouse the suspicions of all sides, and the civil war was continuing. PWE's propaganda campaign, while ostensibly successful outside Yugoslavia, bore little resemblance to the reality within the country and was worse than useless to Mihailović and his followers.

5

PROPAGANDA WARS

A new dimension was added on the propaganda front in mid 1942. From that point, the Soviet Union began to broadcast anti-Mihailović stories and commentaries on Radio Free Yugoslavia, a station purportedly operating from within Yugoslavia, but actually situated in the southern USSR. On 12 August an article appeared in the *Soviet War News*, published by the Soviet Embassy in London, claiming that only the Partisans were resisting the Axis, while Mihailović took no part in the struggle. These stories were taken up by the communist press, first in neutral countries and then in the United States, and eventually found their way into the general press there and in Britain. Croat settlers in the United States, provoked by the wide coverage of Ustasha atrocities in Serbian–American journals there, and not unhappy to redress the balance somewhat, also gave maximum coverage to the anti-Mihailović stories in their own journals.

Up to this point the Soviets had gone along with the British line on propaganda. Stirring stories about Mihailović were as good for morale in the USSR as they were in Britain and occupied Europe; he was also the legitimate representative of the YGE, with whom diplomatic relations had been re-established after the German invasion of the USSR and the Yugoslav revolts. While supporting Mihailović in their propaganda, the Soviets always claimed that they had no contact with, or influence over, the Yugoslav Partisans. This was not the case: a more or less constant radio link with Zagreb had been maintained since January 1940, and in late January or early February 1942 Tito had re-established direct contact with the Comintern. While they were reluctant to admit this, the Soviets were equally reluctant to rock the boat with their British ally by being seen to take a different, and opposing, line on the Yugoslav resistance. Stalin was aware of the fact that he needed aid from the Western Allies for the survival of the Soviet Union, so the Comintern urged the partisans to keep a low political profile and play down the revolutionary nature of their movement. What the Soviets required was concerted action to distract from the Axis attack on the USSR. They accordingly advised Tito and his followers to forge a common resistance movement with the nationalists in Serbia and Croatia, although never actually instructing Tito to come under the direct command of Mihailović, as the British wanted. Tito had, in fact, attempted to make agreements with Mihailović in Serbia and with Maček's Peasant Party supporters in Croatia, but the early excesses of the communists had not aided his case with the nationalists. The Comintern appeared to blame Tito himself for this failure, and to dismiss both the Partisans' allegations that Mihailović and his followers were collaborators and their protests at pro-Mihailović propaganda.[1]

It had become obvious to the British in March 1942 that the civil war was far from over, when military intelligence reported renewed fighting between chetniks and communists; and after Mihailović had re-established fairly regular radio contact with Cairo he complained that the communists were still causing him trouble.[2] Numerous diplomatic approaches were made, in London and Kuibyshev or Moscow, for the Soviets to use their influence with the Partisans to end the conflict, but, as usual, any such influence was denied. However, in July 1942, shortly before the full-scale anti-Mihailović propaganda began, Maisky, the Soviet ambassador in London, informed the FO that his government had no inclination to join the British in attempting to curb the Partisans, since they believed Mihailović was in touch with Nedić and, therefore, was not to be trusted. In reply, Maisky was informed that Mihailović had several times reported to his government that he maintained contact with the Nedić forces, and claimed the loyalty of many of the latter's officers. As there had been no attempt to hide this fact it could hardly be cited as proof of untrustworthiness.[3] This defence proffered by the FO is interesting in the light of events which followed, when, in 1943, contact with the Nedić forces was interpreted by Cairo SOE and the British ambassador to the YGE, as tantamount to collaboration with the Germans.

The question one has to ask, of course, is why the Soviets suddenly switched their propaganda policy so drastically at this precise moment. Responding to the British warning in March 1942, of a massive new German offensive against the USSR, the Red Army launched a pre-emptive strike near Kharkov in Ukraine on 12 May: although a disaster, the action did displace the Germans' timetable for their attack. Ten days later Molotov, the Soviet foreign minister, in London to discuss the Anglo-Soviet Treaty, urged Churchill to open a second front in Europe which could draw off at least forty German divisions from the Eastern front. When Churchill explained the difficulties, Molotov responded by asking what would be Britain's position and attitude if the Red Army were to be defeated in 1942. Churchill replied that Britain and the United States would fight on and ultimately win. However, in the next few weeks the Prime Minister, aware of the serious position of the USSR—and, no doubt, the implications for the Western Allies of a Soviet defeat, or the making of a separate peace—explored all possible avenues for providing diversionary action, even if it were to be a limited exercise, in either France or Norway. On 9 June Molotov visited Britain again, this time armed with a Soviet–US draft on the urgency of creating a second front in Europe in 1942. This seriously alarmed the British, especially Eden, as by this point it had become obvious that major operations into Europe during that year were impracticable. The same evening, Churchill set out for Molotov the problems which precluded an immediate continental offensive, and the following day presented him with an *aide-mémoire* which, in essence, stated that if at all possible, landings would be undertaken in August or September. The document went on to list the various theatres in which Axis forces were being tied down and challenged, and concluded that maximum effort was being concentrated on plans for a large-scale invasion of the continent by British and US forces in 1943.[4]

From Molotov's discussions with Churchill, and the *aide-mémoire*, it must have been obvious that even if the limited operations in Western Europe went ahead, the hoped for distraction of the German offensive on the Eastern front would not be forthcoming on anything like the scale that the Soviets needed. The realization of this made the Soviets view guerrilla activity in occupied Europe with more seriousness than they had done hitherto, and take another look at the trouble the partisans were apparently causing the Axis in Yugoslavia. It is probable that once the Soviets realized that the western Allies were not going to provide the necessary diversion, they felt less compunction in breaking ranks on the common propaganda line. Having appeared only a few months earlier to dismiss Tito's 'proof' of Mihailović's collaboration—indeed, actually reproaching him for the divisiveness of these allegations—the timing of their *volte face* seems to point to this conclusion. In addition, the British were at this time strenuously discouraging the YGE from signing a treaty of mutual assistance with the Soviet Union: the implied mistrust of possible rivalry in post-war Yugoslavia between the British and Soviets could not have been lost on the latter. It may have been no coincidence that the anti-Mihailović article in the *Soviet War News* appeared on the very day, 12 August 1942, that Churchill arrived in Moscow to explain to Stalin in person that there was to be no second front in Europe till 1943, a task Churchill described as 'like carrying a large lump of ice to the North Pole'.[5]

Appeals by the Yugoslav government to the Soviets to cease their propaganda attack on Mihailović elicited much the same response as had British approaches. Continuing to deny any responsibility for the partisans, the Soviet government presented the Yugoslav minister at Kuibyshev with a memorandum, detailing instances of Mihailović's forces collaborating with the Italians in attacks on the partisans, and of his collaboration with Nedić forces and, thus, with the German–Italian occupiers.[6] In addition, the thorny question of the YGE's lack of direct communications with their minister of war was exploited by the Soviets. Whenever the question of relations with Mihailović and the partisans was raised, the YGE was asked whether it had direct and independent communications with its minister of war, and made it clear that if not, the Yugoslav ministers were not qualified to speak for him, with the obvious implication that it was the British—not the YGE—who were in control.

In response to the Kuibyshev memorandum, the YGE presented the Soviet government with a lengthy *aide-mémoire*, refuting all the allegations against its minister of war. For once, the FO was impressed by the YGE's efforts, although doubtful if the Soviets would be moved by them.[7] Jovanović followed this up with a letter to Bogmolov, Soviet minister to the exiled governments, listing the assassinations in Yugoslavia which had resulted from Mihailović identifying traitors whose names had been passed to the BBC, to be broadcast with a letter Z attached to their names to indicate that they were targets for assassination. Jovanović pointed out that the names were those of Nedićists and people who had collaborated with the Germans, thus scotching the suggestion that Mihailović was working for the Axis or its agents. PWE obtained a copy of this letter by 'rather delicate means'.[8]

Eden had also received a copy of the Kuibyshev memorandum from Maisky on 7 August: although he firmly told Maisky that this did not tie in with the information which he possessed, the realization that the Soviets were obviously not disposed to revert to their former position *vis-à-vis* Mihailović caused him considerable consternation. On 7 August Eden minuted the FO Southern Department:

Soviet charges against Mihailović reveal a dangerous difference of opinion between ourselves and the Russians. We support him, they attack him… We ourselves are not altogether clear as to M's singleness of purpose, and I fear that, now the Russians have committed themselves so far in condemning M, it will be extremely difficult to convince them that M and the Partisans can and should make common cause… Either we or the Russians must be wrong about M.[9]

A meeting was convened at the FO on 8 August, at which SOE and SIS were represented. That the Partisans were causing more trouble to the Axis than Mihailović's forces does not appear to have been in dispute. Since March 1942 intelligence reports, which included information provided by intercepted German signals, had indicated that there was considerable activity in areas known to be outside Mihailović's control, while Serbia itself was fairly quiescent. On 2 June Churchill had urgently requested a report on patriotic activity in Yugoslavia—'on not more than two pages'. The report from the DMI stated that the activities of the 'wilder elements' of the Partisans would continue to necessitate considerable Axis garrisons, but had unequivocally backed Mihailović as both a bastion against anarchy and to ensure the maintenance of British influence in the Balkans and the Mediterranean.[10] Orme Sargent concurred with the latter point; he thought supporting the Partisans would be an 'opportunist and short-term policy' while, taking the long view, Mihailović best served British interests. It was essential, however, that the breach with the partisans should be healed, since a continuation of the internal conflict might well lead to Mihailović actually accepting help from, or collaborating with, the Axis forces whether or not he had done so up to that point. The conclusion of the 8 August meeting was that reconciliation should be attempted by yet another approach to the Soviets to influence the partisans. Meanwhile, Hudson should be consulted on reminding Mihailović of the original British condition for helping him: namely, a determined effort on his part to reach an understanding with the partisans. At the same time, the possibility of the British themselves making direct contact with the Partisans was to be examined.[11]

The proposed telegram to Hudson caused friction between the FO and SOE, with some degree of exasperation on the part of SOE at the other's lack of understanding for Hudson's position. Jimmy Pearson was particularly reluctant to ask Hudson to broach the delicate subject of Mihailović making an understanding with the Partisans, and wrote to Douglas Howard at the Southern Department:

You will remember that Hudson made strenuous efforts to bring about a reconciliation between the two parties soon after he got to Jugoslavia and that these efforts very nearly wrecked his entire mission and almost fatally undermined his personal relations with Mihailović. For months he was completely discredited and unable to carry out at all his primary function of helping to organize assistance to the resisting forces.[12]

Pearson pointed out that although Hudson had won back some degree of confidence, his position was still none too secure: if it was HMG's policy to press this issue with Mihailović, then he felt it should be up to the YGE to raise it. Jovanović had just sent Mihailović a telegram assuring him that Hudson and his organization were in no way to blame for the troubles in Cairo, and urging him to co-operate as closely as possible with Hudson. The fact that he had to send such a message is indicative of the mistrust and confusion caused by the decision not to give Mihailović the full story of the Cairo mutiny: it had obviously not helped Hudson's position.

Pearson felt many of the questions in the FO draft telegram were superfluous, since Hudson had already gone to a great deal of trouble to explain the complexities of the situation in telegrams received since the 8 August meeting. The correspondence between Pearson and Howard on the wording of the questions for Hudson reveals a certain degree of scepticism at the FO regarding SOE's attitude to Mihailović's policy of making 'no active attack on the occupiers for the present, but concentration on the restoration of internal order'— which Howard interpreted as 'subduing the Partisans'. Interestingly, what Howard picked out as the greatest problem, was not the possible association between Mihailović's followers and members of the Nedić gendarmerie, or the fact that some indirect support from the Italians had been utilized, but the concentration of Mihailović's principal military effort on the Partisans. It is apparent from Pearson's reluctance to ask Hudson to raise the question of a rapprochement with the partisans that SOE was well aware that it was not possible to reconcile the Yugoslav minister of war with the communist resistance, while the FO continued to pursue this idea as the only possible way to solve their diplomatic problems with the Soviets. Eventually, after lengthy discussion, Pearson and Howard agreed on the wording of the message for Hudson. In essence, he was asked if an Anglo–Soviet appeal to the Partisan leaders would have any effect on either side in Yugoslavia. Who and where was the Partisan leader? And if Mihailović's whole effort to date had been directed at the Partisans, was this likely to continue until they either submitted or were exterminated?[13]

While the FO struggled to find a way around the difficulties of a potential rift between themselves and the Soviets, SOE in London, headed by the conservative Lord Selborne since the British government reshuffle in February 1942, steadfastly promoted the policy of supporting only Mihailović. The DMI shared this position, and produced a map on 23 August which 'shows the bulk of activity is apparently carried out by "Partisans"—alias communists—who do not come under Mihailović's orders and who he, in general, tries to restrain....' However much anti-Axis activity was being carried out by non-Mihailović forces, the DMI was convinced that Mihailović was the leader to back. They thought, or hoped, that some of the activity might be attributable to Maček supporters or other non-political elements.[14]

PWE took a different line: a report produced in the same month from its own sources, gave a similar picture of the amount of activity actually attributable to the forces of General Mihailović, but reached a different conclusion. PWE asserted that SOE's appreciations of the situation in Yugoslavia were 'seen from their point of view alone', with the underlying implication of a bias towards Mihailović in Baker Street, and, to a certain degree reflecting the rivalry between the two bodies. While recognizing the British obligations to Mihailović, PWE warned: 'If the Soviet Ambassador chose to brief himself with the sort of information which we lay before you it might be very difficult… to maintain the thesis that Mihailović was the horse to back.'[15] The difference in these two interpretations might well reflect that PWE's assessment was, to use its own phrase, 'seen from their point of view alone' or, more correctly, from their sources alone, which did not include the secret intercepts from which the DMI worked. The DMI report of 23 August, as well as including maps illustrating areas of Partisan activity, also provided maps showing the location of Mihailović's 'lieutenants', who were gradually establishing his organization all over the country. In addition, their 'most secret sources', while showing that Partisan tactics and organization were improving, also indicated that Axis reprisals caused more damage to the country than the partisans caused to the Axis.

The assumption by PWE that the Soviets did not possess the same sort of information as themselves seems naïve to say the least: the Soviets may have been hard pressed, but their intelligence services were hardly existing in a vacuum. It may possibly have been the case that the Soviets had access to *more* information than PWE. 'Ultra' was limited in circulation to only about thirty people most closely concerned with the running of the war (neither SOE nor PWE was included). The British were very careful not to reveal to the USSR the full extent of their access to German signals, passing on only carefully disguised reports when it was essential that the Soviets be made aware of some particular strategic aspect. In 1964 John Cairncross, who worked at Bletchley Park where Enigma signals were decoded and analyzed, claimed to have passed 'Ultra' documents to the USSR for four years, and he claimed that he was not the only 'mole' there.[16] This seems to be borne out by the fact that the Soviets, who were suspicious on principle of anything emanating from the West, never directly or indirectly probed Eden or anyone else on the subject of Ultra.[17] If it was the case that more than the officially sanctioned information was being passed on, then the intelligence that non-Mihailović forces were causing most concern to the Axis—and, perhaps more importantly, that this was generating interest and debate in Britain—might have been an additional factor in the Soviet propaganda offensive.

While SOE in London continued to advocate a policy of total support for Mihailović, PWE argued that their present propaganda risked bearing little relation to the actual situation in Yugoslavia. It was suggested that a way of providing a basis for unified propaganda with the USSR would be to get Mihailović to modify his—and the YGE's—policy of conserving his forces for future action. In September SOE and PWE agreed that partisan action could no longer be ignored totally, and that it should be mentioned in publicity and propaganda, with the general idea of demonstrating to Mihailović that he was not alone in the field, and it was up to him to continually show proof that he was worthy of the total support of the allied powers.[18] It was hoped thereby to galvanize him into action which could be used to refute Soviet propaganda. Possibly this new line was also a way of hedging their bets if the British did indeed decide to contact the partisans at some future date.

From the end of July 1942 SOE had more success in parachuting Yugoslav agents in to Mihailović, and SIS also sent in a mission consisting of three Yugoslavs.[19] In the first wave of arrivals was one 'Captain Charles Robertson' complete with a W/T set, supposedly to help Hudson with his communications, but of whom, more later. In August 1942, Cairo SOE had received another shake-up. Maxwell was replaced by Lord Glenconner, with Colonel (later Brigadier) C.M. Keble as chief of operations, with an enlarged military staff at their disposal which was reflected in its new name, 'MO4'. Glenconner reorganized the Cairo office on London SOE lines, by creating individual country desks, with John Bennett as head of the Yugoslav desk. An important change entailed SOE finally gaining control over its own communications from SIS.

When Hudson replied to the series of questions agreed between Pearson and Howard, it took the FO a whole month to digest and comment on them. This delay probably reflects the fact that Hudson's reports were not necessarily what the FO wanted to hear. In particular, the FO would not have been pleased to receive Hudson's opinion that the Mihailović-partisan situation was not one that had much chance of being transformed into a united resistance, especially under the leadership of Mihailović, who regarded the partisans as his most immediate and dangerous enemy. While obviously disheartened by Hudson's view that a joint Anglo-Soviet appeal would not effect a reunion unless accompanied by wide-ranging guarantees of post-war political freedom, from both the YGE and Mihailović himself, Pierson Dixon hoped that Hudson might be mistaken in his estimate and the FO did not think it should deter them from trying to agree upon a common policy with the Soviet government. SOE had already decided to send in Bill Bailey, who had just returned from the USA and Canada where he had been recruiting Balkan expatriates for SOE. He was, SOE informed the FO, one of their most experienced agents, with a wide-ranging understanding of Yugoslavia and its politics. In the light of this, Pierson Dixon decided that the FO would wait to hear what Bailey had to say before making another approach to Maisky on the question of a common policy and concluded his reply to Pearson:

When he reaches Yugoslavia, our emissary will be in a better position than Hudson to give us the sort of information which we require regarding Mihailović, and with his thorough knowledge of Yugoslavia, better able to estimate the intentions and capacity of Mihailović and the strength of the various other forces operating in Yugoslavia. We propose, therefore, to review the situation again when our emissary has reached Mihailović's headquarters and has been able to report on the general situation as he sees it.[20]

SOE was rather amused to think of Bailey as an FO emissary; Hambro later noted to Selborne: 'It is not often that a poor agent of SOE is granted so great a dignity of being claimed as a full Foreign Office representative!'[21] In the event, Bailey finally parachuted in to Mihailović's headquarters on Christmas Day 1942, having been variously delayed by an attack of malaria, bad weather, complications with the YGE and the usual problems with aircraft. In the interim, a period of almost three months, FO policy appears to have been in a state of limbo. Every question on Yugoslavia was left in abeyance, and rounded off with the conclusion that matters would become clearer, and decisions made, once Bailey had reported.

One of Bailey's tasks once he reached Yugoslavia was to improve relations with Mihailović by informing him of events outside the country, and how these had largely been responsible for the meagre flow of aid so far. He was also to convince Mihailović that he should fit in with the overall Allied strategy, which included a plan to establish a war station in Yugoslavia as an alternative communications centre for the Balkans (Hungary, Romania, Greece, Bulgaria, Albania and possibly Turkey) in the event of the Allies being forced to evacuate the Middle East.[22] This idea had first taken shape in July 1942 during the 'great flap' when Rommel was threatening Cairo, and SOE personnel were hastily burning documents at Rustem Buildings while the main part of the Cairo office transferred to 'Advance Cairo', i.e. Jerusalem. There was no post-occupational planning for Egypt but Cairo SOE proposed to introduce a relay station into northern Yugoslavia, in Mihailović's territory in order to provide a wireless link with London for its agents.[23] The plan was dependent upon Mihailović expanding his strength and influence sufficiently to secure a large enough area both to establish a secret SOE landing ground and to guarantee the security of the war station. By the end of August 1942, when Bailey's mission was being planned, London SOE had developed the idea still further. Even if the Allies held the Middle East, it was still desirable to set up the war station as a means of establishing a network in Hungary and Albania. It would also simplify SOE's work in Romania and Bulgaria with Bailey co-ordinating all activities in the region from Yugoslavia, which was to become the clearing house for all Balkan activity once more.[24] At the end of September a signals party, consisting of Lieutenant Lofts and two wireless operators, arrived at Mihailović's HQ to form the basis of this new communications system.

When Bailey arrived in Cairo in September one of his stated objects was: 'To extend Mihailović's movement into Albania, Roumania, Bulgaria (and possibly Hungary and Greece) so as to give it a more Balkan character and unite Balkan peoples in their resistance to the Axis.'[25] Cairo SOE was pleased to hear that Bailey would be recognized by the FO as their representative, but whether the FO had agreed on the extension of Mihailović's movement into a Balkan-wide one is uncertain. In early September Mihailović had asked for Dr Georgije Dimitrov, of the Bulgarian Agrarian Party, to be sent in to join him; negotiations on co-ordinating the action of Serbian and Bulgarian Agrarian parties were underway and Dimitrov could make important contributions to the situation on the ground.[26] Cairo responded enthusiastically, Dimitrov was an old friend from pre-war days when SOE was involved with the Serb Peasant Party and Bulgarian Agrarian's plans for Yugoslav-Bulgarian union. With the help of SOE, he had escaped to Istanbul after the Axis attack in 1941 and then made his way to Cairo with Bailey, Tupanjanin and Djonović. Cairo SOE felt that the terms of their treaty with the FO did not necessarily require them to inform the latter of the proposal to send him to Yugoslavia, but 'On the other hand the object of his mission which was to give Mihailović's movement a more Balkan character certainly seemed to raise a question of policy'. Baker Street appreciated this last point but felt strongly that the full purpose of Dimitrov's mission should *not* be disclosed to the FO. They went as far as inventing cover stories to disguise that purpose, but eventually decided that Dimitrov should not go in before Bailey.[27]

By autumn 1942 the FO was becoming increasingly critical of Mihailović. In addition to the fact that he was not as active against the Axis as might be wished, the FO feared that his political ambitions could run to a South Slav Federation, consisting of Serbia and Bulgaria. This was irreconcilable with the British concept of a Balkan federation of *all* the countries in the peninsula that the FO envisaged as the best means of ensuring a stable post-war settlement in the region. Pierson Dixon had been alarmed at Hudson's reports of Mihailović's contacts with the Bulgarians in early June 1942, since Orme Sargent identified Serbia and Bulgaria as the Soviet Union's natural allies in the Balkans. Any Soviet plans for post-war hegemony in the area would be based on a union, or close association, of the two, and the ensuing bloc across the peninsula would leave Greece isolated and powerless. Sargent therefore concluded that Pan-Slavism was a menace to the independence of the Balkan states.[28] So it was not surprising that SOE was keen to keep under its hat the real purpose of sending Dimitrov into Yugoslavia.

In March 1942 Dr Krek, Slovenian deputy prime minister in the YGE, received a letter from Ljubljana that dismissed Mihailović as no longer of any importance in Slovenia. When he read this Orme Sargent had been concerned at the implication that Mihailović was influential only with Serbians, which did not bode well for British

post-war ambitions for the country.[29] The letter had also emphasized that the communists enjoyed a monopoly of positive propaganda in Slovenia. Lord Glenconner probably inadvertently fuelled
these fears. Having studied a paper based on Hudson's reports, he
considered that all hope of reconciling Mihailović and the partisans
should be abandoned, and went on to put a strong case for continuing British support for Mihailović, which included the opinion that
'it is more than doubtful whether the communists would ever agree
to work with us even if we turned completely round and gave
them our full support.' Glenconner gave a fairly realistic assessment
of what Mihailović was and was not capable of achieving, and of his
position regarding British interests as against Serb interests, concluding that the British should recognise that his 'chief preoccupa-
tion will always be to save his country and the system to which he
belongs... we would only disappoint ourselves if we try to build
him up as the leader of a Balkan federation'. It would, therefore, be
necessary to make independent contacts in Croatia and Slovenia, as
well as in Hungary and possibly Bulgaria.[30]

The FO felt there was an undoubted risk in building up Mihailović
morally and materially to the degree that he would be in the strongest position in post-war Yugoslavia, with the result that any British
plans would be dependent upon him.[31] Ironically, exactly the same
fears were to be voiced later by Eden, when discussing the support
given to Tito.[32] Despite reservations, the policy of full support for
Mihailović was to continue, and the situation would be reviewed in
the light of Bailey's reports.

The increased sabotage activity demanded of Mihailović in the
second half of 1942 was presented to him as strategically essential to
help the Allies in North Africa. However, as Rommel's main supply
line ran from Italy and Sicily to Tripoli,[33] it is apparent that the
underlying reason that Mihailović was being pressed into a more
active role was to demonstrate to the Soviets the validity of British
policy in backing him. It was also hoped that Mihailović's activities
might distract German forces from the eastern front. This was not a
signal success: the Soviets acknowledged that Mihailović was doing
more, but complained that the British were only interested in creating diversions of Rommel's supplies, and not supplies destined for
the Russian front.[34]

Whether the change in British propaganda had the desired effect is also questionable, although the FO was convinced that it did. Mihailović seems to have been quite prepared to carry out sabotage, but with two important provisos: first, that there should be some specific reason for it, rather than just stirring up the wrath of the occupiers, and, secondly, that the sabotage should, if possible, be untraceable, so that it would not provoke reprisals against innocent civilians. This, in essence, is what had been agreed between Ilić and Masterson in Cairo before the first SOE missions had been despatched. The problem for Mihailović was that while he still wanted to keep to this original agreement, his British allies wanted much more. Mihailović's second proviso might be seen to be working against him in the propaganda war: his reports of successful sabotage operations always carried a warning to the effect that details should not be broadcast, so that the Germans would not take punitive action against the people.[35] These reports also contrasted with Hudson's, who described Mihailović as evasive on the question of taking action against the main Belgrade-Salonika line, while he was willing to blow up anything outside Serbia he was only prepared to undertake limited and small scale actions within Serbia itself.[36]

The new PWE policy of praising the partisans, not surprisingly, provoked strong protests from Mihailović. Earlier in the year, H.D. Harrison, BBC Balkan editor, had made a contentious broadcast which was agreed by all concerned to be out of line with British policy, and had led to a decree that the Partisans should not be mentioned.[37] Mihailović had reminded his British allies that 'Last Autumn I took cognisance of (information) from British government that Yugoslavs should fight for Yugoslavia and that struggle should not be converted into a communist revolt for Soviet Russia', and warning that Hudson's promises of help had brought about a great crisis: broadcasts glorifying the partisans held the danger of a repeat of that crisis.[38]

The Yugoslav government, who do not appear to have been informed beforehand of the changed propaganda policy, were not unnaturally upset when they realized what was happening. In December 1942, the YGE was in the throes of another cabinet crisis, which they hoped to resolve by reducing the number of members to seven, with Jovanović remaining as premier. Before finalizing the new cabinet, King Peter sought assurance from Eden that Mihailović was to continue to receive the British government's support. Lunching with Peter and his mother Queen Marie, Eden admitted that there had been some suspicions that the General had been devoting his energies to fighting the Partisans, who, by contrast, had been causing trouble for the Axis. However, the foreign secretary agreed that of late Mihailović had been active against the Germans and Italians 'partly due to the exhortations which he had received from us', and told the king and his mother that only in the last few days the British government had decided to continue the fullest possible support for Mihailović.[39]

Despite Eden's assurances, the Yugoslavs were still nervous about the British attitude to Mihailović, and the implications it held for their own position, especially as FO criticisms of their minister of war continued. Their fears appeared to be justified by a conversation Peter Boughey had with Živan Knežević in late December, and their reaction indicates that YGE adherence to Mihailović was conditional on the continuance of British backing. During the course of the conversation, Boughey had apparently told Knežević that SOE was far from satisfied with Mihailović's attitude, and regarded him as no better than Nedić; he was lying about the sabotage he reported; was intriguing with the Italians; and was a pan-Serb and anti-Croat. In view of this, SOE was not inclined to advise HMG to continue support of him, as the Partisans were more active against the Germans. When this was relayed to Jovanović he took it to mean that the British recognition of Mihailović was about to be withdrawn, and told Rendel: 'In these circumstances he could not possibly recommend to King Peter that General Mihailović should be reappointed minister of war in the new cabinet unless he has prior assurances that his impression was wrong and that HMG were in fact continuing to support Mihailović.'[40] After Rendel had discussed this with Orme Sargent and Douglas Howard, and with members of SOE, the YGE was told that no change had taken place in British policy. While this was true at the time, the sincerity of these reassurances seems somewhat questionable: the idea of transferring patronage from Mihailović to the Partisans had been under serious discussion, but was not yet fully decided. At the time, Bailey had been in Yugoslavia for about a week, and Pearson, awaiting his reports, advised that no major decision on policy should be taken until these were received.

Boughey, aware that a transfer of British support to Tito was in the air, had been making a last-ditch attempt to save Mihailović. His conversation with Knežević was meant to be a warning, so that the YGE would bring pressure to bear on Mihailović to take action, thereby making it more difficult for the British government to break with him. Boughey had also given King Peter a discreet warning earlier. However, the Yugoslavs did not react as Boughey had intended: the king approached Eden directly and Knežević went to Rendel to repeat what Boughey had said.[41]

The YGE was not helped by the conflicting and confusing signals the British were putting out at this time. On the one hand the partisans were being praised over the airwaves while Mihailović was being criticized by the FO and now, apparently, by SOE: on the other, they received a message from the British general staff on the anniversary of the foundation of Yugoslavia, full of warm praise for 'the indomitable Cetniks under your heroic Minister of War, General Mihailović'.[42] The Yugoslavs constantly fell prey to their failure to grasp that the British were not a homogeneous entity with one clear-cut policy, but a collection of separate organizations and individuals who could be as confused as themselves. The conflicting signals in fact reflected the divisions and uncertainties in the various British bodies, not to mention the rivalries between and within them.

Only a few days after reassuring King Peter that Mihailović was to continue to receive the fullest possible support, Eden had suggested to Churchill that a strongly-worded telegram should be sent, reminding the Yugoslav minister of war that he was not being furnished with supplies to fight the communists. The British expected in return that he would commit acts of sabotage against the Axis, and create a united front.[43] More than two weeks later, on 3 January 1943, Eden was not pleased to discover that this telegram had not been sent:

We are to go back on the decision we had previously taken (because, it seems, SOE and C-in-C Middle East didn't agree, tho' PM does) and give full backing to Mihailovich tho' he is not fighting our enemies and is being publicly denounced by our Soviet ally. I can see no sense in such a policy and every likelihood that we and the Russians will come to an open clash... I spoke to Cadogan last week and thought he agreed.[44]

Cadogan, however, noted: 'I fear I do not remember you saying anything to me that would necessitate a change.'

While London SOE had agreed with PWE to implement the new propaganda line, it appears that Cairo SOE was either not informed of this agreement, or chose to ignore it. No sooner had the new policy been put into practice in late October, than SOE Cairo asserted both its own independence and its support for Mihailović by setting up Radio Karageorge. This 'freedom station' purported to broadcast from Mihailović's headquarters, and was established to enhance his standing and to counteract the new BBC line and that of Radio Free Yugoslavia. It caused yet more animosity in London towards Cairo SOE on two counts. First, in the August shake-up of Cairo SOE it had been decided at the highest level that control of all propaganda in the Middle East should be handed over to PWE; Paul Vellacott had been despatched to Cairo in November expressly for that reason, but when he told SOE to close down Karageorge they had flatly refused.[45] Secondly, it upset the FO by directly contradicting the new propaganda line which was designed to put pressure on Mihailović to take more aggressive action. Cairo SOE, instead of acting purely as the agents of the Commander-in-Chief Middle East, were actually making their own policy. It was at this point that Glenconner judged that John Bennet was not experienced enough to run his own section: although he knew Yugoslavia well he was too individualistic by temperament. Robert Lethbridge with his knowledge and experience of Yugoslavia would have been Glenconner's first choice but he was unavailable as he had replaced Bailey in the USA and Canada, so Basil Davidson was appointed acting head with an officer to assist him.[46]

When Bailey finally reached Mihailović's headquarters at Gornje Lipovo in Montenegro it did not mean that the time of indecision and suspense at the FO was ended. Nearly six weeks later, Eden was still waiting to hear what Bailey had to say, and was hardly pleased to hear from Selborne that Bailey's interim report was hoped for soon, and that portions of interest to the FO would be communicated to him immediately. It appeared to Eden that SOE—or at least

Selborne—was not totally aware of the importance he and the FO attached to Bailey's mission, nor of the influence his reports may ultimately have on policy in general. Eden wanted *all* Bailey's reports. Selborne quickly reassured the Foreign Secretary that he was already receiving all but the 'domestic details' and went on to assert that he had nothing to hide from him.[47] This was not true. Baker Street was at that very moment conspiring to hide the contents of Bailey's early telegrams from both the FO and SIS. The reason was that Bailey concurred with Hudson's opinion on the impossibility of reconciling Mihailović and the partisans while they were simultaneously attempting to occupy the same territory. There was no point in putting to Mihailović plans for collaborating with groups in Croatia not under his direct command since he was convinced that they were all communists controlled by the USSR, and saw their defeat as the only solution. Furthermore, Trifunović-Birčanin was in complete agreement with Mihailović's assessment of forces other than the Yugoslav Home Army.[48]

In June 1942 a combination of Italian pressure and shortage of supplies had led Tito to the conclusion that Foča was no longer suitable for his headquarters, and the whole Partisan movement had embarked upon the 'long march' to the remote and barren area of western Bosnia. En route the partisans had collected dispossessed Serbs who had lost all in the Ustasha persecutions and young Croats who felt themselves at odds with the Ustasha government of the NDH, and rather than be conscripted into its army preferred to join the Partisans. With expanded numbers, in an area containing no Axis troops and of little or no strategic value, Tito and the communist leadership established the 'Republic of Bihać'. Here they set about creating a new image of a broadly-based movement, with the emphasis on Yugoslav patriotism rather than communism. To further this impression the first session of the Anti-Fascist Council for the National Liberation of Yugoslavia (AVNOJ) was convened on 26 November 1942 and the National Liberation Army (NLA) had been developed throughout 1942 to ensure a wider appeal than the overtly communist Proletarian brigades. In fact both AVNOJ and the NLA were dominated by the Yugoslav Communist Party (CPY). The Politburo and the Supreme Command of the NLA were one and the same, with political commissars attached to all NLA units at every level to ensure maximum control. The discipline imposed by the commissars allowed the leaders, many of whom had fought in the Spanish civil war, to mould the NLA into a much more organized and useful body than the irregular one that had left Serbia in 1941.[49]

Bailey, unaware of these developments, reported that about 4,000 professed communists led by Tito had proclaimed an 'independent republic'. Helping them to hold the area were about another 10,000 fighters whose main interest was resistance to the occupiers and who would probably look to Mihailović's leadership in the long-term. Bailey's main concern was that this area of north-western Bosnia was predominantly Serbian and, as he saw no prospect of compelling Mihailović to make peace with the Partisans, the best solution was to persuade them to leave Serbian lands. His plan was to engineer an agreement between the two sides whereby the Partisans would move north into Croatia proper, allowing Mihailović to move north from Herzegovina. There were, Bailey argued, a number of advantages in this: the unification of 'Serbian nationalists' would upset the Axis policy of ruling by division, and the Germans would be confronted by fresh disturbances in hitherto quiet areas. Once established, the Partisans could link up with their comrades in Austria and Hungary and SOE and SIS could then extend their own links into central Europe. If the Partisans could raise the Croats against the Germans and replace the Pavelić regime it would do much to allay the Serbs' lust for revenge for Ustasha atrocities. Finally, with the threat of attack by the Partisans removed, Mihailović would have no reason for fighting anyone other than the occupiers. Bailey warned that Mihailović would even accept the loss of British support in pursuit of the liquidation of Partisans in Serbian territory. While admitting that his plan meant a 'shift' in policy, Bailey felt that it was worthwhile and, if Mihailović agreed, planned to send Hudson to negotiate with Tito. His only reservation was that Mihailović might refuse on the grounds that it would pose problems regarding the post-war integrity of Yugoslavia.

Cairo SOE was in agreement with Bailey. By supporting Mihailović in his areas of influence and establishing sub-missions there they hoped eventually to be able to control all actions by his forces. As Mihailović did not have strong enough influence in Slovenia and

Croatia any attempt to build him up in those areas would stimulate a resumption of open civil war, benefiting only the Axis. The military argument for SOE to intervene in Slovenia and Croatia was that vital lines of communication ran through both regions and only the guerrillas in these areas could be in a position to take action to disrupt the flow of traffic on those lines. On the political front, it was argued that if SOE did not intervene in these areas then Serbia would become a British sphere of influence while Croatia and Slovenia would come under either Soviet or American influence. The Soviets were already weighing in with propaganda support, while the Americans had a well-organized and vocal expatriate community which was pressing the US State Department to aid Croatia.[50]

Baker Street was *not* in agreement with either Bailey or Cairo, regarding their advice as a *radical change* of policy. Until these differences could be settled so that all three could speak with one voice it was vital that no hint should reach the FO or SIS that these messages had been received from Bailey. In the meantime SOE passed on to the FO edited highlights of Bailey's messages with all contentious points left out as Baker Street was acutely aware that dividing up Yugoslavia on the lines Bailey proposed would not be greeted with joy at the FO.[51]

Given that SOE had built up the expectation that Bailey would be able to produce reports which would immediately make the situation so clear that a major policy change could be decided on the basis of them, it is perhaps unsurprising that Eden and the FO became impatient. Their subsequent attitude probably reflects the 'waiting for Bailey' syndrome, which developed over the three months of SOE consistently advising that nothing should be decided until their man went in: it also reflects their total inability to grasp the complexity of the situation in occupied Yugoslavia, where both war and civil war were raging, with political differences further complicated by ethnic and religious divides. In addition, it appears that Bailey was expected to produce these complicated analyses and encourage Mihailović to be at least as active as the partisans with one hand tied behind his back. An example of this is Bailey's recommendation that BBC broadcasts praising the Partisans should be suspended for a period of six to eight weeks to gauge the effect. As well as putting Mihailović under pressure to step up his activities, these broadcasts were meant to be a bargaining counter for Bailey as Pearson felt that if he should 'deem it advisable for us to change our tone, it would greatly enhance his prestige with the General that it was on his recommendation this was brought about'.[52] However, when SOE wanted to put this into practise, Orme Sargent was not impressed, noting tartly that he could not see what Bailey hoped to gain and that the peasants would hardly flock to Mihailović in their thousands just because all mention of the partisans ceased. More tellingly perhaps, Orme Sargent disagreed with SOE on the issue because it would seem too much like giving in to the YGE and Mihailović,[53] illustrating the depths to which the former's prestige had sunk at the FO, and how closely tied were the YGE and Mihailović. It seems unfortunate for Mihailović that he had as his spokesmen people who, by the winter of 1942–3, had entirely lost the sympathy of their British hosts.

Bailey's early reports indicate that he had got off to a good start with Mihailović, he had been well received and relations were good and set fair for future co-operation, including agreements for receiving British sub-missions and for passing agents into other countries.[54] He was also pleasantly surprised to discover that Hudson's standing with Mihailović was much better than he had anticipated. However, this honeymoon period was not destined to last because in addition to the rejection of Bailey's recommendations on broadcasting, the problematical supply position was not improved. Despite messages emphasizing that supply drops would greatly strengthen his position with Mihailović, and Jovanović's pleas to Eden for arms, the limited aircraft available to SOE Cairo, and their uncertain serviceability, meant that for the first two months of Bailey's mission in Yugoslavia, only two sorties were received. Bailey had obviously been welcomed at Mihailović's headquarters with the hope that the situation would soon improve but, although for no fault of his own, he had failed to come up with the goods. His standing was diminished and his relationship with Mihailović began to deteriorate.

6

YUGOSLAVIA, FROM SIDE-SHOW
TO CENTRE STAGE

During the 'waiting for Bailey' period the war moved on: a number of important developments took place which were to have far-reaching implications for the Yugoslav resistance. Rommel's defeat at El Alamein in early November 1942 had opened the way for the 'Torch' landings of British and American troops in French North Africa. In mid January 1943 Churchill and Roosevelt met in Casablanca for eight days of discussions on all aspects of Anglo-American policy, and while the conference was in progress, Churchill received a telegram from Stalin on 15 January informing him that German forces near Stalingrad were being finished off. Three days later the siege of Leningrad was lifted by the Red Army and on 23 January the Eighth Army entered Tripoli.

One of the most important decisions taken at the Casablanca conference was that in 1943 operations in the Mediterranean should take priority over cross-Channel landings. The rationale was that the elimination of Italy from the war would make the Allied return to northern Europe, when it came, more certain of success. Churchill was also hoping, despite the pessimism of Eden and Attlee, that action in the Mediterranean might yet bring in Turkey on the Allied side. The first move against Italy would be the invasion of Sicily in July. To cover their real intentions the western Allies put in train elaborate deception plans, designed to convince the Axis that the next move would be on Sardinia and the Greek Peloponnese, followed by an advance through the Balkans. In March 1943 the Chiefs of Staff issued a directive to SOE to increase guerrilla activity in the Balkans to strengthen this impression: Yugoslavia, hitherto viewed as of minor significance in the overall conduct of the war, was to take on greater importance as a result.[1]

A commonly held idea is that the deception operation was a major triumph, and that the Germans bought the whole idea and acted upon it. However, Klaus Jürgen Müller argues that this conclusion is based on too limited a reading of sources and too optimistic an appraisal of the Allies ability to deceive the Germans. Using German sources to analyse strategic planning, he argues that their High Command—not unaware of the possibility of Allied deception—was only marginally, or temporarily, influenced by these operations, and continued to rely mainly on their own strategic analysis of what was the next most likely move and, consequently, the longer-term pattern of the conduct of the war. According to Müller, Hitler's main preoccupations in the Balkans were to keep Italy in the war and to secure for the German war machine the vital mineral wealth of the area. Fears and doubts about Italy's commitment to the Axis cause after the loss of north Africa, apparently generated a domino theory: if Italy dropped out then the Balkans and eventually the right flank of the Eastern front would be threatened. The reinforcements sent into the Balkans in spring 1943 were less a response to the idea that the Allies might invade, more a precautionary measure against a vacuum if Italy did indeed withdraw.[2] If Müller is correct, it is arguable that the mere fact of resistance forces existing in the Balkans and *posing* a threat, was as important as any action they engaged in. If so, this raises the question of whether any useful purpose was to be served if the British Chiefs of Staff did manage to increase activity beyond small scale sabotage and disruption, especially given the cost in civilian reprisals.

Whether or not the German High Command and Hitler were deceived, as distinct from the German occupation forces in Yugoslavia, there can be little doubt that both Tito and Mihailović were expecting an Allied landing in Yugoslavia at some stage. The YGE thought the landing was imminent and in February 1943 Jovanović was urgently pressing the FO to agree to the despatch of a number of Yugoslav officers from the Middle East to reinforce Mihailović's Yugoslav Home Army. Bailey was enthusiastic about the idea and the FO agreed, but once again the shortage of aircraft made it impossible.[3] Yugoslavs and occupiers alike were prey to the 'Salonika front fixation', envisaging a repeat of the Allied landings which liberated Serbia in 1918. While both resistance leaders expected such a scenario, each perceived it in a very different light. Mihailović looked forward to the arrival of the Allies as the trigger for the *Ustanak*—the general rising when he and his followers would join forces with the Allies to throw out the Axis. Tito and the communist leadership of the partisans, by contrast, regarded this eventuality as wholly detrimental to their long-term aim of establishing a communist state. They saw the Western Allies as a reactionary force which would naturally unite with similar elements in Yugoslavia— namely Mihailović—to frustrate this aim. One idea common to both was that before any such landing occurred, the other had to be roundly defeated. All the Allied deception did was to give fresh impetus to the civil war, which could only be of benefit to the occupiers.

Early in 1943 the Axis launched another major drive to clear out the Yugoslav resistance once and for all, planning to deal with the Partisans before turning their attention to Mihailović's forces. In January 'Operation Weiss' began against the Partisans, forcing them to move out of their 'independent republic'. Retreating southwards, they attempted to fight their way into the predominantly chetnik areas of Herzegovina, Montenegro and the Sandjak. Even though hard-pressed on all sides by Germans, Italians, Croats and chetniks, Tito perceived the defeat of the latter as the main objective in the light of the expected Allied landing. Tito's solution to this potentially desperate situation was to negotiate with the Germans.

What has subsequently become known as the 'March Negotiations' opened with a proposal for an exchange of prisoners between the partisans and the Germans. There had been a previous exchange in November 1942, at which Glaise von Horstenau, German military plenipotentiary in the NDH, had suggested an agreement whereby the Partisans would be left in peace in their own territory as long as they undertook not to sabotage the transport of vital minerals and foodstuffs. Now three high-ranking Partisan negotiators— Milovan Djilas, Koča Popović and Vladko Velebit—took up this proposal and enlarged upon it at their preliminary meeting with the German general commanding 717 Infantry Division. In addition to Horstenau's straightforward 'truce', the Partisans wanted the Axis to accord them the status of a recognized belligerent. Velebit pointed out that there was no reason to continue hostilities since the Partisans regarded the chetniks as their prime enemy. Furthermore, as the British supported the YGE in London—and, thereby, the chetniks in Yugoslavia—the Partisans would have no compunction in opposing any British landing on the Adriatic coast.[4] This must have looked fairly appealing to the German negotiators. Not only could they cease, or maybe just postpone, their fight with the Partisans, but the latter would destroy the chetniks who were next on the list in the Axis offensive, and fight the British too if they did invade. Encouraging the civil war would result in both sides being weakened and generally make their job easier all round. For the Partisans the agreement—apart from the obvious short-term practical advantages—possibly held a longer-term appeal: to be recognized as a regular belligerent force, even by such dubious means, would enhance their prestige and their standing *vis-à-vis* Moscow. Although Mihailović and the Yugoslav Home Army were included in the Germans' dismissive term 'bandits', the fact that the YGE and the British recognized them gave them something of an advantage in the legitimacy stakes.

The negotiations continued at increasingly high levels, eventually involving German, Croat and Italian authorities in Sarajevo, Zagreb, Vienna, Rome and Berlin. The parley lasted for more than six weeks, during which time a ceasefire was in operation. Velebit, having visited Zagreb with the German intelligence agent Hans Ott to discuss the proposals with Horstenau, travelled to all possible outlying Partisan commands—under German and Croat escort—to assure them that Tito had indeed ordered a ceasefire and prohibited sabotage on the Zagreb-Belgrade railway line. Prisoner exchanges, including the freeing of Tito's common-law wife, went ahead, and Ott and Velebit discussed the possibility of arranging a 'conclusive conversation' between Tito and Kasche, the Nazi diplomatic representative in Zagreb.

It must have come as rather a nasty shock when this temporary peaceful coexistence was brought to an end on Hitler's orders. He had no desire to deal with 'bandits', and instead of playing off the two resistance movements against each other, German troops should destroy them both.[5] Even so, the breathing space had been of considerable benefit to the Partisans. The period of German inactivity had removed the pressure on them, enabling Tito to utilize the forces previously engaged in defensive action against the Germans to penetrate chetnik-held territory.

In early February 1943 Bailey reported the Axis attack on the partisan republic, and the possibility that Bihać was already in German hands: 'Recent hysterical tone of Radio Free Yugoslavia confirms the position is desperate ... Regrettable as might be the Axis success in clearing up the Partisans, it may be the best solution for our long term policy.' He went on to explain this with a detailed history of the relationship of the two resistance movements and the reasons for its irretrievable breakdown, setting out the 'pros and cons' of each side.

Bailey argued that on the one hand, Mihailović had decided on a long-term policy of exhibiting collaborationism as a cover for the development of his organization and received arms and assistance from the Italians—although clearly stating that these would one day be turned against *both* occupiers. On the other, the partisans had lost the support of most of the rural population, due to their hit and run tactics which left the peasants to face the music once the Partisans had moved on, and to their insistence on the republican aspect of their proposed communist state while the majority of the population were loyal monarchists. In addition, in clashes between the two forces, the 'record generally is of Partisan withdrawal before Mihailović' and the former no longer existed as an organized force in any Serb inhabited territory except Bosnia. Bailey concluded:

In my opinion, despite its defects, M's long term policy will serve us best in the long run. After all credit to the Partisans for the trouble they have caused the Axis...M's kinder policy of appeasing the occupiers appeals strongly to the peasants [who are the] strongest source of popular support [although it is] difficult at times to see much difference between this policy and that of Nedic.[6]

Bailey's problem, although he did not perceive it at the time, was his information on the partisans was out of date, and he was unaware of the changes wrought in tactics and organization in Bihać. Bailey reiterated the opinion he shared with Hudson, that the gulf between the two movements was too great ever to be bridged. British influence would not sway Mihailović from attempting to liquidate the partisans but could, if properly exercised, be used to dissuade him from collaborating with the Axis in pursuit of them.

The problem which Bailey perceived all too clearly was that the continuing chronic shortage of aircraft available for SOE operations left him with virtually *no* influence. His inability to provide supplies was steadily eroding his position with Mihailović and souring their relationship. In addition, the BBC broadcasts praising the Partisans—while Mihailović was being attacked by Radio Free Yugoslavia—were, in Glenconner's opinion, driving Mihailović to the conclusion that the British not only lacked faith in his movement but were playing a double game. Glenconner warned that the combination of these factors might soon render Bailey's position untenable. 'Moreover, our influence over Mihailović will be so diminished that he may feel he has no alternative but collaboration with the Italians'. An unidentified FO hand has noted in the margin next to this statement 'He's doing that already.'[7] In November 1942 Hudson had reported peace feelers put out to Mihailović by Birolli, the Italian governor of Montenegro. Pearson thought this might be a useful development, and that it could be the first chink in the Axis armour. Or, as Hudson rather more colourfully, and characteristically phrased it, 'M says if WOPS make peace he will disarm them and hold all WOP occupied zones against BOSH.' Peter Loxley at the FO was not so enthusiastic: SIS had a report of the same incident and it was not clear whether Birolli was offering a separate peace between Italy and the Allies or simply with Mihailović. 'In any case' he concluded rather primly, 'we feel that Mihailović should be fighting the Italians and not negotiating with them.'[8]

The essential problem for Mihailović was his dependence upon the chetnik leaders in the Italian occupied zones. There, early accommodations had been made with the occupiers, to ensure food supplies and to gain Italian supplied weapons to defend the populations against the excesses of the communists. The Italians themselves were fully alive to the long-term danger posed by the chetniks, but without sufficient forces to quell them had no choice but to come to an understanding. These arrangements were already in place before Mihailović and his immediate entourage were driven out of Serbia in the winter of 1941–2. His hosts in Montenegro and the leaders in Herzegovina had already made this accommodation, and since Mihailović's armed strength largely derived from their followers, he had little choice in the matter. British Military

Intelligence was aware of the arrangements in Montenegro and pointed out that while local 'chieftains' Djurisić and Stanisić were prepared to deal with the Italians, there was no doubt that ultimately the weapons supplied by the occupiers would be used against them. By contrast, General Popović was completely collaborating with the Italians and as a result was held in contempt by the other 'chieftains' and Mihailović.[9]

The 'chetnik' movement as a whole was represented by Djukanović, a 'legalized chetnik' at Birolli's HQ in Cetinje. There was no question of direct contact or collaboration between Mihailović and the Italians, but Hudson was fully aware that Mihailović was willing to exploit them as a source of food and arms in Montenegro. Hudson's main gripe was that Mihailović's organization was missing the opportunity to blackmail the Italians and obtain more from them. Bailey and Hudson both had mixed feelings about the Italian connection: while it undoubtedly provided benefits they felt it was sometimes questionable as to who was using whom, and a number of their signals were very critical of the ploy. Baker Street did not share the doubts expressed by Bailey and Hudson and felt that if the two officers were informed of the Allied strategy agreed at Cassablanca—to knock the Italians out of the war in summer 1943—they might perceive Mihailović's relations with the Italians in a different light. Pearson suggested that, as Bailey's communications were secure, he should be informed of this fact. Hambro agreed and felt that Bailey should be given some guidance on the issue, by 'playing discretely' with the Italians Mihailović could get out of them quantities of arms and ammunition on a far greater scale than SOE could ever hope to provide. He might also be in a position to accelerate the Italian withdrawal by means of defeatist propaganda and bribery, but this could only be achieved by remaining on friendly terms with them.[10]

Local chetnik bands had already been planning action against the Partisan republic, and as a result became incorporated in Operation Weiss. In turn, the Partisans, withdrawing to the south, attempted to fight their way into chetnik territory. Hudson put his finger rather nicely on the situation: 'Axis are playing a pretty game by pushing the Partisans down from the north, thus cutting them off from Croatia and forcing the chetniks in the south to defend their territory.'[11] While reporting the attack on the Bihać republic, Bailey had stated that Mihailović's forces, albeit against their wishes, were *not* participating in the anti-Partisan drive. If this was true at the time, it did not long remain so. Mihailović was acutely aware that it was essential to prevent a partisan take-over of the area where the expected Allied landing would occur, and hoped simultaneously to finish off his rivals once and for all. He was just about to depart to join the fray himself when the notorious christening incident took place. On 28 February, at a christening in Lipovo in Montenegro, Mihailović made an impassioned speech highly critical of 'Perfidious Albion', which required the Serbs to fight to their last drop of blood without adequate assistance, while his only source of supply to date had been the Italians. His main enemies were the partisans, Ustashas, Muslims and Croats—in that order—and only when he had dealt with them would he turn his attention to the Germans and Italians.

Bailey's report of this speech caused a furore in London, and brought the collective wrath of both British and Yugoslav governments down upon Mihailović. It took quite some time for the ruffled feathers to be smoothed in the wake of this incident, if ever they entirely were. More than two months later, Rendel was still having to argue against it being evidence of Mihailović's disloyalty.[12] The DMI attributed the speech to Mihailović being badly advised: 'His political confidant, Dr Vasić, was a reactionary pan-Serb of a dangerous type, while two of his principal staff officers Lalatović and Ostojić were decidedly anti-British.'[13] Jovanović, called to account by Eden via Rendel, denied that it reflected any anti-British feelings on the part of Mihailović or that it proved him to be in collaboration with the Italians. It was, he said, obviously made in a moment of great irritation—if he did not know for certain that General Mihailović did not drink, he might have thought it was made under the influence of liquor—and should not be taken so seriously by the British. (In fact, Bailey later stated that everyone present—with the possible exception of the baby—had consumed alcohol in some quantity.) The Yugoslav premier also cited other instances of allies violently abusing each other: the French and the British at the outset of the current war, or the Serbs and the French during the First World War, but neither case had prevented them from acting as loyal allies fighting side by side against the common enemy. While admitting that Mihailović should not have spoken as he did, Jovanović went on to point out that at least some degree of irritation was attributable to recent BBC broadcasts and that independent communications were still denied to the YGE and its minister of war.[14] It was only the Croats and Muslims who worked with the Ustashas that Mihailović regarded as enemies. In December 1942 he had passed on a message to the king from Maček supporters on the Adriatic coast on the 24th anniversary of the creation of Yugoslavia, and informed his PM that he had addressed the Muslim Committee which was working to win Muslims away from the Ustasha. He had gone on to point out that with so many enemies it was impossible to fight them all at once, and that the destruction of Pavelić's Croatia was his priority, both because of the atrocities the Ustasha were committing and because this would 'strike a vital artery of our greatest enemy the Germans'. He asked for propaganda support to win over the Muslims and Croats, and for the Croat members of the YGE to openly condemn the Ustashas and make a distinction between them and innocent Croats.[15]

Bailey had reported the christening speech in order to bring home to the FO the damage being done by the BBC broadcasts and the chronic lack of supplies. He also made a great fuss about it on the spot, feeling that a showdown with Mihailović and company would clear the air and open the way for 'more favourable negotiations', although it meant some uncomfortable moments. Presumably 'favourable' here meant Mihailović falling in with British plans for Yugoslav resistance. To make his point, Bailey withdrew to his own quarters, remaining there for a few days to allow Mihailović to stew. Bailey assessed that his behaviour had 'given rise to a gratifying apprehension at Mihailović's headquarters', which he thought would strengthen his negotiating hand. Another member of the British mission, Major Greenlees, however, maintained regular contact.[16]

Bailey's plan backfired in *both* directions. Bailey wanted the incident to be used to put pressure on the YGE to get Mihailović to co-operate with the British mission, but in the event the whole episode seems to have been blown up far beyond what he intended.[17] The incident was taken very seriously in London: Churchill sent Jovanović a stiff note, warning that unless Mihailović changed his policy the British might no longer favour him to the exclusion of other resistance movements. Baker Street had expressed reservations on the wisdom of passing on Bailey's report of the 'outburst' to the YGE in case it further undermined his relationship with Mihailović. Cairo was more gung-ho and advised that the more rigorously the FO prosecuted the matter, the better for both long and short-term SOE programmes, no matter how unpleasant the immediate consequences might be.[18] While at Mihailović's HQ the 'apprehension' did not have the desired effect either, it simply set the seal on the poor relations between the British mission and its Yugoslav hosts. Months later it was not unusual for the two to be semi-incommunicado, with only the trusty Greenlees keeping open channels of communication.[19]

The breakdown in the relationship between Bailey and Mihailović led to a lack of confidence on both sides. When the latter suddenly departed on 16 March without telling Bailey where he was going, Bailey thought the most likely explanation was that 'He might be assuming personal command of operations against Partisans'. However, having recently heard of attempts by the Germans, Italians and Ljotić, leader of the Serbian fascists, to arrange a meeting with Mihailović, Bailey did not consider it an impossibility that this might be a secondary reason for his absence. Mihailović had in fact gone to fight the Partisans, but did not want Bailey to know it. Bailey was suspicious, and perhaps a little nervous, and on 23 March, with Mihailović still away and reports that the fighting was going against the chetniks, he thought it possible that the SOE mission might have been abandoned—as Hudson had been previously. In this eventuality he told Cairo not to heed any appeals from Mihailović for supplies unless they were guaranteed by Bailey's correct code signature. Bailey's signals, some of which seem to contradict each other, reflect his uncertainty as to what exactly was happening. Shortly after fearing that Mihailović might be meeting Germans, Italians and Ljotić, he sent a telegram clearly indicating that Mihailović would have no truck with the Germans.[20] Mihailović himself had already informed Jovanović of two German approaches. The first, on 26 February was from a local commander; the second, on 1 March, was by the Gestapo chief in Yugoslavia who wanted Mihailović to meet Hitler's special envoy. The deal on offer was that all German and Bulgarian forces would withdraw from Yugoslavia, leaving Mihailović in charge as long as he guaranteed free rail passage to the south and to Bulgaria. This proposal had been turned down flat. Mihailović's opinion was that the Axis authorities were attempting to exploit the adverse publicity he had been receiving in Allied countries.[21]

The Bailey-Mihailović relationship was patched up after Jovanović sent a telegram to his minister of war, instructing him to receive Bailey at once, and a new broadcasting policy was arranged between SOE, PWE and the BBC to tone down praise for the partisans. The situation appeared to be improving until the BBC went back on the agreement and began to broadcast pro-partisan items again, embarrassing Bailey who had taken credit for the change.[22]

While everyone was getting so indignant over the christening speech, the Partisans—who in turn regarded Mihailović and his adherents as their primary enemy—were making their arrangements with the Germans. Mihailović had some intelligence of this, although not all the details: Bailey reported on 22 March that 'most reliable sources' had informed Mihailović that the Partisans in Bosnia were parleying with the Germans, and gave some details of the participants in Sarajevo, although the object of the negotiations was unknown. He asked if SOE had any confirmation of this. Rendel drew this information to the attention of Douglas Howard, and reminded him that one of Bailey's reports had indicated that the partisans had recently obtained a good deal of German war material. While admitting the fact that the information came from Mihailović sources, therefore possibly rendering it suspect, and doubting that the Partisans would closely co-operate with the 'Huns', Rendel felt it was interesting in the light of the great play being made of Mihailović's contacts with the Italians.[23]

An accusation constantly levelled at SOE, particularly by the FO, was that of taking only the short-term view regarding Yugoslavia. Hudson's comment that 'I remain convinced that we should attempt to persuade Mihailović to think more as a soldier than a politician' was interpreted by Rendel as an illustration of the fundamental difference between SOE and the FO. The very nature of SOE, he felt, meant that short-term expedients were inevitable, while the FO looked to the long-term consequences of any actions. Obviously winning the war was the most important consideration:

But my own impression is that no military action on the part of Mihailović can possibly tip the scale in favour of an Allied victory, and that the war will be won in quite different areas, and by military operations on an infinitely vaster scale. Mihailović's movement in fact seems to me to be of comparatively little military importance, but of very great potential political importance. I cannot help feeling therefore that the time is coming when we shall have to decide whether the political or military aspect of his movement should come first.[24]

This was largely in line with Bailey's conclusions: one of his early messages stated 'German intentions to liquidate Mihailović are directed much more against his movement as a political factor in Serbia than against him personally as a military opponent.'[25] Nevertheless, Bailey did regard the Yugoslav Home Army as a military organization of great potential usefulness, and had ideas on how to strengthen it, including the addition of the Yugoslav officers from the Middle East to improve the calibre of the Staff. An SOE analysis, produced in January 1943, which advocated unqualified support for Mihailović—mythologizing him if necessary—was greeted at the FO with a degree of scepticism, if not downright antagonism.[26] It appears that the FO interpretation of 'long-term' planning was tinged with a certain lack of realism and a large amount of wishful thinking. The FO wanted to appease the Soviets, while keeping them out of Yugoslavia; *and* they wanted a resistance leader charismatic enough to inspire his followers, but at the same time lacking any long-term political ambitions of his own, easily bent to the British will, and who would reunite Yugoslavia at the war's end. If such a creature existed, SOE had not found it: they appear to have been trying to make the best of what they had, which the FO found unsatisfactory.

In early 1943, London SOE were putting forward what in their judgement was the best long-term option politically. However, while Baker Street was attempting to convince the FO that the greatest long-term advantage was to be gained from not only continuing but increasing support for Mihailović, there were other ideas taking shape in SOE's Cairo offices. As 1942 drew to a close an internal feud was raging there between those who wanted to replace Mihailović with the partisans, and those who adhered to the idea that supporting Mihailović meant that SOE should only have dealings with forces deemed to be loyal to him: the battle between the 'Children of Light and the Children of Darkness', as Basil Davidson rather picturesquely termed it.[27]

Basil Davidson had remained in charge of the Yugoslav desk with James Klugmann assisting him. These two were very firmly in the 'Children of Light' camp, and between them have probably done more than anyone else to fuel the flames of conspiracy theories: this is due in great measure to Davidson's account in his *Special Operations Europe* which is lively, biased, and not untouched by artistic license, and the fact that Klugmann was subsequently revealed to be a prominent member of the British communist party. It was to Davidson, and later also to Captain Bill Deakin, that Colonel 'Bolo' Keble, Glenconner's Chief of Staff, chose to reveal his big secret— namely, that he had access to bootleg secret information to which SOE was not officially privy.

The usual explanation of how Keble got hold of this is that he had access to it in his previous post in intelligence, and that by some bureaucratic oversight he was left on the list of people cleared to receive secret information. The origin of the information is a matter of dispute. Davidson confidently claims it was derived from 'Ultra',[28] while people who worked on the Enigma decrypts staunchly deny that this could be possible and claim that it could only have been low grade 'sigint' (signals intelligence) from German forces in Yugoslavia.[39] Michael Stenton, in his study of PWE, suggests that it is possible that SIS, feeling SOE was woefully ill-informed on events in Yugoslavia, decided to bring MO4 up to date by allowing access to *Sicherheitsdienst* decrypts which had previously been withheld, possibly maliciously.[29] Whatever its origins, the use to which this secret information was put is not in dispute. From early January 1943 Davidson and Deakin, with the aid of the intercepts, plotted a map which indicated the extent of Partisan activity, confirming the idea that these people were being unjustly ignored. It was not long before the 'Children of Light' were able to make telling use of their information, by what appeared to them to be a stroke of extreme good fortune.

After the Casablanca conference Churchill stopped in Cairo for four days, and while there had lunch with Deakin, who had been his research assistant when he was writing his *Life of Marlborough*. On the same evening, 28 January, Churchill met Keble and Deakin for a half-hour briefing on the situation in Yugoslavia, during which they showed him the map of Partisan activity. The result was that Churchill demanded a memo on the whole subject. Keble demurred and said that this should go through Baker Street. 'But he replied in his own inimical [*sic*] way that he was PM and could demand whatever he liked from whoever he chose.'[30] So Keble gave him a copy of a memo he had already prepared for the Chiefs of Staff and sent a copy by 'fast bag' to London: on 9 February the document reached Selborne, who was furious at not being kept informed of what was afoot.

While stating that aid to Mihailović was as necessary as ever, Keble's memo pointed out that the areas in which he was known to be active were occupied by three German and six Bulgarian divisions. This in effect, meant only Serbia. 'Other resisting elements', in Slovenia and Croatia were holding down thirty divisions in areas known to be vital to both Italian and German communications, without having received any external aid at all. The leadership was politically 'extreme left', but the rank and file—who included Croats, Slovenes and Serbs—were 'not necessarily politically minded'; in northern Croatia some still came under the leadership of Maček. Therefore, it was not accurate to adopt the German technique of branding the whole movement 'communist'.

At the present time no aid from any quarter is reaching these elements. If this situation continues, either the RUSSIANS or the AMERICANS will, for different reasons, take a practical interest. This will inevitably lead to the weakening of the whole BRITISH position. His Majesty's Government will, and is in fact already being accused of supporting a reactionary Pan-SERB leader, who commands no universal support within the country as a whole. *The prospect of two members of the United Nations backing mutually antagonistic groups within JUGOSLAVIA could only have lamentable consequences.*[31]

The memo offered what looked like an ideal solution; if SOE officers were to be with both sides they could use their influence not only to maximize Yugoslav resistance but also reconcile Mihailović and the partisans. Apparently the only thing preventing this being achieved was the want of a few long-range Liberators. It concluded with the latest telegram from Bailey, warning of the dangers of not supplying material assistance. Baker Street was inclined initially to view Keble's report as a neat ruse for obtaining more aircraft for SOE operations, rather than a major change in policy regarding the Yugoslav resistance movements. However, Keble's memo was essentially a revamp of Bailey's suggestions for supporting Mihailović in Serbian lands, and partisans and others in Slovenia and Croatia, but with some of Bailey's more contentious ideas edited out, such as the Yugoslav communist Partisans being able to link up with their comrades in Austria and Hungary. Bailey's analysis was an important part of the document presented to Churchill. His ideas about supporting both strands of resistance in separate areas was exactly what was being so hotly debated in Baker Street where it was felt that "Cairo are advocating a radical change of policy which we, at present, disagree with."[32] At the time Glenconner was in London discussing the position with Masterson in an attempt to co-ordinate the views of MO4 and Baker Street while the latter attempted to conceal the debate from the FO. It was hardly surprising that Selborne was so cross.

Keble's memo did not contain any radically new revelations for Churchill. Enigma decrypts had for some time been revealing the extent of the partisan activities and the fact that they were often doing more than Mihailović's forces. Since the summer and autumn of 1942 the PM's weekly reports from Hut 3 at Bletchley Park recommended that the Partisans should receive support: 'From the material we had from the Germans it appeared that Tito was the best bet.'[33] The DMI reports to Churchill also contained information on Partisan activities and the fact that at times they were more overtly active than the Mihailović followers, but had always advocated caution in the British attitude to these forces because of their apparent communism.

Churchill's enthusiasm for Keble's maps and memo was not because a veil had suddenly been lifted from his eyes. He simply needed all the Balkan guerrillas he could get, given Stalin's anticipated reaction to the news that Husky (the codename for the Sicily landing) was to take precedence over the cross-Channel landings. Churchill and Roosevelt had sent a joint telegram to Stalin informing him of what had been decided at Casablanca, expressing as their 'main desire' the diversion of German forces from the Russian front. American and British forces would be concentrated in Britain to prepare for an entry to the continent 'as soon as possible'. These concentrations would be known to the enemy, but not their eventual destination or purpose, thus the Axis would have to divert forces to France, the Low Countries, Corsica, Sardinia, Sicily, the heel of Italy, Yugoslavia, mainland Greece, Crete and the Dodecanese. It must have been plain to Stalin that this was not the second front in Western Europe that he had been promised for 1943, Churchill was painfully alive to this

Nothing in the world will be accepted by Stalin as an alternative to our placing 50 or 60 Divisions in France by the spring of this year. I think he will be disappointed and furious with the joint message.[34]

The prime minister was also acutely aware that Stalin was facing 185 German divisions while the British and American forces would not be engaging any Axis forces until Husky, which was scheduled for June. In the light of this, he used the Cairo memo to try to whip up enthusiasm for pressing ahead with contacting the partisans. He must have known that MO4's claim that the Partisans were holding down thirty Axis divisions was erroneous: there were actually thirty-one Axis divisions in the whole of Yugoslavia according to Baker Street, nineteen Italian, seven German and five Hungarian. At that time three Italian and four German divisions were engaged in Operation Weiss.[35] However, this was rather immaterial, as Churchill was more inclined to get involved with the *idea* of things rather than the mundane details. In Cairo he had been presented with a document selling the idea of a great guerrilla force, and he made an immediate start on trying to obtain the much-needed aircraft with an approach to Eisenhower in Algiers in the hope of persuading the Americans to provide the Liberators.

On 11 February Keble's memo was circulated to the Chiefs of Staff Committee "for information and any action which they may consider necessary".[36] As the Chiefs of Staff also received Hut 3's weekly reports based on Enigma, it did not tell *them* anything new either, and appears to have had no immediate impact upon them as they favoured continuing exclusive support of Mihailović. At a meeting on 4 March at which they discussed a memorandum by the FO on policy in Yugoslavia, accompanied by minutes from Eden, Selborne and Orme Sargent, they concluded that they could not divert any Liberators for Yugoslavia as they were all needed elsewhere but, anxious to help Eden and SOE, they could spare four Halifaxes. Having considered the alternative policies set out in the FO memorandum, they did not feel qualified to express a strong view on the intricate political issues involved. 'In principle, however, they are inclined to the view that it would be a mistake to adopt a policy of supporting both sides'—not least because the available aircraft were hardly sufficient to give effective support to either.[37] By 20 March, when the COS issued a new directive for SOE, they had obviously changed their minds, due to detailed information on Operation Weiss gleaned from Ultra decrypts.

At a high level meeting between the FO, SIS and SOE on 20 February representatives of SIS disputed Bailey's information on Mihailović's strength, claiming that it was exaggerated. In general SIS pressed the Partisans' case and emphasized their resistance in eastern Bosnia and western Serbia.[38] Obviously SIS was also basing its analysis on Ultra information.

This meeting and Keble's memo heightened the debate between the FO and SOE on their respective attitudes to the Partisans, as revealed in the correspondence between Sir Charles Hambro and Orme Sargent who had both attended the meeting. Hambro defended Mihailović against the charge of being Pan-Serb, anti-Croat and anti-Partisan. Basing his argument on telegrams from Bailey and Hudson dating from the middle of February 1943, he pointed out that Mihailović was now abstaining from fighting the partisans and from collaborating with the Italians. The possibility of SOE co-operating with the Partisans had never been excluded, the failure to do so only because they had not been successful in establishing a British officer with them. SOE's policy of backing Mihailović was not based on considerations of post-war interests but on current military ones. He went on to say 'we are in full agreement with backing both sides' but with a number of provisos. Bailey's opinion was that the Serbian population was in a position to make a greater contribution than the Slovenes or Croats and it therefore followed that Mihailović, as head of the most important para-military organization in Serbia, Montenegro, Herzegovina and south-west Bosnia, should have priority. It was technically impossible to give support to anyone until they had a British officer to organize it, and any such support must never be allowed to jeopardize the excellent relations SOE had with Mihailović's movement. Hambro concluded that the eventual decision to back both sides rested with the FO, but this would involve a modification of present policy which was to support Mihailović, infiltrate officers to other resistance elements, and support these others if the resulting information justified it.

Orme Sargent agreed with this, but pointed out that it already implied a change of policy. The FO was always 'influenced by post-war interest in the Balkans and not entirely on the short-term policy of military advantage', Orme Sargent stated, setting out the objections to Bailey's plan to separate the two contending factions by moving the partisans into Croatia. While this seems to have appealed to SOE as the most sensible solution to the clashes between the two, it represented the worst of all possible worlds to the FO, who viewed it as the first step towards the ultimate disintegration of Yugoslavia. Having disagreed with the idea that Mihailović should always receive priority, Orme Sargent also contended that once the other elements had been contacted it might well 'serve our immediate purpose' to give them priority in certain circumstances.[39] Ironically, he did not appear to perceive any discrepancy between his statements on post-war interests and immediate purposes.

This was all part of a spat between SOE and the FO over who should call the shots: Orme Sargent had told Glenconner that while SOE was entirely free to contact anyone they wanted to work with, to do sabotage and stir up disaffection, the terms of the FO-SOE agreement of June 1942 meant that the FO always had first say on contact with individuals or organizations with political ambitions. Glenconner, not without some degree of logic, pointed out that 'the very people we either co-operate with or assist are just those who are concerned with the organization of political movements and activities.'[40] Hambro was even more indignant: 'As usual Orme Sargent is playing departmental grab.' Selbourne was prepared to be more conciliatory, but Hambro pointed out that if SOE even touched anyone not in line with exiled governments elsewhere then the FO made a huge stink, and yet here they were pushing for the partisans in Yugoslavia.[41]

In Cairo SOE the champions of Mihailović fought a rearguard action, producing a memorandum on 6 March which backed him to the hilt, arguing that 'We should only praise or back the partisans if he fails to play after we have given him material support.'[42] The memorandum, presumably penned by the 'Children of Darkness', warned that to back both sides simultaneously would only fan the flames of civil war. It went on to put forward suggestions on how to get Mihailović to agree to British proposals. Douglas Howard described this as 'sensible', acknowledging Mihailović's faults and the Partisans' good points: 'The conclusions, however, do not in every respect coincide with our views.' A questionnaire, based on the 6 March memorandum, was sent to Bailey, who took a more critical line than the Mihailović backers in Cairo, but recommended stronger support for Mihailović if he would agree to act in accord with SOE requirements.[43]

There appeared to be different perceptions within the pro-Mihailović camp on whether the 'other elements' SOE had agreed to contact included the partisans. The 6 March memo wanted to extend missions to Croatia and Slovenia, but cautioned that 'the communists would not suit us'. While the discussion was going on, the FO changed the idea of *contacting* the partisans into one of *supporting* them, a move that SOE viewed as not only precipitate but shortsighted. At a meeting of the FO-SOE Committee on 9 March, Orme Sargent stated: 'It had been decided as a matter of policy to support all resistance groups in Yugoslavia.' Pearson pointed out that it was impossible to agree to this without first discovering the long-term aims of other resistance groups.[44]

The Cairo memo supporting Mihailović ended with the claim that PWE was in substantial agreement with its content. This was not entirely true; in February Cairo PWE had drafted its own memorandum which was very similar in content to the one Keble gave Churchill but very much more antagonistic in its references to Mihailović. Keble felt a number of modifications to this memorandum were necessary before it was sent to London, he particularly wanted some of the strongly anti-Mihailović references toned down, and more positive aspects of his contribution included. He also wanted references to 'Partisans' to be changed to 'Croats and Slovenes'.[45] These modifications indicate that Keble was in favour of maximum support continuing to go to Mihailović, but at the same time very much in favour of supporting the partisans, even if they had to be disguised as simply Croats and Slovenes. While he had given the 'Children of Light' their ammunition, he does not, from this showing, appear to have shared their ultimate goal of switching support from Mihailović to the Partisans. In London meanwhile, PWE and SOE continued to be at loggerheads over PWE's propaganda, which SOE felt had taken on far too much of a pro-partisan stance since they had reluctantly agreed to PWE's changes in autumn 1942. Hambro wrote to Robert Bruce Lockhart to complain that this was antagonizing Mihailović and making life difficult for the British mission; he also noted that certain elements at the BBC were said to be personally enthusiastic about the Partisans.[46]

Rendel joined the argument, reminding Orme Sargent that it was the British who had played up Mihailović in the early days, and pressed the YGE to give him unequivocal support. In his conversation with the British ambassador, Jovanović had drawn an analogy between the Russian attitude towards the Mihailović-Partisan situation and their attitude towards the war in the west. The Soviets always took the line that the Partisans did all the fighting while Mihailović stood idly by; similarly only on the Russian front was the war being waged seriously while the Western Allies equally stood idly by. This, Rendel felt, was a reasonable line: Mihailović was no more anxious to strike prematurely than were the Allies.[47] Selborne thought Orme Sargent was taking 'an unusually pessimistic view of the amount of sabotage that Mihailović had actually executed' and sent him a list of actions for the past six months, which Orme Sargent noted was 'certainly more encouraging than we had thought'.[48] Into the midst of this debate came Bailey's report of the christening speech. This obviously did little to further the case for Mihailović, but essentially made little difference overall, since the FO had been moving inexorably towards taking up the Partisans for some considerable time. Eden and the FO had decided, in view of the fact that nothing could be done to persuade the Soviets to use their influence with the partisans to form a united resistance, that the only alternative was for the British to establish direct contact. The efforts of Sir Archibald Clark-Kerr, British ambassador to the USSR, had fallen on stony ground, as had all previous appeals. Clark-Kerr proposed that, in view of the British association with Mihailović, an Anglo-Soviet mission to the partisans might be suggested to allay Soviet suspicions. This was not greeted warmly by the FO, who felt it would commit the British too far, and that there was no reason for the Soviets to be suspicious unless *they* had ulterior motives for preventing British-partisan contact. In which case, it was preferable to go ahead without Soviet aid or involvement.[49]

Having agonized over long and short-term interests, the FO had finally decided to try to combine the two.[50] It was hoped that by increasing British influence it would be possible to prevent the establishment of a communist regime in Yugoslavia and thus obviate the possibility of communism taking hold in Austria and Hungary. The fact that SOE Cairo judged that the Partisans were not all communist was also no doubt a favourable factor, but it seems that none of the British intelligence sources had any idea of the degree of control Tito and the Partisan leadership had managed to establish. Or if they did, they did not say so.

Clark-Kerr welcomed the news. He told Orme Sargent that 'our SOE man here' had been hard put to meet attacks from his Russian opposite numbers, who were baffled by British determination to support someone known to be in touch with the Yugoslav Quisling when they might be helping the gallant partisans. Douglas Howard warned him against taking such a simplistic view of the situation, pointing out that Mihailović was as far from black and reactionary as the Partisans were from being all red.[51] Apparently Clark-Kerr relied quite heavily on the advice of Brigadier Hill—'our SOE man', who appears to have been something of a shady character, and who enjoyed an interesting relationship with the NKVD. British diplomats in Moscow and Kuibyshev were also influenced by the opinions of Simić, the Yugoslav minister to the USSR, who was at odds with the YGE over the question of the Partisans. He felt it unlikely that the partisans were communist, but was not averse to supporting them even if they *were*, as long as they were fighting the Axis.[52] Eden later wondered just how hard Clark-Kerr had tried to get an agreement with the Soviets.

The COS March directive to SOE, setting out what was required in 1943 to distract German forces from the Eastern front and give cover to the Mediterranean operations, gave as one of their main objectives the encouragement of large-scale revolts in the Balkans.

It is of the greatest importance that all resources at your disposal should be employed to the full to strengthen guerrilla warfare and direct the efforts of all resistance groups in Yugoslavia against the enemy....It may be necessary at a later date to co-ordinate the actions of all Yugoslav and Albanian guerrillas with the operations of Allied forces but this should not be allowed to detract from the fullest exploitation of guerrilla warfare from now onwards.[53]

It was only in the Balkans that large-scale guerrilla warfare was required: diversionary activity on a lesser scale was planned in Norway, while other areas, such as France and the Low Countries were to concentrate on sabotage and preparations for acting in support of Allied strategy. The co-ordination with Allied forces referred only to possible small-scale forces being established in the Balkans, to act in conjunction with the resistance forces against communications and the Romanian oilfields. While the COS were aware that guerrilla forces always had political objectives and that external control and manipulation were never easy, on purely pragmatic grounds the Partisans were too good a military advantage to miss. In the light of the success of 'Operation Harling' in Greece in November 1942, in which communists and non-communists had co-operated in blowing up the Gorgopotamos bridge, the COS had convinced themselves that the same thing could be achieved in Yugoslavia. This flew in the face of Bailey and Hudson's opinion that the two factions could never be reconciled. The COS's change of attitude between 4 and 20 March reflects the influence of military intelligence, including Ultra decrypts, which gave much more detailed information than that available to SOE. DMI reports had intelligence of joint actions between chetnik and partisan forces in some parts of Bosnia. Military sources also told them that Mihailović's organization was not inactive but more inclined to acts of sabotage, while the partisans were actually fighting.[54]

Orme Sargent wrote to Selborne, in effect asking what he thought the COS directive meant. Did they really want to depart from British policy of discouraging premature revolts, or did they simply intend to tune up existing guerrillas to be ready when the signal for action was given? He hoped that the COS did *not* mean to encourage an immediate rising because this would cause problems with supply and would require future political promises. Selborne's reaction to the COS directive was guarded: he felt that the COS could not possibly want to encourage activity that would play into Axis hands and prematurely break up Balkan resistance. He argued against supporting both resistance movements in Yugoslavia with the current resources, and for increased support for Mihailović's organization. This would not only bring about political and military agreement with Mihailović, but also win over the Slovenes and Croats, thus leaving the Partisans with only hard-core communists who had little popular support and were of no value to the British. He doubted if the COS had really thought through the implications, but 'if they really want immediate action and results then indeed we should have to study seriously the question of collaborating with and building up the Partisans, since they alone, in return for promises of assistance from us, might be sufficiently desperate and fanatical to be ready to start a guerrilla war at once.'[55]

Hambro regarded the directive as an opportunity to obtain a new charter for SOE, in the hope of freeing the organization from 'interdepartmental grab and deliberate misinterpretations', now that its role was to be a link between regular armies and resistance.[56] He did not agree, however, to Glenconner's proposal for greater autonomy for MO4; the Cairo office had already caused too many difficulties and embarrassments to risk that.

Pearson warned the FO that any attempt to back both sides would simply result in falling between two stools, but the FO did not want political advice from SOE, and Baker Street eventually agreed, albeit half-heartedly. Howard felt that they had no choice, in the light of the evidence against Mihailović, and Bailey's report of the christening incident had brought things to a head. This, combined with the COS March directive, had produced a 'sudden and unexpected change' in SOE's attitude which brought their policy into line with that of the FO. The new policy was to 'slow down' with Mihailović and contact others outside his sphere of influence.[57] It might be difficult to see *how* it was possible to slow down any further with Mihailović, since the paucity of supplies had been one of the main problems for Bailey who—time after time—had emphasized that if anything was to be achieved supplies had to be increased. Lack of any substantial aid from the British, and the continuing reliance on having to get what he could from the Italians, was, after all, the cause of the christening outburst which was now being used in evidence against him.

Bailey had expected the Mihailović forces to disperse the partisans, albeit at a cost, but he looked forward to vigorous action against the Axis from some of the younger commanders once the Partisans had been liquidated.[58] In the event, Bailey's predictions were wrong: the partisan-German truce, although short-lived, had given the Partisans enough breathing space to survive the battle on the Neretva river, probably one of the most decisive events in the war in Yugoslavia. If Mihailović had defeated them there his position would have been strengthened considerably: a once-and-for-all defeat of the Partisans by Mihailović was often viewed by the FO as an alternative to a united resistance. While the debate on whether or not to contact and support the partisans was raging in London and Cairo, events in Yugoslavia were making this eventuality inevitable.

7

CONTACTING THE PARTISANS

Once Cairo SOE had the green light to contact the Partisans, there was no problem on whom to send. Already in Cairo was a group of Yugoslav émigrés from Canada and the United States who had been trained by SOE at 'Camp X' on the Canadian-United States border. Both countries were fertile ground for SOE and SIS looking for European immigrants to train and return to their homelands. The economic situation in Europe during the 1920s and 1930s had led many to cross the Atlantic in search of employment, while others had made the crossing to escape political repression. Many of the latter naturally tended to be left wing and had escaped Europe as fascism expanded its hold, and also following Franco's victory in Spain.

One of the earliest Yugoslavs to be recruited and returned to his homeland was not a signal success for anyone concerned. Branislav Radojević, a veteran of the Spanish civil war, was discovered in a Quebec prison, where he was serving a sentence for inciting a strike, by William Stuart of SIS in October 1941. Stuart assessed Radojević to be a Yugoslav patriot, in exile because of his leftist sympathies, who would be useful in view of his previous employment as a telegraphist.[1] Radojević arrived in Cairo on 28 January 1942 to be trained as a W/T operator to be sent to the Partisans. At the end of March the first attempt to parachute in failed, as did several subsequent attempts, due to the usual problems with weather and aircraft mechanical troubles. All the exploratory missions in the early months of 1942 who did not have a pre-arranged rendezvous went astray, so in late July Cairo SOE decided that the most effective way to get Radojević into Yugoslavia was to drop him to Mihailović's headquarters. This would kill several birds with one stone. Radojević was to ascertain whether Hudson's transmissions were genuine, as his security check was missing from his messages, and to help him re-establish secure wireless contact with SOE. Radojević was also meant to gain information on the partisans and to help Hudson and Mihailović to settle any problems with the partisans by acting as a mediator between the two factions.[2]

By the time Radojević arrived at Mihailović's HQ he had been commissioned as a captain in the British army and renamed Charles Robertson. According to Hudson, this was because he had refused to return to Yugoslavia as a civilian: he was also disguising the fact that he was originally a Serb from Shumadija by speaking French. Mihailović was not informed of Robertson's background or asked for permission for his infiltration, as Cairo 'thought that to give details of Robertson's history would be to court a negative reply'. Hudson had been told of Robertson's left-wing background, but had been assured that as an officer, and on his own word of honour, he would not get involved in politics.[3]

Baker Street was a little uneasy about the situation and asked Cairo for the terms of Robertson's briefing, and for assurance that he was fully informed on British policy and that under no circumstances should he attempt to co-operate with the partisans. Cairo gave the required assurance that Robertson would not contact the Partisans unless ordered to do so. Baker Street also wanted to know why Robertson's signals were in French, and were informed that this was because he did not know English: Cairo does not seem to have told them that it was because he was disguising his origins. Mihailović and his people were aware that Robertson was not French as Mihailović spoke excellent French himself, but they were not aware that he was Yugoslav.[4]

To complicate the situation further, Robertson appears to have been somewhat unstable. He did not stick to the agreement regarding the Partisans: on 31 October he cabled Cairo to say that only the Partisans were fighting and that he wanted to escape to them. At this point Cairo seems to have picked up on the fact that there was a divergence in both style and content between his and Hudson's messages, and asked the latter to explain why this was so. It transpired that Hudson, despite living in the same house, was unaware of the contents of Robertson's signals as it had never occurred to him to ask to see them. Many of these had been highly critical of

Mihailović, and Robertson was not helping Hudson's position, which was still rather a delicate one following his recent re-admittance to Mihailović's company. Robertson's messages became increasingly hysterical: he claimed that Mihailović's threats to him were daily becoming more menacing and that he was in fear of his life. Hudson said that this was entirely imaginary, as there was no threat from Mihailović and that Robertson should stay put. It appears that Hudson was possibly more of a menace to Robertson, as by this time he had so irritated Hudson that one day he threw Robertson from a first floor window of the house they shared.

Eventually matters came to a head when Robertson attempted to bribe two soldiers to defect to the Partisans with him. Up to this point Mihailović had ignored his strange behaviour because he was a member of the British mission; but, when confronted, Robertson finally admitted that he was a Yugoslav and Mihailović issued a written threat of court martial. Hudson described this as 'a pretentious document', but admitted that Robertson's behaviour had been 'undignified'. Having protested about Robertson's conduct, Mihailović eventually demanded Hudson put him under arrest before his men executed their own justice. Baker Street was distressed that despite his assurances, Robertson had, after all, become embroiled in political disputes and suggested that Cairo send apologies to Mihailović through Hudson.[5]

Robertson was still causing problems when Bailey arrived at the end of 1942. Bailey tried to get him out of his hair by sending him to the British sub-mission established in 1943 with Major Dragutin Keserović, Mihailović's commander in the Kopaonik area.[6] Robertson left the mission in August in the company of Major Neil Selby and his wireless operator, to attempt to negotiate a settlement between Keserović's forces and some nearby partisans. Shortly afterwards Selby and his W/T operator were captured by Ljotićists and handed over to the Gestapo, but Robertson escaped and subsequently attempted to re-establish contact with Cairo via other British officers. He did not succeed in this, but did eventually reach the Partisans in the Lim valley. He was not entirely welcome there either: the political commissar, Dobrica Ćosić, was highly suspicious of Robertson's political loyalties since he had fought with the anarchists rather than the communists in Spain. It seems likely that

Robertson was executed by the Partisans on the grounds that he was a Trotskyite.[7]

It is uncertain if MO4 genuinely thought that Robertson could mediate between the two resistance movements. Whether or not he was sent in good faith because MO4 accepted his assurances regarding politics, he certainly caused bad feeling between the British and Mihailović and his posting to the latter seems inept to say the least. It also gave conspiracy theorists the idea that he had been infiltrated deliberately by the Cairo 'reds' precisely to undermine Mihailović: a suspicion furthered by the fact that he was given a new name and instructed to speak French. The fact that Robertson escaped while Selby was captured also raised the question of whether Robertson had betrayed that unfortunate officer who eventually perished in a vain attempt to escape from the Gestapo.

Further fuel was added to the conspiracy theories by the Camp X graduates, but they were an altogether more straightforward group: they were communists and made no bones about it. They had been recruited in late 1941 and early 1942, by Bailey for SOE and Captain William Stuart for SIS. One of the seemingly enduring mysteries, and a major cause of suspicion, is why Bailey sought out only left-wing Balkan émigrés—or 'radical groups' as he termed them—on his mission to New York and Canada. The various accounts seem to be contradictory at times and in some cases involve virtually every mole or spy—suspected or proven to be—in action at the time. Mike Lees even asks: 'Could Bailey have been a mole?'[8]

All agree that the British Security Council (BSC), headed by William Stephenson in New York, played a part. Bailey's 'Terms of Reference in America' stated that he was to act as political adviser to Stephenson on all east European and Balkan matters, including the selection and vetting of recruits from the Balkan émigré groups for training in subversive work and subsequent return to occupied Europe. SOE in New York had already been asked to find potential recruits so Bailey was not starting from scratch, and by the time he arrived at the end of December there were fourteen prospective agents: three Greeks and eleven Yugoslavs. In reply to an enquiry on security vetting, Bailey told London that he had checked them out in all available British files and would do the same in American records. He also added that all fourteen had been 'introduced through contact recommended to us by DONOVAN personally.'[9] This contact was Milton Woolf, an American communist and Spanish civil war veteran, as were the majority of the fourteen potential recruits, which meant that they already had some military experience. Spanish veterans helped to form the backbone of Tito's movement when it took on a more military aspect. Given that Donovan was personally anti-communist, his relationship with Milton Woolf is interesting in that it probably reflects the OSS chief's domestic problems, which in many respects were not dissimilar to those encountered by SOE in its early days—namely, antagonism from the establishment.

All except one of the fourteen were selected by the end of January 1942 and sent to Britain in June for further training, finally arriving in Cairo in February 1943. In May 1942 Bailey moved on to Canada. There Kosta Todorov, of the Bulgarian Agrarian Party and an old friend of SOE, introduced him to three members of the Canadian Communist Party (CPC): Paul Phillips, a Ukrainian and treasurer of the CPC; Nikola Kovačević, a Montenegrin and Soviet agent; and a member of the Croatian CP. Woolf continued to advise Bailey on 'radical groups', while Tommy Drew-Brook, the official BSC representative in Toronto, also helped out: according to David Stafford he advertised for recruits in *Novosti*, a left-wing Serbo-Croatian journal.[10] Officials in the Canadian Department of External Affairs were also helpful, and McClellan, head of the RCMP, provided names from his list of illegal immigrants and possible subversives. In the summer of 1942 Bailey was replaced by Robert Lethbridge who selected further groups of Yugoslavs in Canada, whom he described as 'largely communists'.[11] From early 1943 all recruits were enlisted into the Canadian army, having agreed to transfer to the British army when requested.

SOE told neither the YGE nor its consul-general in Montreal what was going on. Bailey's mission to the USA and Canada coincided with the crisis in the Yugoslav military in the Middle East when the YGE made a number of protests to the FO at the 'unsuitable' people being returned to Yugoslavia by the British secret services. The news that SOE was recruiting communists in North America would not have been greeted with enthusiasm by the YGE. Given the files full of protests which Rendel passed on to the FO Southern Department on their behalf, one would certainly expect to find something on this matter, had they known of it. Deakin tells us that the consul-general got wind of the recruitment, but not of its underlying purpose.[12]

The fact that *predominantly* communists were recruited a very long time before the meeting at the FO on 8 August 1942, at which the possibility of eventually contacting the Partisans was agreed, also stoked the conspiracy theories. The recruits themselves thought it unusual: Kovačević, who became their spokesman, apparently asked Bailey why he was recruiting them when plenty of pro-royalist Yugoslavs were available. According to Stafford 'Bailey replied that the royalists were collaborating in Yugoslavia and only the Communists were fighting'. Stafford says this was possibly designed to please the Yugoslavs but thinks it 'unlikely', although he does not explain why. The British seem to have made a previous approach to Stanković, of the Croatian Peasant Party (HSS). When the first Camp X graduates arrived with the Partisans they claimed that the British had at first attempted to recruit Croats loyal to Maček, and that it was only after this had come to nothing that 'progressive elements' in the British intelligence services looked to the CPC for volunteers.[13] Although this is the only mention of such a move, it would seem to be a logical one for the British to make, given that all branches of British intelligence were convinced there were guerrilla forces loyal to Maček operating within Croatia.

The recruitment for Camp X began shortly after Hudson reported the existence of communist guerrillas while SOE was attempting to contact all resistance groups, and before Mihailović had been recognized as the leader of Yugoslav resistance. Dalton was still in charge of SOE until February 1942, and recruiting communists would fit in very well with his concept of stirring up left-wing revolutions throughout occupied Europe, an idea which probably lingered for some time after he had been replaced by the more conservative Selborne. While the communist recruits were still training, the Soviets started the anti-Mihailović propaganda which eventually led to the FO decision to hold in reserve the possibility of establishing contact with the partisans.

Once they had arrived in Cairo, the left-wing Yugoslavs were looked after by Lieutenant James Klugmann, who was a 'conducting officer' in the Yugoslav section at the time; his job seems to have been to look after the general welfare of agents about to go into the field. Mike Lees remembered how Klugmann 'fussed around us like a mother hen. He was charming, solicitous, and enormously helpful in tending to all our needs: for louse powder, for cyanide suicide pills, for secret maps, and for any other paraphernalia that we required or that he thought to be necessary.'[14] Klugmann was very firmly in Basil Davidson's 'Children of Light' camp.

The battle in Cairo SOE between the Children of Light and the Children of Darkness was ongoing: it was probably a member of the latter that caused the Camp X graduates serious alarm with the suggestion that they might be sent to Mihailović, telling them this was their best bet as the partisans had been annihilated.[15] Presumably the officer was basing his view on information received from Bailey in early February that the defeat of the partisans was imminent. The Yugoslavs took this seriously, and took a dim view of it as they had joined up to fight with the Partisans, and had no intention at all of joining the royalist resistance, but they were soon reassured by Davidson and Klugmann. In fact, the intention had always been to send them to areas where Mihailović's writ did not run: according to Deakin the planning for infiltrating these men into Croatia had begun in the autumn of 1942, before any high-level decisions had been taken.

The only member of the first missions to the partisans who genuinely thought he was destined for Mihailović was Alexander Simić-Stevens, an Anglo-Yugoslav who had been Atherton's assistant editor on the *South Slav Herald* for five years in pre-war Belgrade. Simić-Stevens, now in the British army, had volunteered his services as a Serbo-Croatian speaker in April 1940. It was not until eighteen months later that he was taken up on this, when 'a Col. Bailey presumed I knew all about a legendary Mihailović and his ghost army of Chetniks heroically opposing the invaders of his country in the Serbian mountains.'[16] This encounter throws some interesting light on Bailey's motivation. Simić-Stevens was not a communist, although he had left-wing sympathies, so Bailey was not exclusively recruiting communists before he left for the United States, although he seems to have been happy to go along with the existing arrangements once he arrived there. It is also apparent that Bailey was enlisting people to contact *all* resistance groups. The fact that he mentioned Mihailović to Simić possibly indicates that he thought Simić's sympathies might lie with the chetniks. If this is so, it might put into context his remark to Kovačević about 'only the communists fighting' while he was trying to enlist the Yugoslavs in Canada. At that stage of the war, and of the development of SOE, when suitable people who could be infiltrated into occupied territory were hard to come by, telling potential agents what they wanted to hear might have been a useful ploy.

Simić-Stevens met the Yugoslavs from Camp X, and Bill Deakin, at an SOE training school in Britain. On board ship from Liverpool to West Africa en route to Cairo, his Yugoslav companions informed him that Mihailović and the chetniks were collaborating and fighting against the communist-led resistance of Tito and the partisans. Somewhat shocked by this intelligence, Simić-Stevens, when interviewed by James Klugmann in Cairo, demanded to know the truth: Klugmann told him that 'the reports seem to be fairly accurate', but that he should not worry, as he was going to be dropped to 'a chap called Tito who led an army of Partizans'. Before this was accomplished Simić-Stevens seems to have caught the off-shots of the battle between the Children of Light and Darkness. It had been proposed that he should be commissioned before his departure, but instead of meeting Keble, 'who was heart and soul in favour of the project', he saw Colonel Tamplin whose first question was 'What do you want to go to those bloody Reds for?' Simić-Stevens—without his commission—parachuted 'blind', namely without a prearranged rendezvous, into western Croatia with Petar Erdeljac and Paul Pavlić on the night of 20–21 April 1943; this was the 'Fungus' mission.

On the same night the 'Hoathley 1' mission, made up of Stevan Serdar, George Diclić and Milan Družić were also dropped blind into eastern Bosnia, landing near Seković. The Fungus mission was picked up by local peasants who passed them on to partisan divisional HQ at Brinje, whence they were transported to partisan HQ for Croatia. There Erdeljac was immediately recognized as an old comrade from Spain by the Croat GHQ commander, Ivan Rukovina. Simić-Stevens on the other hand was closely questioned by the political commissar, Dr Vladimir Bakarić: he tells us that 'for a full week I was held incommunicado, albeit treated with the utmost courtesy and friendliness and allowed to question all and sundry the while'. In this case 'all and sundry' should probably be read as 'loyal partisans', bearing in mind that when Atherton earlier contacted the Partisans he was carefully isolated from the local population.

Croat HQ immediately sent a cable to Tito, advising him of their arrival and asking for advice on how to proceed. The cable also informed him of the Hoathley 1 mission, supposed to be landing near Bihać and bringing a communication signed by 'Alexander, commander of the near east'.[17] Neither group of agents bore a message from General Alexander: any such formal communication would have been premature, as these two missions were purely exploratory.

Tito told Croatian HQ to keep the new arrivals there, to look after them, and to ensure that they did not, as Atherton had done earlier 'undertake some provocation which would compromise the Partisans in the eyes of the international public'. Atherton was very much in the minds of the partisans with this new approach from the British: they suspected Atherton's arrival, sudden departure and murder to have been part of some dark plot against them by the YGE, possibly with the connivance of the British.[18]

The Comintern was informed of the new arrivals and asked to check on their identity through the Canadian Communist Party. On 28 April Tito cabled the Comintern with further information, namely that in Canada 'Filipo' (Paul Phillips) had worked with 'Lesbric' (Lethbridge) in assembling the members of the mission. The agents at Croatian HQ had said that the British would furnish aid to the Partisans as soon as they requested it; their mission was to supply information on the occupying forces and the Partisan movement. The Comintern did not reply until 5 May, and then denied all knowledge of the Communist Party's involvement with the recruiting of agents in Canada, cautioning Tito to act with the greatest care in establishing the true identity of the mission and on no account to give them any information on the internal affairs or plans of the Partisans.[19] This advice was somewhat superfluous, since Tito *was* acting with the utmost caution, and the missions had been received with considerable suspicion.

The Comintern's denial appears to demonstrate that the Soviets were no more enthusiastic about unilateral British involvement with the Yugoslav partisans than the British were about the prospect of Soviet intervention. Presumably the Comintern hoped to put the partisans off accepting this proffered aid by raising doubts about the new arrivals. Nevertheless, Tito had the political foresight to take what was on offer. On 28 April he allowed Simić-Stevens to broadcast, although ensuring that the partisans had control over the contents of the messages. Once communications were established, Cairo asked whether the Partisans would receive a sabotage team to disrupt railway lines used to transport Axis war material and petrol. Thus it was that the first uniformed mission, consisting of Major William Jones, Captain Hunter and Sergeant Ron Jephson, arrived on 18–19 May.

Jones, a 50-year-old Canadian veteran of the First World War, who had the use of only one eye, was very brave by all accounts and not a little eccentric, immediately fell in love with the whole Partisan movement. The admiration seems to have been mutual in this case: Jones was described by the Partisans as the most popular Allied officer in Yugoslavia, and was fondly remembered long after the war. He was not so well appreciated by MO4, to whom he sent telegrams of such great length, and written in such hyperbolic terms that Cairo eventually gave up deciphering them. Jones' immediate enthusiasm led him to jump the gun regarding British policy: his requests for explosives, enough equipment for four partisan divisions, and the proposal that a partisan delegate from Croatian HQ should be sent to Cairo to negotiate, far exceeded his remit. To agree to any of these would have implied a commitment to the future support of the Partisans.[20] The Comintern was no more enthusiastic regarding such proposals, and after further communications with 'Grandad' (Georgi Dimitrov, General secretary of the Comintern), Tito ordered the Croatian HQ not to contemplate sending a delegate to Cairo; such a move would be decided by him, when and if it became possible. It was doubtful anyway whether SOE could have extracted any representative of the Partisans at that time: parachuting agents into Yugoslavia was one thing, getting them out was quite another until after the Allies had moved into Italy.

Fungus and Hoathley 1 were purely exploratory missions; the addition to Fungus of Jones and company was specifically to sound out the possibility of committing acts of sabotage. As these had apparently been favourably received, Cairo proposed a further mission to Partisan supreme headquarters to which Tito agreed on 17 May. This was two days after the Axis began 'Operation Schwarz', the resumption of the offensive against the resistance. The message Tito relayed through the Fungus mission in Croatia agreeing to receive a liaison officer, requested that he land at once near Durmitor in Montenegro; it also asked that the RAF should bomb specific towns which were the bases from which the fresh Axis attack was being launched. The 'Typical' mission, which was a joint SOE-SIS affair, headed by Bill Deakin and William Stuart respectively, arrived on 28 May, although it had originally attempted to come on 25 May, just as the Axis circle was drawing perilously tight around the Partisans.

It was at this juncture that Tito decided to introduce ranks into the NLA. Dedijer noted this innovation on 24 May, adding 'We are becoming a regular army'. Tito's ambition was to have the NLA recognized as an official belligerent: the Germans had turned down this proposal in the March negotiations, and he was probably hoping for better luck with the British now that the first official mission was on its way. Dedijer observed: 'There is no doubt that the coming of this mission, albeit exclusively military, means a great victory', and went on: 'The English are realists. We should be realists too.' He also noted that Deakin was a personal friend of Churchill.

The choice of Deakin as the first SOE liaison officer to be despatched to Tito's HQ is an interesting one, especially in the light of the fact that he knew about the intercepts of German signals. Official SOE policy was to ensure that anyone going into the field where they risked capture should not be the bearer of sensitive secret information. He was certainly not the only officer available. Major Jasper Rootham was on hand, and hoped that he might get the job: he had earlier proposed that, because he spoke fluent Russian, he should be dropped in to contact the Partisans in the company of a Soviet officer. Rootham had taken a course in Serbo–Croatian, been trained in demolitions and had travelled extensively throughout Croatia, Dalmatia, Bosnia and Herzegovina a few years before the war. However, when he suggested this might be a useful background for making the first official SOE contact with Tito, he was told the post was filled.[21] Deakin himself admits: 'I was no out-standing specialist on Yugoslav affairs, but had been directly engaged in studying the situation in the country for some time, and now in Cairo, had been closely connected with the recent opera-tions.'[22] Churchill received Keble's memorandum recommending contact with the partisans at the end of January 1943, the COS Directive to SOE was issued on 20 March, and Cairo SOE had been planning to establish contact since the end of 1942. In view of this timescale, it is somewhat surprising that Tito's message of 17 May, agreeing to receive the military mission, appears to have caught SOE unawares. They had, according to Deakin, neither briefed nor selected members of the mission. The joint SOE-SIS party was now 'hastily assembled', some twenty months after the Bullseye mission had also been hastily assembled with its attendant omissions: if Deakin's account is accurate it appears that SOE's organizational skills had not improved in the interim. In addition to straightforward inefficiency, the pro- and anti-Partisan dispute added confusion to the question of what supplies Deakin and Stuart were to take with them. Much needed medical supplies were cancelled at the last minute, leading Deakin to wonder if the failure of 'Typi-cal' was regarded in some British quarters as a means of avoiding complications.[23]

Events had, it seems, moved so swiftly that neither London SOE nor the FO had been informed beforehand of the despatch of the first exploratory missions to the Partisans. Considering the ongoing debate, and the high level of anxiety existing in both these bodies, it was hardly of little import to them. The Typical mission, the first official mission to Partisan GHQ also departed before London SOE had been told of it; Churchill asked to see Deakin for a further briefing on Yugoslavia only to be informed that he was already in that country.[24]

Deakin and Stuart parachuted into a very perilous situation: Tito and the Partisans were almost encircled by the Axis forces in the area of Mount Durmitor in Montenegro, where, according to Dedijer's diary entry for 24 May, they had delayed their departure in order to meet the British mission. As the Partisans attempted to battle their way out of the Axis ring, Stuart was killed on 9 June in an air attack which also slightly wounded Tito and Deakin. The prologue of

Deakin's *Embattled Mountain* is given over to a graphic account of their desperate escape; perhaps not unnaturally, Deakin, who was experiencing guerrilla warfare for the first time, felt that 'as a stranger, I had taken on by stages a binding and absolute identity with those around me.'

Stuart's death left the Typical mission with only one Serbo-Croatian speaker, Starčević, who was one of the Yugoslavs from Canada. Deakin was warm in his appreciation of the people who made up the original mission, not least of Starčević:

I was ill-qualified in Serbo-Croat, and he was nominally allotted to me as an interpreter. If he had any other duties, I never discovered them. There were many times during the coming months when I was grateful for his presence.[25]

It might seem incongruous that the head of the first official military mission to partisan headquarters admitted that one of the men under his command might have 'other duties' of which he knew nothing. The other members of Typical were Corporal Walter Wroughton, Sergeant John Campbell and Sergeant Rose who was Stuart's wireless operator. 'Rose' was actually Peretz Rosenberg, who also worked for the Jewish Agency.

Baker Street treated the information available from the first missions to the Partisans with caution. On 25 May Pearson sent Howard a short memorandum whose subject was 'The Partisan Movement in Yugoslavia', based on telegrams received from the Hoathley 1 mission in Croatia, with the warning that he should bear in mind that this was composed of three Canadian Yugoslavs 'who though intelligent, are certainly biased to the left'.[26] He also warned that the information emanated from partisan sources and was therefore hearsay evidence. Much information from Bailey was discounted on these grounds, and the same caution should be applied when forming any opinion on the basis of telegrams from missions with the partisans. SOE was awaiting further information before coming to any conclusions themselves, but meanwhile Cairo was arranging to drop supplies to Croatia and to partisan headquarters. Pearson did not mention, since he did not know it, that Cairo was just about to drop Deakin and Stuart into Yugoslavia.

Baker Street was furious when they did hear of Deakin's despatch, since they regarded the whole question of support for the

Partisans as still under discussion. While Cairo had informed them that such a mission was at the planning stage they had not consulted London or the FO on actually going ahead with it. Although Baker Street was happy to contact individual resistance groups outside Mihailović's areas, and to supply aid if the liaison officers thought it worthwhile, the problem with the Typical mission was that it was sent to what Deakin called 'the southern sector' *and* it was sent to partisan GHQ. By their action MO4 implied recognition of the Partisan movement as a whole rather than individual and separate groups within limited and defined areas in Slovenia and Croatia, thereby giving evidence of their intention to support a movement that was openly hostile to both the YGE and its minister of war. The fact that it went to 'the southern sector', namely Montenegro, was regarded by MO4 as the first step to supporting the Partisans in western Serbia. Both of these moves were divergent from the new policy agreed between the FO and Baker Street and should not have been made without proper discussions and agreement with the FO.[27] The area where Typical had been dropped was the very one that the Partisans had fought their way into—and from which Mihailović forces were being pushed out.

Bailey had recommended that supporting the Partisans in non-Serb areas was the optimum way to avoid conflict between the two resistance forces, but MO4 was now flying in the face of that by proposing to support the Partisans in western Serbia. MO4 had also decided that, as they were now treating the Partisan movement as a whole, in addition to Croatia and Slovenia they would also support them in Montenegro, Herzegovina, Bosnia and Dalmatia. In accordance with this decision, MO4 sent Bailey a telegram on 24 May, informing him that in all these areas chetnik commanders who claimed Mihailović leadership, were 'known to be working with the Axis exclusively against Partisans. This is not, rpt not, open to doubt.'[28] The message went on to advise that Mihailović could only clear his name by denouncing these commanders in a detailed message broadcast by the BBC in Serbo-Croatian which should be coupled with immediate action against the Axis. This advice contained a number of major drawbacks as far as Mihailović was concerned. To denounce out of hand the various leaders who, in most cases, did not actually come under his direct orders, but were generally in sympathy with his aims and upon whose long-term support he depended for the planned *Ustanak*, would immediately lose him that support and undermine his often fragile power-base. It would also leave him with only his commanders in Serbia, not a position he wanted to entertain as Yugoslav minister of war and therefore head of the armed forces for the whole country. The possible effects of Cairo's telegram were recognized by London SOE, as were the complexities facing some of the chetnik leaders that MO4 wanted Mihailović to disown. In May Bailey reported that Mashan Djurović, who was notorious for collaborating with both Germans and Bulgars, had been liquidated on Mihailović's orders. Djurović had fallen out with the Bulgars and so attempted to reinsure himself by allying with Mihailović who wanted nothing to do with the collaborator, but did want his men for the Yugoslav Home Army. In the light of this, Baker Street felt that they might have judged Mihailović harshly, without taking full account of the difficult political situation he faced. Cairo SOE claimed that the telegram demanding Mihailović disown these leaders had been to exonerate him, and also to help 'a mission which is to go to partisan HQ soon'. This was Deakin's mission, of which MO4 had not yet informed Baker Street.[29]

A further attempt to confine Mihailović's influence to Serbia was made on 28 May, when Glenconner sent Bailey a telegram instructing Mihailović to move to the east of the Ibar river.[30] If he complied with this, he would receive ample air support in the new area. Apparently MO4, having heard from Bailey that Mihailović was moving east under pressure from the new Axis attack had decided that the Ibar river would make a good dividing line between the opposing forces. Bailey protested to Cairo that their telegram had not been well received by Mihailović, and that it contradicted the directive from the YGE which had only just been delivered, he also told Cairo that Mihailović knew that agents and supplies had been dropped to the partisans, which 'I was unable to deny or confirm.' Rejecting Bailey's opinion on the contradiction between the two messages, Cairo told him that SOE was now officially supporting the whole Partisan movement in order to comply with the COS's directive; Mihailović meanwhile was to concentrate on southern and eastern Serbia and to remain east of the Ibar. This was the policy they had recommended to London.[31]

They might have recommended it to London, but it had certainly not been approved there. There was uproar at the FO when it was discovered that Glenconner had sent this telegram to Bailey without reference either to themselves or Baker Street. These instructions were not only at variance with their own and London SOE's views, but also cut across the message that the FO, in conjunction with the YGE, had just sent to Mihailović, setting out conditions for continued support and plans for co-ordinating his actions with the C-in-C Middle East.[32] This joint directive had taken over a month to put together and there had been considerable discussions at all levels, involving the YGE, FO, COS and SOE, and all had agreed on the importance of the directive in order to fully utlize the Yugoslav Home Army in meeting the demands of the COS March directive. By the time it was finally despatched Mihailović was on the move and Bailey had been ill with malaria, with the result that the YGE directive and Glenconner's telegram reached Mihailović at almost the same time. He was furious at receiving these two contradictory messages, which he attributed to 'foreign interference'. The FO was equally furious with Cairo SOE and with Bailey for repeating the whole telegram to Mihailovic, 'when it was clear to all but the totally blind that only one portion was intended for his sight.'[33] Glenconner was told to send a further message to Mihailović in an attempt to put things right before returning to London to 'explain the muddle', although Howard feared that so much bad blood had been spilled that it might be difficult to rectify the situation.

The YGE and King Peter had also reacted badly on hearing of the 'muddle', *and* on hearing that the British had sent liaison officers to the partisans. Rendel had informed Jovanović on 7 May, reassuring him that this did not mean any diminution of support for Mihailović and that the partisans were not receiving any arms which might be used against him.[34] However, Rendel had decided to hold back for a few days the telegram Mihailović had sent about the arrival of British missions to the partisans,[35] in case Jovanović thought this was the only reason he was being informed of them now. It transpired that King Peter had already seen this telegram and two others from Mihailović protesting about the conflicting instructions, which had not yet reached London SOE.[36] Douglas Howard thought it likely that Mihailović's telegrams, when received and translated in Cairo, might easily have come into the hands of Colonel Putnik, of the Yugoslav military in Cairo, who was forwarding them directly to King Peter. The question of how Putnik could pass messages to King Peter faster than MO4 could pass them to Baker Street seems to have taken second place to the old question of preventing direct communications between Mihailović and the YGE. Hambro was detailed to investigate and plug the leak.[37]

At the Trident conference in Washington in May 1943, Churchill and Roosevelt had agreed that the cross-Channel landings would be in the spring of 1944. The conference coincided with the Axis surrender in North Africa, and at its conclusion Churchill flew from Washington to Algiers to discuss the Sicily landing and subsequent actions. General Eisenhower, Commander of all US forces in the European theatre, stated that if Sicily were to be 'polished off easily', he would be willing to go straight on to Italy. This upbeat assessment encouraged Churchill's idea that once in Italy the Allies could 'do something in the Balkans'—not invade, but certainly take the opportunity to supply the Balkan guerrillas across the Adriatic, especially since large quantities of captured small arms and ammunition were now available from North Africa. It was probably with this in mind that he asked for Deakin to be sent to him to provide an update on the situation in Yugoslavia.

In reply to the PM's request, Cairo SOE sent a brief note to say that Deakin was already in the country, and an account of 'SOE activities in Yugoslavia', dated 1 June 1943.[38] As Deakin had only just arrived, this three page report obviously was not based on information received from him. Its contents were very similar to Glenconner's telegram and concluded that, as Mihailović was now only effective in eastern and central Serbia, the present plan was to persuade him to keep to the east of the river Ibar. The report missed Churchill in Algiers, but it caused quite a stir. Desmond Morton, the PM's intelligence adviser, 'though no expert on the complicated Yugoslav situation, felt at once that the reports were not in line with what I understood to be FO policy'.[39] He was quite right. Morton consulted the FO and Baker Street on 9 June and both agreed that the facts, recommendations and conclusions were not only spurious but opposed to the policy of the FO, SOE, YGE and COS. After much discussion, it was decided that the PM should not be presented with this document but that Colin Gubbins would produce another, more suitable, version on behalf of Baker Street and with the agreement of the FO and DMI.[40]

Churchill was anxious to hear news of Deakin and on 18 June Selborne forwarded to him SOE's appreciation of the situation in Yugoslavia, giving the strength and disposition of the resistance forces as far as it was known and a brief account of their activities. The report also brought out the extent to which the shortage of aircraft had diminished British influence in Yugoslavia, and Selborne made a direct appeal for 'any sympathy that can be extended to me in this matter'.[41] He concluded with the news that since the appreciation and map had been drawn up, Tito's HQ and army had been disintegrated by the Axis drive, a factor which might alter the whole 'set-up'. He feared that Deakin was with Tito, and nothing had been heard of him for a week. The PM reacted swiftly to the appeal for aircraft. On 22 June he sent SOE's appreciation to General Ismay, head of Churchill's Defence Office, with a minute for the COS Committee, emphasizing the importance of supplying aircraft for SOE 'and that this demand has priority even over the bombing of Germany.'[42]

Selborne was invited to discuss the paper at 10 Downing Street the following evening. In his letter to the PM, he had stated that his sympathy was definitely with Mihailović, who had kept the flag flying since 1941 with very little in the way of practical assistance from the British: he felt that the COS were not sufficiently aware of the difficulties facing Mihailović. There was a degree of truth in this. At a COS meeting on 6 May Lord Louis Mountbatten expressed doubts about the military advantage of backing Mihailović, whose loyalty he thought to be questionable in view of his known collaboration with the Italians. In addition, the danger inherent in continuing to back Mihailović while the 'Russians' supported the partisans, might imperil relations between the British and Soviets, a fact which he thought ought to be brought to the attention of the FO.[43] As the FO had been keenly aware of this dilemma for the past year, Mountbatten's advice might be viewed as somewhat superfluous. Eden noted dryly in the margin of the meeting's minutes: 'Curiously enough, we had thought of that.' More tellingly, it is an indication of how little attention had been paid to Yugoslavia up to this point by those who were not directly involved in Yugoslav affairs.

Although Glenconner was getting the blame for the idea to confine Mihailović to the east of the Ibar, the telegram to Bailey had
not been sent on his own initiative, but at the behest of the Middle
East Defence Committee (MEDC), who wanted immediate action
in Yugoslavia, regardless of the longer-term political consequences.
Glenconner had been caught between the conflicting demands of
London SOE and the MEDC, and had eventually given in to pressure from the latter. Despite the upset at the FO, the MEDC sent a
telegram to the COS, Eden and London SOE, reiterating the policy
they had pressed upon Glenconner. The FO and SOE wanted to
limit support of the partisans to the supply of sabotage and medical
material until they had made an agreement to co-operate with
Mihailović. The COS favoured the MEDC plan, advocating the
immediate supply of war material to the partisans and favouring the
recognition of the two resistance movements within territorial
boundaries.[44] Eventually a compromise was reached: there would
be no recognition of separate groups in specific territories, which
would lead to the disintegration of Yugoslavia, but the partisans
would be supplied with war material as long as they agreed not to
act against Mihailović's forces except in self-defence. The last point
was the greatest concession by the FO, and was a far cry from persuading the partisans to co-operate with Mihailović and form a
united front against the Axis.

On 24 June Eden sent the PM what was in effect the new British
policy towards Yugoslavia, having been asked by the COS to give
the FO views on the situation. These were briefly summed up as

(1) that we should continue to support Mihailović provided he accepts certain conditions which have now been put to him; (2) that the Croatian guerrillas and Communist Partisans should forthwith be supplied with war material
on condition that those Partisans operating in close proximity to Mihailović's
forces should be required first to give an assurance that no operations will
be carried out against Mihailović. This is also one of the conditions which
we have put to Mihailović; and (3) that the suggestion that each group
should be recognised in a certain territorial district should not be adopted.
This would in my view have strong political objections. By dividing Yugoslavia into areas and recognising certain political elements as predominant
in those districts we should be taking the first step towards breaking up the
unity of the country which it is our policy to maintain. The principal

change in policy with which I hope you will agree is that we are now recommending that the Communist Partisans and the Croat guerrillas should
henceforth receive our military support.[45]

This new line was communicated to C-in-C Middle East on
27 June. The British were now going to back both sides as 'resistance to Axis is of paramount importance'. The ultimate objective
was to unify all resistance in Yugoslavia: accordingly SOE was to
instruct Bailey and the other liaison officers to arrange, if possible,
political non-aggression between Mihailović and the Partisans.[46]

Deakin's feeling of binding and absolute identity with the Partisans as they desperately fought their way out of the encirclement on
Mount Durmitor was not wholly reciprocated. The Partisans were
pleased to have been noticed at last, but were not going to be over-
whelmed; they heeded not only the Comintern's warning to be
careful in their dealings with these new friends, but also their own
deep suspicions of 'Perfidious Albion'. The delayed arrival of the
Typical mission was regarded as suspect—was it a deliberate ploy so
that the Partisans would be destroyed while awaiting its arrival?[47]
During the first few months of the Typical mission Dedijer records
numerous complaints about expected supply drops not arriving or,
when they did, of the inappropriateness, meagreness or uselessness
of the contents. However, much more important than the contents
themselves was the fact that they arrived at all: his diary entry for 12
July 1943 observes 'We have no particular material advantage from
the things they send, but they are politically useful, particularly
about here'. ('About here' was eastern Bosnia, an area only just
vacated by Mihailović and one where the partisans needed to establish themselves as his replacement.) The political dimension of
material support was recognized by both sides as being the most
important factor: receiving supplies and the presence of British—
and later American—officers conferred legitimacy on the resistance
group thus favoured, and helped secure the support of the local
population. Deakin himself was not unaware of this fact.

The Typical mission was supplemented by three additional members on 25 July, although Stuart was not replaced until 15 August
when SIS sent in Kenneth Syers, a 'Cambridge communist' who
had worked for the British Council in pre-war Yugoslavia.[48] In the

interim Deakin was presumably filling both roles of establishing operational co-operation with the partisans and providing intelligence. In addition, extra missions had been dropped in Mihailović territory in accordance with the agreements Bailey had made with Mihailović. This sudden upsurge of interest and the arrival of more liaison officers appeared to be an indicator that an Allied landing in the Balkans was indeed impending. This impression was reinforced in early June when the partisans really did receive a message from General Alexander, C-in-C Middle East, which told them: 'Hang on...the second front is not a dream...your struggle will gain significance in coming months.'[49]

Now that the Partisans had an official British mission, the possibility of having to fight against the Allies when they landed might be thought to have receded somewhat, although certainly not entirely. A new possibility had opened up but the Partisans could not afford to relax, nor could they afford to be an *additional* guerrilla movement, simply aiding the strategic objectives of the Allies. Their long-term plans were much more ambitious. Deakin had the following impression:

Underlying these frequent discussions was, latent and unexpressed, the conviction that the British and Americans would land in the Balkans, beginning on the Adriatic coast, before they had recognized the Partisans as their formal allies and broken with the chetnik movement.[50]

As Deakin was the Partisans' main channel to the Western Allies, he was undoubtedly perceived as their only chance to effect this formal recognition. He had been enormously impressed by the Partisan military muscle displayed in escaping the Axis encirclement; as soon as he had been able to establish radio contact with Cairo he had recommended that they should receive all possible aid. The first step in achieving official recognition was on the way to being accomplished. The second—a British break with Mihailović's movement—was a larger leap and would take longer, although of course at this time the partisans did not know how *much* time they had to accomplish it, especially when news of the Sicily landings on 8 July reached them.

In the light of this presumed urgency, the Partisans lost no time in trying to convince Deakin that Mihailović and his followers were collaborators. As they were escaping from Mount Durmitor, the

Partisans pointed out the 'vultures' of Mihailović, when fired on by chetniks. Apparently the British were rather surprised, though quite why they should have been is difficult to see, when the fact that there was civil war between the two resistance movements was one of the main problems confronting all concerned. Deakin did not seem to be aware that the Axis action was not directed solely at the partisans, but was a general mopping up operation of all resistance groups. Mihailović himself had only just managed to escape and head for Serbia. The Croat Supreme Staff later set up a meeting between the British and a chetnik, who stated he was *not* fighting on the orders of Mihailović. He also claimed that the general was collaborating with the Italians and in agreement with Nedić, with the primary aim of saving the Serbs from communism.[51] The partisans continued to provide Deakin with proof of chetnik collaboration, which he duly reported to Cairo. According to his own account, Deakin generally seems to have been satisfied to accept the word of the partisans on this matter. Later, when MO4 asked him tactfully to investigate allegations that the partisans were making accommodations with the Ustashas he replied that this was 'plainly silly' and 'impertinent propaganda'. He also noted that the partisans had invited him to witness what they claimed to be Mihailović's chetniks fighting under German command—an invitation he refused as he had no one available, and anyway he considered 'further credence of this type unnecessary'.[52]

In August the British mission and the Partisans had a welcome respite after the constant moving on which had made it difficult to arrange pinpoint dropping grounds for supplies. A base was established on Petrovo Polje plateau, where they stayed for two weeks while waiting to move into Bosnia to establish a new 'free territory' centred on Jajce. Over these two weeks Deakin was presented with documentary evidence of chetnik collaboration, in the form of captured German, Italian and chetnik papers.[53] Deakin and Vlatko Velebit, who was attached to the British mission as a liaison officer, became quite close. On 16 August Basil Davidson arrived at Petrovo Polje and he describes the idyllic scene of Deakin and Velebit's daily meetings by a riverside in a ravine, where they

> … sat naked in the sun looking at dreary documents captured from chetnik commanders which proved their complicity with the occupiers,

and when we were tired of doing that we would swim in a pool, and afterwards begin again with Vlatko's evidence of what the partisans had done to help the United Nations.[54]

Velebit has described it thus:

My system of indoctrinating Deakin was to take him to a stream nearby, very nice and cool and fresh water where we used to bathe in the whole afternoon: I always took a bunch of captured documents with me... I think the course of indoctrination, if I may call it that, worked very well because Deakin got more and more convinced that the Mihailovic movement was really no good at all, and was really a kind of fifth column supporting the enemy rather than a resistance force.[55]

This was an interesting role for Velebit, bearing in mind that he was a member of the high ranking partisan delegation involved in the March negotiations with the Germans: a fact of which Deakin was blissfully unaware.

8

TUNING UP THE BALKANS

The aim of supporting both resistance movements in Yugoslavia was to create, if not a united resistance, then one that would concentrate on the Axis rather than internal enemies, and the British thought that the best way to achieve this was to take control themselves. To this end, a high-status mission would be established at both Mihailović's and Tito's headquarters. The original plan was that these missions would eventually consist of all branches of the services, including a representative of the FO. As the immediate purpose was military, it was proposed that each should be headed by a regular officer with the rank of brigadier, backed by a political adviser and a staff who would co-ordinate resistance in Yugoslavia with Allied military policy and strategy. By running the show themselves the British thought they could be sure of maximizing guerrilla activity while keeping a finger on the Yugoslav political pulse.

Although from the outset SOE had been trying to contact all potential resisters in Yugoslavia and had been formulating plans to work into neighbouring countries from Yugoslav territory, it was only during 1943 that either became feasible. The Axis defeat in North Africa in May 1943 provided the opportunity to expand SOE activities in the Balkans, while captured Axis armaments provided a ready-made stockpile to be transported to guerrilla forces. Extra military personnel were now also available and at last SOE had an increased number of aircraft at their disposal. In the spring Churchill obtained ten Halifax bombers to add to the four Liberators, and at the end of July the COS agreed to increase the total aircraft allotted to SOE to thirty-six, albeit they did not all become available until the autumn.

By the end of 1942 SOE had established a large stay-behind team for Persia and Iraq and the rest of the Arab world, but once the

Germans had been pushed back from Stalingrad and the danger of a German breakthrough diminished, these people could be used for missions in Greece and Yugoslavia.[1] Military personnel from regular units were sent to the SOE training school in Palestine to be instructed in demolitions, small-arms use, self-defence and silent killing. Some aspects of the training were more useful than others: for example, the tips on how to make contact with other agents included complicated arrangements for meeting at a certain park, on a certain day of the week, at a certain time of day, where—on a certain bench—a chap was to be found reading a certain newspaper. This might have been a useful arrangement in a city in north west Europe, but had limited possibilities in the wilds of occupied Yugoslavia.[2] Those not from airborne divisions were given parachute training and all took a crash course in Serbo-Croat. Preparations were rounded off by a trip to Jasper Maskelyne's escape school to be issued with a set of nice little gimmicks, such as silk maps and compass trouser buttons. W/T operators were also recruited in large numbers and as well as intensive physical training they were taught how to use high speed morse and codes. One had responded to a message on his mess notice board that read 'Two W/T ops wanted for dangerous and hazardous mission'.[3]

From April 1943 sub-missions were established with Mihailović's commanders throughout Serbia, as agreed with Bailey when he first arrived. Once it was decided that SOE would also work with the partisans, from late June sub-missions were sent to local partisan commanders in the same way, including the partisans in Slovenia where Major William Jones' Fungus mission was sent. By December 1943 there were sixty-five agents with Mihailović's forces, including five Yugoslavs and three Americans, and 107 agents with Tito's forces, including thirty-six Yugoslavs and seven Americans.[4]

In expansionist mode SOE had agreed to allow American OSS officers to join their missions—with the strict proviso that these officers were to be under SOE control: and this included the insistence that the Americans use British communications—both ciphers and W/T sets.[5] The agreement to take the American officers was, presumably, to circumvent OSS establishing their own independent missions in summer 1943: rumours that the Americans and Yugoslavs in the Middle East had been in negotiation over this possibility had alarmed Cairo SOE.[6] They did not want the Americans muscling in on their show, if they had to let them in then SOE wanted to be as much in control of their American allies as of their Yugoslav allies. During the summer of 1942 SOE's main anxiety about Donovan's plans for OSS had been that they would attempt to work with the Arabs, which SOE definitely regarded as a British preserve: they felt that American participation in the already complicated Arab situation 'would be nothing short of a disaster'.[7] By the turn of the year the Americans seemed to have lost interest in the Arabs, but were now very keen on the Balkans. Glenconner feared that OSS wanted to dabble in Balkan politics, economics and propaganda, as well as in SOE and SIS affairs, and felt that the Americans needed reminding of their agreement on spheres of interest and activity. He was willing to let OSS participate, but only if he and SOE called the shots and as long as they avoided independent contacts with the Greek or Yugoslav governments or their high commands.[8] On 18 August Captain Mansfield of OSS joined Bailey's mission in western Serbia and three days later Lieutenant M.O. Benson joined Deakin's 'Typical' mission at Petrovo Polje.[9]

One of the reasons SOE was so keen to ensure that Mihailović and the YGE did not have independent communications was because if they could communicate freely then nothing could prevent them from arranging operations with the Americans, thus cutting SOE out of the loop.[10] Keble's capitals and underlining of 'the AMERICANS or the RUSSIANS' in the report Churchill was given in February was not an empty dramatic gesture, but represented a real anxiety in Cairo SOE of being supplanted by the Americans.

Infiltrating increased numbers of agents into occupied Yugoslavia was no simple matter. The first mission to be arranged by Bailey was that led by Major Eric Greenwood, who was destined for eastern Serbia with plans to halt the flow of oil and other supplies to the Axis war machine by sabotaging and disrupting traffic on the Danube. Greenwood made his first attempt to parachute into Yugoslavia in January, but was foiled by bad weather. At that time Suez was the departure point for the British Liaison Officers (BLOs)—some 13 or 14 hours' flying time from Yugoslavia. Greenwood made another attempt in February and two more in March, all aborted because of bad weather or mechanical problems. Eventually Derna airfield in Libya became operational, cutting the journey by three to four hours, and from there Greenwood—fifth time lucky—finally departed in mid April. While Derna shortened the flying time, it could still take up to three days to travel to the airfield over-land from Cairo, plus there was always an unspecified period of just hanging around, never quite knowing when it would be time to go, and there was still no guarantee of a straightforward flight and a successful parachute jump once at the destination. In late May Deakin flew from Derna, only to have a round trip before success-fully repeating the journey to Yugoslavia three days later. Finally, there was the jump into darkness and the unknown, with only the lights of the signal fires to guide them into the mountainous terrain below, and perhaps some uncertainty about exactly *who* would be waiting there.

On the ground meanwhile the waiting BLO would organize fires set out in a prearranged pattern known only to him and the air crew. It was no mean feat for the pilots and navigators to find their way to these pinpoint dropping zones, and if cloud cover rendered the fires invisible, their passengers had to return to Derna and wait for another try. Just to be quite sure the reception committee was the genuine article, recognition signals between it and the aircraft were exchanged before the men or supplies were despatched. Major Archie Jack had a close call at his first attempt to parachute in: although the wrong signal was given from the ground, Jack was keen to jump but the pilot refused to allow him to go. It later transpired that the dropping ground had been over-run by Bulgars who had found the fires and lit them, but fortunately did not know the correct ground to air signal when the aircraft arrived.[11]

Greenwood was joined in eastern Serbia on 20 May by Major Jasper Rootham, Lieutenant Hargreaves and their W/T operator, Hall. Hargreaves, having decided to cut a dash, jumped in his full dress uniform and monacle—unluckily he landed in the middle of one of the signal bonfires, which rather diminished the effect he had hoped to create.[12] More seriously, Captain Vercoe and Corporal Scott, who joined the mission in September were badly injured on landing. Archie Jack had a second lucky escape in a later attempt when his pilot, nervous of flying over the high mountain ranges, made him jump out at a much greater altitude than was usual. What initially seemed inconsiderate saved Jack's life as his parachute 'candlesticked', the ropes twisting around each other in a narrow vertical space and preventing the canopy from opening. Thanks to the time allowed by the extra height—and a very cool head indeed—Jack managed to untangle the strings in mid-air: his parachute opened and he landed in one piece. On the same flight was Major Albert Seitz, an OSS officer who, on landing, burst into joyous 'yee-haw' cowboy-style whoops, to the amazement and delight of the Yugoslav welcoming party.[13]

Once on terra firma the perils were far from over. While Deakin was fighting his way out of the Axis encirclement with the partisans, Captain Mike Lees, who flew in the night after Deakin, immediately found himself in the midst of a combined German and Bulgar mopping up operation against Mihailović's forces. Lees, his second-in-command Lieutenant Tomlinson and W/T operator Thompson, were bound for Macedonia to replace Major Morgan's mission which had been captured by the Bulgars after dropping blind into the area. To avoid a repeat of this, Lees and his mission dropped further north where Major John Sehmer, the BLO with Major Radoslav Djurić's forces, arranged a reception party. On his second morning in Yugoslavia Lees and his companions were surprised by a Bulgarian dawn raid. Lees managed to escape—ensuring that he took with him the mission's bag of gold sovereigns—but a number of Djurić's men and four members of the SOE mission perished and Tomlinson was wounded. Lees was not impressed by Djurić—commander of southern Serbia, and supposedly responsible for both his own men and the SOE party—who was first through the door when the Bulgars attacked. Lees' opinion of Djurić did not improve on further acquaintance, especially as Djurić went on to cause a great deal of trouble and upset.[14]

While the changed situation in North Africa had facilitated the expansion of SOE operations, the rate at which BLOs were sent into both camps in Yugoslavia soon outpaced SOE's supplies and organizational capabilities. From the outset the new and enlarged missions were confronted with the same problem that had made Bailey's situation problematical, namely the meagre supplies that the British were able to deliver. The extra aircraft made available were not adequate to service the additional missions established with either Mihailović forces or the partisans. Greenwood noted that in the early days of his mission the quality of supplies was quite good but, as the year wore on, he had the impression that the quarter-masters in Cairo were sending anything that came to hand.[15] By December 1943 the missions in Slovenia had not had a sortie for two months and the partisans there were beginning to think that the game was not worth the candle in view of this limited aid.[16] Cairo SOE simply did not have the back-up organization in place: their men were dropped into Yugoslavia without proper communications or supply networks to support them adequately. Extra men were added to existing missions in the face of advice from officers on the ground that this was pointless without sending the arms and explosives which would enable them to accomplish something when they got there. In early June Rootham was incensed when Cairo told him that all sorties for that month were cancelled but they were sending one aeroplane with personnel only, including a Pole who was going to pretend to be an Englishman. Rootham sent Cairo a strongly-worded message concerning the 'flaming Pole', but Cairo despatched him anyway with a few supplies: Rootham felt that the cancelled sorties led to a drop in British prestige in his area.[17] In the event, the 'flaming Pole'—or 'Nash' as he was now known—turned out to be a very courageous member of the Polish underground who had come to organize resistance among a group of his countrymen who had escaped from forced labour in the Bor mines, and soon became respected and regarded as a friend by the British mission. Missions to the partisans that arrived without having had proper clearance from Tito were not allowed to do anything or use their transmitters until proper authorization had been granted.[18]

One of the first problems to confront the liaison officers was that of communications. Their suitcase radio sets were heavy, delicate and cumbersome, with batteries that needed frequent recharging; Greenwood's petrol driven charging motor was smashed as it was dropped from the air, which meant that as soon as his batteries ran down he was incommunicado. There was a shortage of charging motors and the only alternative was hours of hand-charging or pedalling before any signals could be sent. Less than two weeks after Rootham arrived he was having trouble with his batteries and everyone at his mission had to take turns pedalling for him to send messages to Cairo until his charging motor was sent a month later. Arthur Marlow, an enterprising SIS man in Slovenia, decided against pedalling and ordered a fishing line from HQ to tap into overhead electricity lines to send his signals. There were no direct communications between the various sub-missions, all messages went through Cairo and were then transmitted back into Yugoslavia. This rather creaky arrangement was further hampered by the fact that the rapid increase in numbers of men and wireless sets had not been replicated in Cairo, where there were not enough cipher clerks to handle the extra wireless traffic engendered. By contrast Mihailović's communications system, based on home-made and improvised radio sets, allowed his whole organization to be constantly in touch with each other: this surprised the BLOs who were having the most terrible trouble trying to communicate. It was not unusual to spend days travelling to the next sub-mission to confer with another BLO, only to find him away from his HQ or having moved camp altogether. Such journeys were no picnic when they were through occupied territory, sometimes on foot sometimes on horseback, and in winter, often through deep snow.

The greatest disaster to befall the communications network occurred on 14 July 1943. Greenlees and Lieutenant Maynard, with a reception committee, were awaiting a delivery of stores at Ravna Gora when they were attacked by German troops. There were no casualties, but the Germans captured code books and both SOE and RAF ciphers, patterns for fire signals, and ground-to-air and air-to-ground identification signals. In addition, the captured material probably gave them the names and locations of nearly all the BLOs with Mihailović's forces and the names of the commanders of those forces, as well as SOE's opinions on the trustworthiness of some of them. All manner of other sensitive information, such as projected targets, plans for sabotage, arrangements for the evacuation of Hudson and assessments of the effects of BBC propaganda, had all fallen into enemy hands. According to Cairo, also lost to the Germans was a list of Yugoslavs who were due to be parachuted in, with remarks about a private code to be brought in by them for communication between Mihailović and the YGE. MO4 blamed Bailey, Mihailović and the FO for the catastrophe. Bailey was supposed to destroy all records of signals and their cipher workings as soon as they were sent (Bailey later explained that, as he was away from HQ at the time, the signals had been retained by the other two BLOs for him to see on his return). Mihailović was at fault for his 'stubborn refusal' to accept Cairo's advice to move to the east of the Ibar river, although SOE Cairo did not enlarge upon *why* the mission would have been any safer from German attack there than at Ravna Gora. As for the FO, 'Glenconner could not help pointing out that events had justified the advice... the disaster might have been averted if the Foreign Office, instead of making difficulties, had backed us up'. Not surprisingly, news of these lost ciphers was 'to be kept from Yugoslav ears'.[19]

The idea of the British taking control and organizing Yugoslavia on purely military lines was not such a straightforward solution, since it disregarded the fact that the two resistance movements were on home ground and had their own perceptions of how best to achieve their long-term political aims. This should have been apparent from nearly two years experience of dealing with Mihailović; while Tito had made it abundantly clear to the Fungus mission that he would not tolerate a situation such as that existing in Greece, where the British were directing operations. Simić-Stevens claimed that he certainly passed this intelligence on to Cairo.[20] It is uncertain whether this warning was passed on as high up the scale of decision making as it should have been: Selborne appeared to have been unaware of it when he told Eden that Tito had made it plain to Deakin that he was willing to accept guidance from the Commander-in-Chief Middle East and SOE regarding military dispositions and sabotage respectively.[21]

Bailey welcomed the new policy of establishing high status missions at both GHQs, but with the proviso that the brigadier selected for Mihailović's HQ was of the right calibre, and that the mission should avoid giving the impression that it was attempting to subordinate Mihailović to British control. He also warned that it would be unwise to expect a situation comparable with that prevailing in Greece, where Brigadier Eddie Myers, head of the SOE mission, had persuaded the three main guerrilla organizations to put aside their differences and operate as 'the National Bands of Greek Guerrillas' under the command of GHQ Middle East.[22]

A major limiting factor in the efficient operation of the British missions was that most BLOs were given very vague briefings which hardly, if ever, touched on the political situation in Yugoslavia. This was a particularly odd state of affairs, since the officer in Cairo responsible for briefing agents was Hugh Seton-Watson, an expert on all aspects of the Balkans. Seton-Watson was also in charge of collating and interpreting political intelligence from Yugoslavia and producing appreciations for future action, so he should have been ideally placed for giving comprehensive information.[23] The general line seems to have been that the BLOs were to fulfil a purely military role: it was only on their arrival that most became aware of the vital part politics played in the job they were meant to do. It might not have been so bad if the liaison and co-ordination between the political advisers with the two camps had been carried out as planned: Bailey attempted this, but was prevented from achieving it by orders from Cairo[24] and a total lack of reciprocal action from the mission with Tito. Baker Street felt that it was unfortunate that Cairo's directive for Deakin did not include instructions to maintain contact with Bailey through Cairo, and that Bailey had not been told that Cairo had specifically instructed Deakin not to communicate with him either directly or indirectly.[25]

It eventually became apparent to London that simply telling the BLOs not to get embroiled in local politics was a woefully inadequate policy. On 12 August the FO conceded this point and told Baker Street that the Minister of State Middle East would henceforth be responsible for advising liaison officers on political matters.[26] There is little evidence that any improvement was made as a result; officers sent into Yugoslavia after this date were still told not to worry about politics, and that theirs was a purely military job. At least the officers were told what their destination was to be, other ranks were not always so fortunate: the W/T operator with the Brasenose mission in Macedonia had no idea of where he was going until he landed.[27]

The BLOs' scant briefing on the political background to their mission was compounded by the lack of solid information provided by Cairo once they were they were on the ground, and was a serious handicap and embarrassment when dealing with the Yugoslavs. Initially the BLOs with Mihailović's forces were not told that SOE was also supporting the partisans: Hargreaves, when informed of this by the Yugoslavs he was with in eastern Serbia, denied it because he did not know that it was true. When the mission in Homolje was told that a brigadier was coming in to Mihailović's HQ to co-ordinate all SOE missions, Rootham and Greenwood thought it an excellent idea, but they were not told that a new head of mission with equal rank was also to be appointed to SOE missions with Tito's forces. Later Rootham was to read of Tito's formation of an alternative government in *Novo Vreme*, while the local leader he was with had heard of it on the BBC three days earlier, and was amazed that Rootham did not know. He noted rather bitterly in his diary: 'Another instance of the way Cairo supports its officers in the field.'[28] BLOs with the Partisans did not fare any better, when he arrived in Slovenia Peter Wilkinson found most of the SOE people there were in the dark about developments elsewhere that directly concerned them. When he sent his impressions of the situation in Slovenia to Gubbins in London he noted 'Cairo has done very poorly about keeping chaps in the picture.'[29]

In June 1943 there was yet another change in the YGE when Jovanović, disillusioned by the continuing disunity in his government, resigned and was replaced by Miloš Trifunović. Responding to the idea that Mihailović should not retain his post as Minister of War in the new cabinet, Bailey pointed out that British recognition of Mihailović as head of the Yugoslav armed forces was neither here nor there in Serbia where he was loved. The Serbs saw him as the embodiment of their own individuality and nationality. To reduce his standing would simply be a gift to Axis propaganda while reducing the popularity of the British, especially 'in view of the rapidly growing conviction among Serbs that England has sold them to the Russians' due to BBC broadcasts praising the partisans.[30] Hanging over the whole question of politics within Yugoslavia was the relationship with the Soviet Union. Nazi propaganda made the most of the change of government and caused consternation in Serbia by circulating the idea that the YGE had resigned under Russian pressure, and that the whole issue was connected with the Soviet Union's plans for an outlet on the Adriatic. No wonder that Rootham concluded 'Blast politics!'[31]

The Partisans also attempted to make capital out of the new government and in early July contacted Mihailović's commander in

Herzegovina to ask for a parley. With Mihailović's consent Bačević sent a representative to meet Milovan Djilas, chief political officer to Tito, who stated that the British had abandoned Mihailović and that he would probably not remain in the government because of his 'Greater Serbian' policy. Djilas went on to point out that the partisans had a British mission with them in Montenegro, and although they had been partly destroyed in the Axis onslaught, with British aid the Partisans would quickly recover, and as soon as Mihailović was abandoned the rift between his followers and the Partisans would evaporate. Bailey protested to MO4 about this and asked them to get Deakin to ensure the Partisans stopped trying to win over the chetniks in Montenegro and Herzegovina, by personal attacks on Mihailović and attempts to undermine his authority.[32]

Mike Lees ran into political complications of which he knew nothing, when he made contact with a group just south of Priština in Kosovo. They were a mixture of Albanians from Albania and Kosovo, right-wing supporters of the exiled King Zog. They were all armed and eager to set up an anti-Axis resistance movement and gain recognition from the Allies. Lees was delighted as they could field up to 4,000 men in a matter of weeks and many more in the longer term, and had already demonstrated their fighting skills against the Bulgars. MO4 also seemed pleased at first and promised him supplies for them (they particularly wanted American ciga-rettes).[33] But the supplies were never forthcoming because recognition of this group would imply recognition of a post-war united Albania and Kosovo, which ran contra to FO policy. The trouble was that no one told Lees this and he constantly hoped for a 'plane-load for his Albanians.

BLOs with the Partisans certainly could not escape politics. Tito and his associates were in the process of creating a whole new com-munist Yugoslavia, the success of which depended upon winning hearts and minds as well as the war against both the Axis and their internal enemies. Even pro-Partisan liaison officers sometimes found the rigid political control exercized by the commissars hard to take, and were occasionally affronted by the hostility displayed towards the British and Americans and an all too obvious prefer-ence for the Soviets. Some were particularly irritated by claims that SOE supplies either emanated from—or at least were funded by—

the USSR. Lindsay Rogers, a New Zealand surgeon who served at partisan hospitals on the island of Viš and in Bosnia, Croatia and Slovenia, was heart and soul for the partisans, full of admiration for their courage and fighting spirit, and impressed by Tito's charisma and the loyalty he commanded. But Rogers was rather cross about the spurious claims of Russian supplies, and was amused by the story he heard of a British naval commander who crossed the Adriatic with hundreds of tons of supplies for the Partisans. On landing at Dubrovnik the commander encountered the local commissar who insisted that they were 'Russian stores', despite the commander's assertion that they were British. After spending some time in fruitless argument the commander eventually lost patience: 'Well, I've come to the wrong bloody port—cast off for'ard', said he and sailed back to Italy.[34] It was probably an apocryphal tale, but demonstrates rather neatly the reaction of some BLOs to credit not being given where it was due.

All the missions constantly called on Cairo to increase supplies, warning that they were being placed in an impossibly embarrassing situation. Both resistance movements thought the British—with their empire—to be rich and well organized, and read some dark undertone that was designed to work against them, into the thin dribble of arms and equipment. The Partisans took this attitude from the outset and some of Mihailović's commanders began to look more cautiously upon the extra BLOs as they failed to produce supplies. The Allied missions were not universally welcomed by either side, but were regarded as useful *if* they could provide matériel. A message from Benson at the OSS Turnpike mission sums up the situation "The weather has changed from cold to damn cold and the attitude of PARTISAN Staff Fourth zone has changed from cool to cooler. Reason for latter might be the absence of promised sorties."[35] The Americans at Mihailović's HQ were also acutely aware that the very limited amount of supplies furnished by the British was never likely to encourage Mihailović to change his policy to one of becoming overtly active against the Axis forces. Mansfield and Seitz identified the chronic shortage of available British aircraft as the major limiting factor, and suggested that as the USA was producing large numbers of aircraft every month, some of these might be brought into play to alleviate the situation. The

Serbs, they said, were well-disposed to the Americans, and 'Any aid now, like that given by FRANCE in the last war, would not be forgotten'—demonstrating that at least some of SOE's fears of American desire to gain post-war influence in Yugoslavia were not without foundation.[36]

A new YGE-British directive to Mihailović, following the confusion of the two conflicting messages at the end of May which had caused such bad feeling, promised him maximum support as long as he would take action against the Axis and agree not to employ his forces against the Partisans. Liaison officers with both resistance movements were instructed to ensure that the two did not clash, by granting sorties to those who refrained from fighting each other, and withholding them from those who did not. Attempts to put this into practice in Serbia were defeated by Cairo SOE, who failed to supply local commanders who did not fight the Partisans and who had agreed to undertake anti-Axis activity, sometimes in defiance of Mihailović's orders.[37] Conversely, when Major Sehmer warned Djurić that if he continued his attack on the partisans on the Radan, then air support would cease. MO4 immediately sent four sorties leaving Sehmer with no bargaining counter to fulfil his own military briefing.[38] This seems to have been exclusively a problem for the British with the Mihailović commanders, as there is little evidence that any BLOs with the Partisans ever tried to implement the policy. In the Homolje area, Greenwood and Rootham convened a conference with all their local commanders and a delegate from Mihailović's HQ at which they had a showdown, demanding that plans for forthcoming action be made at once. The conference concluded with the bald ultimatum 'No action, no support', but when they reported this to Cairo they received a rebuke for their efforts and were told that this was likely to embarrass the brigadier who was coming in and would disturb higher-level negotiations. They were given three days to backtrack on their ultimatum—saving face if they could—at which time sorties would have to be received. They duly informed their hosts that supplies were on the way, then the 'planes did not arrive, which did little for the face-saving.[39]

Cairo SOE's attempt to prevent clashes after Djurić and his men fought with Partisans encroaching on their area, ended in disaster for the BLO concerned. Major Neil Selby was instructed to contact the partisans in an effort to end the local conflict and persuade them to concentrate their efforts on the Axis: as a 'safety precaution' neither Selby nor Bailey were to tell Mihailović's people or any other BLOs until it was a *fait accompli*.[40] The general idea was that Sehmer in Djurić's camp, and Selby with the Partisans, should decide who was the aggressor and allocate sorties accordingly, a plan Sehmer thought 'most impractical'. Sehmer never found out whether he was right or not in this estimation, as only three days later Selby and his wireless operator, whether by misfortune or betrayal, were captured by Axis forces.

As well as lack of supplies and political complications, the question of reprisals was a continuing problem for BLOs attempting to stimulate action in Serbia. Some thought, as did Mihailović, that precipitate action was pointless and cruel. Archie Jack, on his travels in Serbia, tore down posters which listed the names and home villages of people shot by the Germans in retaliation for any activity against the occupying forces, on the grounds that they were bad for morale. He did not engage much in sabotage himself but collected a vast amount of useful information, such as plans of the inside of mines and industrial sites, all obtained from agents employed by these enterprises, as well as blueprints of turbines and other heavy plant. He had also, as a qualified engineer, made a number of detailed technical drawings of potential targets such as road and rail bridges, all of which he felt should be blown up as the Germans were in retreat through the Balkans—thus maximizing the impact and, because of the general chaos that would prevail, minimizing the scope for reprisals. Jack was sometimes accompanied on his reconnoitres by H.C. Mueller, popularly known as 'Chika Pera' (Uncle Peter) because of his white hair and beard. Mueller was a German who had settled in Slovenia in order to escape from Nazi Germany in the 1930s; unfortunately Nazi Germany caught up with him in 1941, and, although he managed to send his children and his English wife to safety in Britain, he had got trapped in Yugoslavia himself. He had been serving with Mihailović's forces since the summer uprisings in 1941 and was an extremely supportive companion to Jack, once the latter had overcome his suspicions at being approached by a German in occupied territory. These were entirely dispelled when Jack discovered that he and Mueller had both been married in the same church in India and concluded that even the most enterprising German intelligence officer would not have been able to come up with such an obscure coincidence as a cover story for an agent.[41]

In addition to the aim of stepping up activity within Yugoslavia, other missions were infiltrated into all parts of Yugoslavia to contact neighbouring countries. By the same flight as Rootham's 'flaming Pole' came David Russell and his W/T operator Nicolae Turcanu, who constituted 'Operation Ranji', and were destined for Romania. After spending some time with Rootham, the two crossed the Danube on 2 August, their purpose being to establish contact with Maniu, the Romanian liberal politician and long-time SOE associate. Cairo received messages on 12 and 13 August to the effect that they had contacted Maniu, but Russell was murdered on 4 September, probably by a local bandit motivated by greed since his gold and possessions were stolen, but the mission itself had not been betrayed and Turcanu survived and continued to send intermittent messages.[42] On 22 July David Thomas arrived at Rootham's mission, also bound for Romania; Rootham noted in his diary that his would be a hard job since he had little in the way of support from Cairo. There was no resistance movement in Romania, but SOE and PWE had created a fictional Romanian Mihailović figure called Vliaica to sow confusion in Bucharest.[43]

Peter Wilkinson was in Cairo in July 1943 and took the opportunity to catch up with the situation in the Yugoslav section. He was delighted by the news that SOE missions were to be established in Croatia and Slovenia. The decision to support the partisans in Slovenia had produced more irritation in Baker Street at the FO attitude. Douglas Howard's opinion that not enough was known about the situation in Slovenia was dismissed by Pearson as nonsense. It was known that Novak, commander of the Yugoslav Home Army in Slovenia, had collaborated with the Italians—albeit as a means of self defence—while the Partisans were in areas containing Axis lines of communications. Pearson felt that time was 'too pressing to have endless arguments with the FO', and at a meeting between SOE, SIS and the FO on 19 July it was agreed to support the Slovene partisans as long as they agreed not to fight their neighbours and to come under the command of C-in-C Middle East. The consensus at the meeting was that 'the importance of Slovenia could hardly be overestimated.'[44] Its importance was not lost on Wilkinson who perceived it as 'the back door into central Europe for which I had been searching for the past two years'.[45] Back in London he immediately set to work on a planning paper which recommended working into Austria from Slovenia and was to result in the Clowder mission, which was ultimately to be as ill-fated as Ranji. In August Basil Davidson joined Deakin with the plan to cross the Danube into Hungarian occupied Vojvodina with the aim of continuing the work that he had started in Hungary before the whole area had fallen under the Axis mantle. In mid August Tito decided that as the partisans had overcome the most dangerous attempt yet to annihilate them, they could now cease straightforward military operations and concentrate upon guerrilla warfare and sabotage on lines of communication and Axis controlled industries. Partisans at Vojvodina HQ whose operational area also included Srem, Baranija, the Bačka and the Banat, were ordered to attack Axis rail and river transport. A specialist rail sabotage group was to be based at Papuk and Davidson was to cooperate with this group.[46]

Reports from these SOE missions from July to September indicate that there was a good deal of sabotage going on, the bulk of it being carried out by partisan forces. The Mihailović forces were doing a reasonable amount, but the Homolje mission reported that the commanders in their area, while resolute and capable, preferred secret sabotage action to overt military activity to avoid needless reprisals; they had large numbers of volunteers in eastern Serbia but were in need of arms. Many BLOs reported that large numbers of volunteers were available for both the Partisans and the Yugoslav Home Army, and in the Priština area the BLO reported at the end of July that Serbs were arriving in the forests in droves to volunteer for action; they just needed weapons.

Reports from the field also indicated that the civil war was continuing unabated. In early July Bailey signalled that Major Fehim Musa Kadić, one of Mihailović's commanders in Bosnia-Herzegovina, had been captured with three of his men by Partisan Lieutenant Ratomir Hamović. All four had been executed and Hamović had made off with about 500 SOE gold sovereigns. Musa Kadić, well known to Bailey and Huson as an able and loyal Muslim, was in the Kalinovik area organizing Muslims for anti-Axis action and Bailey wanted Deakin to take up the case with Tito. He felt that a partisan investigation and disciplinary action against Hamović would greatly improve the partisan image in Serbia, and promote co-existence and tolerance between the two forces, which Bailey thought was far from a hopeless proposition.[47]

In August the Neronian mission reported an unprovoked attack by the partisans, while Fungus in Croatia reported that the partisans claimed Mihailović's forces were not only collaborating but consisted purely of Serbs, and so no co-operation was possible. The Ballinclay mission with the Partisans in the Drvar area on 1 and 8 August sent reports of a pitched battle between chetniks and Partisans in which the former came off worse. Their leader, Jovo Plećaš, had been killed and among his personal effects were Italian and German identity passes allowing him to travel in occupied territory, although as they have different dates and places of birth they were possibly forged or obtained clandestinely. Plećaš also had in his possession an order to organize attacks on the partisans in the Glamoč, Drvar and Petrovac areas to pave the way for an Allied landing in September, which was, according to the BLO, signed by Mihailović and Lalatović and dated 1 August 1943. MO4 queried the dates and was informed by Ballinclay that the battle had lasted from 27 July until 1 August; the 1 August document was not signed by Mihailović, but his name was typed at the end, but another document found on Plećaš, dated 27 July, was signed by Mihailović.

In late August a series of telegrams from Deakin's Typical mission informed MO4 that he had seen captured documents proving chetnik collaboration with Germans, Italians *et al* and even with Pavelić, although a later telegram said 'For Pavelić read Nedić': presumably these were the documents that Velebit produced for Deakin and Davidson to peruse between their swims. Deakin's conclusion reinforced the opinion from the Fungus mission that the Partisans simply could not be expected to co-operate with Mihailović.[48] By the summer of 1943 the COS had not only tuned up the Balkans, but had also tuned up the Yugoslav civil war.

9

BACKING BOTH SIDES: TWO BRIGADIERS AND 'EQUAL SUPPORT'

While SOE was building up the network of agents within Yugoslavia the process of selecting the brigadiers who were to command the high status missions at both HQs was in train. Keble thought that appointing two regular brigadiers with a proven military record was an obvious way of maximizing the efficiency of the whole show. Less kind commentators have suggested that having two brigadiers under his command would also increase his own status and possibly lead to promotion. Keble recommended to Glenconner that Brigadier Charles Armstrong should go to Partisan HQ while Brigadier Nicholls should take over as head of mission from Bailey at Mihailović's HQ: he felt that it was time to have a first class soldier fulfilling this role rather than an 'amateur', then suggested Brigadier Orr when Nicholls was unavailable.[1] The best laid plans often go awry, and so it was with Keble's brigadiers. While he was sorting out the military side Orme Sargent was helpfully putting forward the name of Captain Fitzroy Maclean as a possible political advisor, to be Bailey's counterpart at Tito's HQ.[2]

Maclean, a Conservative MP, a captain in the SAS, and late of the FO himself, appeared to be an excellent choice, particularly at the FO, which had never been entirely happy with SOE's assessments and advice. The FO would now have the benefit of having one of their 'own' men on the spot. According to the plan, and Maclean's original brief, he was to be seconded to SOE to act as political adviser to the brigadier appointed head of the mission. Maclean was to maintain contact with Bailey, the senior political adviser for the whole of Yugoslavia, to enable the minister of state in Cairo to keep abreast of any political complications arising from differences in the assessments of the two advisers.[3] However, Maclean did not long remain second-in-command of the projected mission, despite objections from SOE.

Maclean gave his own account of his appointment at a conference in 1973 which, no doubt due to artistic license, is somewhat different to that gleaned from FO and SOE documents. He omitted the fact that he was initially to be second-in-command and cut straight to Churchill summoning him to 'command the mission with the rank of brigadier and also to be his personal representative with the Partisan command'.[4] Maclean went on to detail the dirty tricks SOE tried to prevent him going to Tito. These included a bogus telegram to Churchill purporting to come from Jumbo Wilson to the effect that he considered Maclean unsuitable for the job; a 'whispering campaign' in Cairo that Paul Vellacot of PWE was asked to set in motion insinuating that Maclean was a homosexual and a drunkard; and a concerted effort to delay his departure for Cairo. Even if Maclean's account of these SOE machinations was accurate, it would have made no difference; Churchill had already decided that this was his man. It has been suggested that Churchill's choice of the colourful Fitzroy Maclean was a ruse to disguise the fact that the British were reading German Enigma signals and that he was basing his judgements on information from this source.[5] Whether or not this was the case, the PM recommended to Eden that Maclean—as an ideal 'ambassador-leader to these hardy and hunted guerrillas'—should be head of the new mission, and asked the foreign secretary 'to use my influence, for what it is worth'.[6] Charles Hambro preferred to keep the military and political functions of the mission separate, in accordance with the original plan. The Middle East Defence Committee was also against the idea of combining the roles of political advisor and head of mission, arguing that suitability for one role did not necessarily demonstrate suitability for the other, and they did not think that the political advisors should be part of the chain of command. Glenconner, Baker Street and Orme Sargent all concurred.[7] But Eden agreed with the PM.

Selborne weighed in with a sensible argument: while he recognized Maclean's qualities and felt his independent spirit made him admirably suited to the role of political adviser, he thought that to tie Maclean to Tito's headquarters would limit his ability to move around and get a clear picture of the situation in Yugoslavia. Selborne also had reservations regarding the military side: 'I do see considerable difficulties in putting an officer who, however brilliant he might be, has only one year's service as a captain, in a position where he will be expected to give military advice to a commander of a force of 65,000 men and to furnish strategic appreciations to C-in-C Middle East Forces.'[8] He was also concerned about Bailey's position. Hambro had offered Bailey the post of brigadier when the plan was first mooted, but Bailey had replied that he felt he was not qualified to advise Mihailović on the conduct of military operations, and that a regular officer was more appropriate in this role while he concentrated on the long-term political aspects of the mission.[9] Fitzroy Maclean appears to have had no such doubts about his own capabilities. He favoured the PM's plan, arguing that the C-in-C Middle East was not particularly interested in the Yugoslav venture, and the SOE were planning to send in people they wanted to get rid of; he felt it would be difficult for him to work with these 'inefficient officers' who would be senior to him. What the basis of this argument was it is difficult to tell, since Keble was keen to get a high level mission in to the Partisans and the C-in-C Middle East was equally keen to make maximum use of them.

Although still adhering to his reservations, Selborne was forced to acquiesce on 6 August, as Churchill and Eden felt so strongly about the matter, and he did not want to hold things up. This was fairly academic as Churchill had already sent a telegram to General Wilson informing him that Maclean was his choice as head of the mission and there was 'no question of his being put under a Brigadier'. On being sent a copy of this, and Eden's draft letter to Wilson, Selborne essentially had no choice.[10]

In the summer of 1943, Cairo SOE was again coming under fire for independent actions which were not in keeping with FO and military policy. The main complaints stemmed from problems arising from SOE's involvement with Greece, which only a short time earlier had been held up as a major success story. The political advisor to Eddie Myers' mission had sent a series of telegrams which MO4 had failed to deliver to Rex Leeper, British ambassador to the exiled Greek government. Then Myers had brought out six guerrillas who demanded that the Greek king should not return to the country until there had been a plebiscite on the future of the monarchy. In addition, SOE was proceeding faster with the Yugoslav partisans than the FO wanted, particularly in regard to propaganda, and taking to themselves authority that the FO thought inappropriate. They were sharply told that the FO and London SOE were to be the arbiters on any changes of policy. The FO particularly objected to Cairo raising the question of the Anglo-Soviet political background and references to the AVNOJ, nor did they want the word 'Partisans' plugged: their favoured phrase was 'Yugoslav guerrillas', to promote the idea of the Yugoslav resistance as a whole. MO4 had also been rather precipitate in supplying matériel to the Partisans before obtaining an agreement that they would refrain from fighting Mihailović's forces.[11]

The FO was not taken by General Wilson's suggestion that yet another co-ordinating committee should be established 'to see that SOE play the game in future', but preferred the idea of MO4 being taken over by the regular military. Their attitude was no doubt reinforced by the reception accorded Fitzroy Maclean in Cairo. Glenconner and Keble openly told him that they disliked his appointment and were working to reverse it, and in the meantime, according to Maclean, erecting obstacles to prevent his departure for Yugoslavia. Cairo SOE had taken on a rather more formidable opponent than they had bargained for in Maclean, and the attempt to undermine him backfired and provided more evidence in the case against them, leading Wilson to the conclusion that 'the whole organization was rotten.'[12] Maclean himself was able to use it to escape the authority of SOE and, citing the handling of messages from Greece, ensured that he would have independent communications that did not go through SOE channels.[13] Glenconner's subsequent attempts to pacify Maclean met with a stony response.

SOE Cairo narrowly escaped being taken over by the military, largely it seems, due to the intercession of Mountbatten, whose aid had been sought by Colin Gubbins, who replaced Hambro as executive head of SOE in September. Mountbatten had been a supporter of SOE since its creation and regarded its continued presence in the Middle East as important to his position in south-east Asia.[14] Nevertheless, SOE Cairo had lost this particular battle. Maclean rose from captain to brigadier, and was to be both political and military head of the mission with direct communications to the Minister of State, Lord Moyne, and General Wilson in Cairo. All of this made Bailey's position as chief political adviser in Yugoslavia somewhat meaningless.

The appointment of the new head of the military mission to Mihailović was a much less dramatic affair and was made in accordance with the original plan. The brigadier selected was Charles Armstrong, the regular officer whom Keble had originally earmarked as a suitable head of mission to Tito. Armstrong was not designated Churchill's personal representative, or 'ambassador-leader', or given his own independent communications, having to rely instead on the vagaries of Cairo SOE. As Maclean had put up such a strong argument against Cairo SOE's handling of messages from the field, this seems to have been a major oversight on the part of those who apparently wanted to make the best possible use of all resistance in Yugoslavia, and it did, in fact, turn out to be a handicap for Armstrong. He *could* have had direct communications with London, as shortly after Bailey's arrival in Yugoslavia, in early 1943 trials for direct radio contact with the SOE war station in Britain had been successful. Contact was broken when Bailey had to move due to enemy action, but there was no reason not to re-establish the link. Cairo blocked that possibility, insisting that all messages should first come to them.[15]

Mihailović had agreed, under the terms of the British-YGE directive, to step up anti-Axis activity and to refrain from fighting the partisans in return for maximum support, but he was still reluctant to take any action which might provoke reprisals. In an attempt to galvanize him into sabotaging the north-south lines of communication in the Ibar and Vardar valleys, Bailey took matters into his own hands by delivering an ultimatum which he claimed came from the C-in-C Middle East. This earned him a rebuke from Cairo, but a few days later Bailey sent out a long telegram, illustrating the depths of desperation which had driven him to take independent action. It begins: 'Herewith reasons for my failure…in hope that you [Cairo SOE] and Brigadier Armstrong may profit from them and so ensure success his mission.'[16] Emphasizing that he did not wish to cast blame on anyone, Bailey set out both his own and Mihailović's shortcomings: the problems of supply and propaganda, coupled with the fact that he himself did not appear to enjoy the confidence of his superiors, was hampering the whole operation. He was also distressed by Cairo's lack of understanding of the situation in Yugoslavia.

This last point was apparent in the response Bailey's telegram elicited in Cairo, where it was interpreted as evidence against Mihailović—quite the opposite of what Bailey seems to have been trying to achieve. At a meeting between the minister of state, Glenconner and the Director of Military Operations, Mihailović's reply to the British-YGE directive and to Bailey's ultimatum were deemed unsatisfactory, and a 'show down' with the Yugoslav minister of war was recommended. This provoked a furious response from Eden who, in accord with London SOE, had assessed Mihailović's replies to both as quite in order:

> The fact is, I am sure, that S.O.E., Cairo (plus the Minister of State) do not *want* us to come to a satisfactory arrangement with Mihailović. We have been on the verge of doing so many times, but on each occasion a spanner has been thrown in to prevent us.[17]

He went on to enumerate examples, including Glenconner's 'bludgeoning' telegram, and argued that Mihailović should at least be given a fair chance before a negative judgement was assumed, which seemed to him 'a typical SOE way of doing things'. Douglas Howard and Orme Sargent both agreed with Eden's opinion that MO4 and the minister of state, Cairo, were definitely against reaching an agreement with Mihailović. The minister of state had particularly objected to Mihailović's response to British support of forces other than his own, yet only two days earlier, on 4 September, MO4 had forwarded to Baker Street Bailey's report which stated: 'Mihailović accepts our right to support other elements of resistance.'

At about the same time that Cairo SOE was arguing that Mihailović's response was unsatisfactory, and complaining about his lack of activity, they stopped Mike Lees carrying out a sabotage operation on the grounds that it had not been sanctioned by Mihailović. Cairo later apologised for the series of 'stop-go-stop-go' messages which had led to the cancellation, but it was only one of a number of confusing and conflicting signals which halted sabotage just as local commanders had agreed to carry it out. When these signals were followed up by orders for immediate action, the moment had often passed.[18]

Before either brigadier arrived to take up his command, the armistice with Italy was announced on 8 September 1943. What form the expected Italian surrender should take and how it should be handled in the Balkans, had been under discussion for nearly two months before it finally occurred. In the interim, the coup that deposed Mussolini and made Marshal Badoglio Italian prime minister, brought the moment closer. Unsure of whether the Italians in the Balkans would surrender to anyone other than a British officer, the COS, FO and SOE had considered the possibility of SOE officers on the ground taking charge. In Yugoslavia, it was thought that the Italians might be more likely to negotiate with Mihailović forces and chetniks than with Partisans, and it was hoped that instead of being disarmed and evacuated, some Italian forces could be persuaded to come over to the Allies.[19]

All parties in Yugoslavia were aware that Italy was about to drop out of the war and made their plans accordingly. The Germans prepared to disarm the Italians and fill the vacuum with their own troops, Tito produced the terms of an armistice,[20] and Mihailović had been waiting to take the Italian arms and positions since 1942. In the event, despite Mihailović's long-term plans, the Partisans managed to obtain the bulk of the arms that the Germans failed to take. The British missions were not given prior notification of the date of the armistice, but Keble perceived the expected Italian collapse as an ideal opportunity for resistance forces to obtain Italian supplies. Great secrecy surrounded the exact date for fear of a German move against Badaglio's government in Rome. The French were not given advance notice at all, much to the chagrin of de Gaulle. A state of high tension existed among the British and Americans in the Middle East over whether Badoglio *would* broadcast his announcement of the armistice as agreed, and contingency plans had been made in case he did not. In the event, it seems that both Deakin and Bailey first heard of the armistice on the radio when Badoglio made his broadcast. A few hours later the British missions in Yugoslavia received a signal from GHQ Middle East:

Get in touch with Italian commanders in your area. Insist implementation armistice terms and enlist aid against Germans. If Italians unable to fight Germans take possession arms, aircraft, other military stores.[21]

Deakin appears to have been unable to recall the exact text of the signal he received, or whether it was 'similar' or 'the same' as the one sent to Bailey. He only recalled it telling him to 'carry out the disarming of the nearest Italian division', while his W/T operator noted in his diary 'We have been told to arrange armistice locally'.[22] Whatever the precise wording, Deakin received a dusty reply when he relayed the message to Tito, who made it clear that no British officer would assume the responsibility of conducting negotiations with the Italians whose armaments rightly belonged to the Partisans. Obviously Tito would wear no outside interference, so it would have done Deakin no good to push the matter, even if he had been inclined to do so. There was a great difference between Deakin's relationship with Tito and Bailey's with Mihailović. Deakin had arrived well-disposed towards the Partisan movement, having worked closely with Davidson and Keble on producing the memo of which Churchill was given a copy in Cairo. The circumstances of his arrival and subsequent experiences seem to have coloured his perception to the point of accepting Tito's authority as supreme. By contrast, Bailey, who was an old Yugoslav hand, had taken a much tougher line—and a much more sceptical approach—to Mihailović, and remained first and foremost governed by orders from British HQ in Cairo.

The experience of the Italian armistice is a clear illustration of the different positions of the two chiefs of mission. After his confrontation with Tito, Deakin suggested that he be allowed to accompany General Koča Popović, commander of the First Proletarian Division, to Split to witness the Italian surrender. While there Deakin rebuffed an attempt by General Becuzzi, commander of the Bergamo Division, to discuss the armistice with him personally, making it clear that this was a partisan show. Later Deakin tried to mediate between the Bergamo Division and Popović to reach an agreement on the Italian forces joining the Partisans as whole units, but the latter had little enthusiasm for this idea and were willing to accept Italian recruits only as individuals. At about the same time Bailey set out for Montenegro with Lukačević, one of Mihailović's commanders, to negotiate with the Venezia Division. At Prijepolje Lukačević's forces fought with and defeated the Germans who had already disarmed the Italians there. On reaching Berane, the Venezia

Division's headquarters, Bailey—following instructions from Cairo—had a private discussion with the commander, General Oxilia, who agreed to co-ordinate his division's actions with those of the resistance: namely, to come over lock stock and barrel to the Allied side. Bailey had to dissuade the Mihailović forces from disarming the Italians, but eventually an agreement was reached whereby the administration of the area would be taken over by the Yugoslavs and the Venezia Division would fight against the Germans.[23]

The arrangement reached in Berane was the optimum outcome from the Allied point of view; unfortunately this mutually beneficial arrangement was not destined to last. While the Split and Berane discussions were still proceeding, Deakin and Bailey were informed of the imminent arrival of their new heads of mission and hastened back to their respective headquarters to meet the brigadiers. The Lim Valley around Berane was Mihailović territory, with no Partisans in the area: before Bailey departed to meet Armstrong, he contacted Cairo and told them to inform Tito of the position there, and ask him to restrain his troops from moving into the Sandjak and Montenegro.[24] It seems that Cairo was unable to secure such co-operation from Tito. Partisans in large numbers, under Peko Dapčević, commander of the Second Proletarian Division, were rushed to the Lim valley, where they attempted by both force of arms and persuasion to win General Oxilia and the Venezia Division away from the already-concluded agreement with Mihailović's forces. General Oxilia, after attempting to unite the two opposing forces, finally succumbed to Partisan pressure but did manage to arrange safe passage out of the area for the Mihailović men.[25] This must have been a bitter blow for Mihailović and his followers, as they had been counting on obtaining Italian arms for the *Ustanak*: not only had they lost the arms, but the Partisans had managed to move in force into Montenegro and the Sandjak.

The reported presence of British officers who finally helped persuade Oxilia that the Partisans were the only official Allied representatives, calls into question whether Cairo really tried to secure co-operation from the Partisans. Lees tells us that one officer was Major Hunter of the Fungus mission; Deakin says that the 'ghost of the British officers at Berane' was an invention of Mihailović's HQ, offering as proof the fact that Hunter was established in the area only on 1 January 1944. This does not, of course, preclude Hunter's presence in Berane in September. Another possibility is that the 'British colonel and major' were Partisans in British uniform; Dedijer had pulled off this trick already, when a large force of Italians surrendered to a much smaller group of partisans in the belief that Dedijer was a British officer.[26]

Immediately after the Italian armistice, Mihailović sent out a general order to his commanders throughout Yugoslavia to attack lines of communication and German troops. Widespread sabotage was achieved and a number of towns and villages taken from the Germans. The action was in full flow when Armstrong's arrival added weight to the general belief that the Allied invasion was at hand and the time ripe for the general rising. This aggressive action was further encouraged by the message Armstrong brought from General Wilson, promising military supplies on a much larger scale. Armstrong wired to Cairo that Mihailović was 'more pugnacious against the Germans' and gave details of the fighting and sabotage. Four railway bridges around Mokra Gora were blown up in a single day and about 100 Bulgar troops were killed. On 5 October Armstrong was at Ostojić's HQ waiting for the attack on the German garrison in the town of Višegrad at 03.00 hours. If the town was taken and if Ostojić cut the throat of the German commander, then Armstrong—a teetotaller—had promised to drink a glass of raki: 'Don't like Raki, but like Germans less.'[27] Mihailović assembled about 4,000 guerrillas and after heavy fighting Višegrad fell to his forces and the railway bridge there was destroyed. Major Archie Jack who laid the charges was particularly proud of this action as it was the longest single-span bridge to be blown up in south-eastern Europe during the war.

The BLOs with the various sub-missions were pleased to hear of Armstrong's arrival; they too thought this would presage better organization and supplies, and improve their chances of achieving more positive action. This turned out to be an illusion: the supply situation did not improve at all, but deteriorated in both frequency and quality, and eventually Armstrong himself was reduced to sending desperate messages to Cairo. Expected sorties were cancelled at short notice or simply did not materialize, and when the BLOs with Mihailović's forces protested, they were told this was unfortunate but beyond Cairo's control. They were also told that BLOs with the partisans were receiving only minimum sorties.[28] This was not true: supplies to the partisans steadily increased following the arrival of Maclean, possibly due to pro-Partisan elements in Cairo, but more likely attributable to the fact that SOE had already received a bloody nose from Maclean and were anxious not to cross him again. The Partisans were the main beneficiaries of the extra aircraft that were made available to SOE in early autumn, and when it became possible to transport supplies across the Adriatic by boat the Partisans were the *only* beneficiaries. Between June and December missions with the Partisans received 224 tons of airborne supplies, while those with Mihailović forces had 228 tons during the whole of 1943. In October and November Partisan missions were also sent 2,050 tons of seaborne aid.[29]

The suspicion gradually took hold, in the minds of both the Mihailović BLOs and their hosts, that the Partisans were receiving their sorties. The suspicions were hardly allayed by the arrival of two mysterious missions in November. 'Monkeywrench', headed by Major Dugmore, joined the Partisans in eastern Serbia, and 'Mulligatawny', led by Major Mostyn Davies, dropped in to partisans to the east of Lake Ohrid. When Major Sehmer asked Cairo SOE for information on the Mulligatawny mission, Cairo denied its existence, but was caught out by the fact that Davies had already been in contact with Captain Robert Purvis, another BLO with Mihailović's forces. The mission was in need of assistance which Purvis was trying to arrange, until he was told by Cairo to leave Mulligatawny alone, as they were on a very special mission. Furthermore he was instructed to keep their presence secret. This, Sehmer concluded, was ludicrous, since all the local people already knew, and had informed *him* of Mulligatawny's arrival.[30] The Mihailović BLOs were in an impossible situation—either they looked foolish for not knowing about Davies' presence with the Partisans, or treacherous for not acknowledging it. Purvis felt Cairo had displayed a lack of confidence by not warning him of the mission's passage through his area; it was also detrimental to the task of preventing clashes between the local resistance and Partisans. The situation was made worse a few days later when Davies received a sortie so close to Purvis' own position that the signal flares were visible: feelings were already running high and 'the result of course was a battle'.[31]

The 'special mission' was an attempt to get in touch with the Bulgarian partisans. A 'Captain Patterson' had already joined Jasper Rootham in eastern Serbia on 20 September for the same reason. Rootham noted in his diary that Patterson was 'really a Russian' but in reality he was Captain W. Petro-Pavlovsy, a Bulgarian. SOE's massive efforts to make contact with Bulgaria were because of the possibility that the Italian armistice might stimulate a Bulgarian coup or persuade the government to change sides. Since this would probably have meant that the Germans would take over in Bulgaria, it opened the possibility of stimulating resistance there also—and, as usual, SOE felt that it was they who should be orchestrating it. Colonel Pavlović, the local commander in Homolje, had initially been willing to help Patterson, but his enthusiasm had apparently waned when he heard whom Patterson wanted to contact. He insisted that Mihailović's permission had to be given before any infiltration into Bulgaria might be contemplated, while advising that the Bulgarian Agrarian Party was a better bet than the Bulgarian Partisans.[32]

Mostyn Davies was later joined by Major Frank Thompson, elder brother of the social historian E.P. Thompson; both Davies and Thompson were to perish in their attempts to organize Bulgarian resistance. While waiting to contact the Bulgarians, Davies remained with the small band of Partisans in the south, with Svetožar Vukmanović—'Tempo', a member of partisan Supreme Command. Cairo sent sorties to this mission, and to Dugmore's Monkey-wrench mission, despite the policy of GHQ Middle East that arms would not be supplied to either Mihailović or Partisan forces in areas of 'debated ground' where the two were in close proximity to each other.

To make matters worse, if this were possible, all the action taken by Mihailović's forces, including the success at Višegrad and Mokra Gora, was attributed to the Partisans in BBC broadcasts.[33] Misattribution of each side's activity was not an uncommon feature of broadcasts, it had provoked protests from the Partisans too, and caused embarrassment to the BLOs with Tito's forces. The problem with these particular mistaken attributions was that Mihailović had at last taken overt action, as opposed to covert acts of sabotage to avoid reprisals, and received no credit. The mistake was compounded by the fact that the attendant reprisals, costing many hundreds of

Yugoslav lives, were not given air coverage, while the BBC made
great play of four victims of reprisals in Norway resulting from
resistance activity there. On 13 October the BBC announced that
the Partisans had taken Berane, omitting to mention that they had
taken it from Mihailović forces, not the Axis.[34] These blunders, if
such they were, coupled with declining supplies and the Venezia
affair, convinced Mihailović that 'the British had sold him down
the river to Stalin' as Mansfield later reported to OSS. Having co-
operated with the British, and had insult added to injury for his
pains, Mihailović seems to have concluded that he should return to
his own policy regarding both occupiers and Partisans. The result
was a swift decline in relations between Armstrong and Mihailović.
At times the two were not even on speaking terms, and once again
it was only thanks to the personal efforts of Major Kenneth Green-
less that any channels of communication were kept open between
them.

In addition, Armstrong appears to have alienated the American
members of the mission at Mihailović's HQ by excluding them
from any important discussions and treating them as inferiors. He
also insisted on seeing all the telegrams they wished to send out,
while denying them access to his own. A protest to Cairo from the
Americans simply brought a confirmation that they were under
Armstrong's command.[35] Armstrong was only following instructions from Cairo, who had agreed to allow OSS participation in
British missions as long as they did not interfere. Eventually Colonel
Seitz and Captain Mansfield, the OSS officers, became so frustrated
at kicking their heels that they departed on a tour of inspection
around Serbia.

Subsequently, various people—including some members of Mihailović's forces—questioned the wisdom of selecting Armstrong for this
mission, even suggesting that he was deliberately chosen because of
his unsuitability. While this is not the case, it is undeniable that it
was not a fortunate choice: he was a regular officer with no experience of guerrilla warfare, was given to sticking to military discipline
and 'proper' conduct, and had stated openly before he arrived that
he wanted no truck with matters political. Furthermore, as a non-
smoking teetotaller, he was far from being at home in meetings at
which raki was regularly passed around and a thick fog developed

from the heavy-smoking Serbs around him. Word soon reached the sub-missions that Armstrong was not a success, Jasper Rootham heard that he was the 'worst type of Col. Blimp, fussy and domineering' but was pleasantly surprised when he finally met Armstrong 'although he was clearly a fish out of water in this mainly political job'.[36]

Fitzroy Maclean was a very different character. He and Tito seem to have got on well from the start, perhaps recognizing a certain degree of kindred spirit in each other. At his meeting with Churchill, the PM had told Maclean not to bother unduly about the political colouring of the resistance he was to join—this was something for future consideration. Churchill's own enthusiasm for the Partisans, made apparent in his phraseology, had given Maclean the keynote for his mission and he appears to have determined to make a success of it from the outset. Maclean's background reading seems to have reinforced the romanticised and idealized conception of the 'hardy and hunted guerrillas' he was about to join. Free from the constraints of SOE, Maclean was able to make good use of both his own initiative and personal contacts.

There was a great difference in the attitude of the British with Tito and those with Mihailović. While the latter delivered orders and ultimatums to Mihailović and fell out with him, Maclean treated Tito with kid gloves, often warning that 'deep offence' would be caused if things did not go exactly in accordance with Tito's wishes. In one of his early reports Maclean described the partisans as 'a far more considerable military and political force than we had imagined' and likely to be the decisive force in Yugoslavia. In the light of this he urged that the go-ahead be granted for a Partisan delegation to come to the Middle East: failure to grant this risked offending the partisans and might undermine the chance of the British to strengthen *their* position with Tito and his movement.[37] Armstrong sent Mihailović a number of letters warning him to desist from fighting the partisans, but there are no equivalent letters from Maclean to Tito. When the two missions were asked to sound out Mihailović and Tito on the possibility of establishing a neutral zone between them to lessen the risk of clashes, the mission with Mihailović indicated that he would accept such an arrangement, while that with Tito refused even to pose the question, 'as it would involve a withdrawal by him from territory now in his occupation'.[38] The territory in question was the area of Montenegro and the Sandjak that the partisans had acquired as a result of Bailey following Cairo's instructions after the Italian armistice. Although Armstrong had protested to Cairo that Mihailović had been severely provoked there, and that Tito was to blame for the confrontation this was bound to produce, no pressure was to be brought to bear on Tito. Instead, Cairo SOE sent Armstrong a warning that Mihailović's positioning of his HQ on the extreme western edge of his territory was 'highly precarious' and advised *him* to move. To which Armstrong replied Mihailović was currently operating against the 'Huns' in western Serbia, with a friendly population and Nedić neutral; if he were to leave this area, as MO4 suggested, the Partisans would immediately enter, and they would have to fight the 'Huns' and Nedić forces, with the local population against them and Mihailović at best hostile. The large scale reprisals that were going on in Serbia were already bound to impair Mihailović's popularity and Armstrong argued against diminishing it further by introducing Partisans to Serbia. The end result would be to lose the whole point of backing both sides.[39]

In November Cairo SOE told Armstrong that in view of this situation, an agreement had been reached with Tito that any BLOs who might be captured by the Partisans would be treated as members of the Allied army and sent to Maclean's mission for evacuation.[40] Two questions spring to mind here: how else should they have been treated, and what had happened to the British organizing and co-ordinating the resistance? The answer to the second point is to be found in Maclean's statement:

There is, of course, no question of any Allied officer or other outside authority conducting the operations of the National Liberation Army or in any way directing its strategy.[41]

Tito had agreed that it would be 'useful' for Maclean to keep him informed of the main lines of Allied policy, and he had undertaken to do what he could to further Allied plans. Maclean thought this co-operation would be in direct proportion to the amount of material help supplied. The British knew that Mihailović had no-one else to turn to: he constantly hoped for aid from the USA but, although the Americans were sympathetic, SOE had made it clear to them that Yugoslavia was a British sphere of influence, and had taken pains to ensure that it stayed that way. By contrast, the British were constantly aware that Tito could turn to the Soviets; they probably overestimated Soviet interest and intentions to begin with, but it was a possibility which coloured British perceptions. It played an important part in Maclean's recommendations which were largely designed to win Tito and the Partisans away from their primary loyalty to the USSR.

Having formed a favourable impression of Tito and his movement, and discussed the best way of increasing supplies to them, Maclean set out for the coast, walking most of the way, to explore possible landing places for seaborne supplies. After a not-so-brief sojourn on the island of Korčula, during which time a boat bearing aid for the partisans arrived, Maclean made the return journey to Tito's HQ at Jajce. On 5 October, 19 days after his first arrival in Yugoslavia, the ambassador-leader set out for the coast once more to make his way, via the islands of Hvar and Vis, to Italy by sea and from there to Cairo. Maclean's journeys take up three whole chapters in his colourful, entertaining and swashbuckling autobiographical *Eastern Approaches*. By 5 November Maclean was back in Cairo where he met Sir Alexander Cadogan and Anthony Eden, who were returning from the Foreign Ministers' Conference in Moscow. He presented Eden with a written report on the situation in Yugoslavia, to be passed on to Churchill before he left England to attend first the Cairo Conference with Roosevelt, and then the Teheran Conference of 'the Big Three'.

This report—'the blockbuster'—was probably the most influential document produced by any British officer in Yugoslavia during the war.[42] That fact makes it all the more unfortunate that it was so inaccurate. The reason for its inaccuracy was that it was based entirely on Partisan sources. During Maclean's brief time in Yugoslavia, which he mainly seems to have spent 'yomping' between Jajce and the coast, he simply had not covered enough ground or gained enough first-hand intelligence to produce an accurate and impartial assessment.

The 'blockbuster' proved Selborne's doubts about whether Maclean had the experience to be both political and military adviser to the commander of 65,000 guerrillas, to have been well-founded. The first point to note is that these 65,000 had apparently risen to 220,000. The numbers game is a feature of Yugoslav wartime history, whether it be the number of Serbs massacred by their collective enemies, or, as in this case, the number of Partisans at Tito's disposal. There are so many—and such disparate—estimates of Partisan numbers that the only positive statement to be made on the subject is that no-one, other than possibly the Partisans themselves, really had any idea of the exact figure. That Maclean's estimate is far too high is borne out by his own subsequent accounts, which contain a number of different figures, but never again reached 220,000. His early reports state that partisans forces increased by 60,000 between 8 and 20 September—about 5,000 per day—to a total of 180,000. In *Eastern Approaches* he gave Partisan strength variously as 'over 100,000' and 'about 150,000, perhaps more' and in *Disputed Barricades*, published eight years later he quotes German estimates as 111,000 Partisans.

Maclean's claim that, when engaging the enemy, the Partisans counted on losing only one fighter for every five Germans killed, and one dead Partisan for every ten Ustashas or chetniks, reads like something from an ancient heroic Balkan ballad. According to the blockbuster, the Partisans were also between ten and twenty times more numerous than Mihailović's forces, and 'infinitely better organized, better equipped and better disciplined'. The Partisans were certainly better equipped after their gains from the Italians—and Maclean was on the way to increasing the discrepancy by ensuring that they received the lion's share of supplies; the organization and discipline ensured by communist control might well have been superior, but ten or twenty times more numerous was wildly inaccurate, as was the claim that there were 30,000 partisans in Serbia itself. Major Dugmore gave the far more realistic assessment of around 1,700 partisans in eastern Serbia in November 1943.[43] This misinformation reflects the fact that neither Maclean nor Deakin, who supplied all the information for the report,[44] had had any contact with Mihailović-controlled areas, specifically Serbia, or made the slightest attempt to liaise with Bailey and compare notes with him. Bailey's suggestion that he should go to Partisan headquarters to do just that had been deemed unsuitable by Cairo, as it would arouse the suspicions of both Mihailović and Tito, and would also be 'premature until Fitzroy Maclean is established and we have his opinions'.[45] This was in spite of the original plan for supporting both sides emphasizing the importance of the political advisers with the two resistance leaders maintaining contact with each other.

Politically, Maclean's blockbuster assessed the Partisans to be the most important element in Yugoslavia, both in terms of reconstituting the state after the war, and for organizing it on a federal basis where racial harmony would prevail; the YGE was composed of 'traitors and deserters' whose aim was to restore the old régime with all its abuses; and King Peter was compromised by his support of Mihailović, although the partisans had 'scrupulously refrained' from attacking him. Members of the Croat Peasant Party who had not thrown in their lot with the Ustashas had joined the Partisans (thus finally knocking on the head the long-cherished illusion of Maček guerrillas), while Maček himself was regarded as a traitor by the Partisans. Mihailović was a Pan-Serb, compromised by collaboration, whose organization only continued to exist by means of British support. Withdrawing that support and concentrating resources on the Partisans, Maclean argued, would produce immediate military benefits and simultaneously reduce Soviet influence. It would also, at a stroke, end the civil war, since without British aid Mihailović's movement would wither and his followers would transfer to the Partisans. This last point was exactly what Selborne had argued, but in reverse. Both were wrong because they had an oversimplistic view of the motivation of the two resistance movements and an over-optimistic view of British influence. Some Mihailović people did go over to the Partisans later, but the eventual withdrawal of British support did not mean the end of his movement.

Maclean's political assessment is also obviously based only upon partisan sources, and again reflects the fact that he had not seen enough of the country or its people. Mansfield, of the OSS, reported almost universal support for Mihailović in Serbia, where romantic songs were sung about him and 'they talk of him as one would of the Messiah',[46] because Mihailović was perceived as standing for the king and democracy. Bailey had also made this crystal clear in a number of his messages from the field. Maclean patently had no idea of the Serbian loyalty to King Peter or his minister of war, and the partisans would hardly tell him of this, although they were very much aware of it themselves. They had not attacked the king in their propaganda because they knew this would have done them no good in Serbia where they must establish themselves if they were indeed to be the future rulers of Yugoslavia.

Armstrong and Bailey also produced a report.[47] This was not a blockbuster, but a carefully weighed and considered analysis of the situation which set out the problems with Mihailović and the best way to overcome them. Although it was despatched only one day later than the date of Maclean's report it did not enjoy the same swift channels of transmission, only arriving at the FO on 23 November bearing the date of origin as 18 November. On 27 November, the British Embassy to Yugoslavia in Cairo informed the FO that 'we now learn from SOE that the date of the report itself was actually 7th November.'[48] This was explained by it being a lengthy report that took many days to transmit: it *was* lengthy—92 parts in all—and had taken quite a few of the liaison officers at Mihailović's HQ a good deal of time to encode and transmit: *not* 16 days, however. The hold-up could only have occurred in Cairo SOE. This was despite the fact that when it had been agreed that Maclean should have a direct line of communication with the minister of state in Cairo, similar arrangements were also supposed to apply to political telegrams to and from Bailey.

The Armstrong–Bailey analysis missed Eden by a hair's breadth as he was leaving London to join the PM in Cairo for the Sextant Conference; Eden later told Bailey that he had never seen it at all.[49] It missed Churchill by a mile: he had left on 12 November to embark for Cairo on the battleship *Renown*. Even if it had arrived in time, it would probably have made little difference; Churchill's mind was already made up in favour of the Partisans. The discrepancies and exaggeration in Maclean's figures had been picked up at the FO, where E.M. Rose of the Southern Department minuted on the blockbuster that if the figures for resistance forces in Serbia were true, then the Partisans would already have mopped up Mihailović's men, and that the claimed ratio of two to one was 'fantastic'. Churchill presumably should have spotted the wild inaccuracy of the numbers compared to information available from Enigma decrypts: whether or not he was using the blockbuster to disguise the existence of 'Ultra', he used Maclean's figures as a basis for all his discussions in November 1943.

The *Renown* put in at Malta en route, and at a meeting on 18 November with the commanders of the Mediterranean forces, Churchill spoke of the 'unsatisfactory situation' in the Balkans where the Germans had recovered their balance after the collapse of Italy and were now pressing back the Partisans. Churchill does not appear to have questioned how this might be, given the attrition rate of five to one claimed by Maclean for German-Partisan fighting. The slow Allied advance through Italy had allowed the Germans to transfer several divisions to the Russian front. The Western Allies had not only failed to take the weight off the Soviets but also failed to provide proper support for the partisans in Yugoslavia and Albania, despite the fact that "they are containing as many divisions as the British and American Armies put together." At the Sextant Conference with Roosevelt in Cairo between 23 and 25 November, Churchill made the same point, again quoting Maclean's figures. In the interim, the COS had managed to convince the PM that it was unnecessary to open a bridgehead on the Dalmatian coast and Churchill now asserted that there was no need for regular formations in Yugoslavia. 'All that was needed there was a generous packet of supplies, of air support, and possibly a few Commandos.'[50]

The COS, JIC and Chief of Air Staff had discussed Maclean's blockbuster on 16 November. When the Chief of Air Staff asked if Maclean was 'a reliable observer, or like many people who go on such missions, a fanatic?', Victor Cavendish-Bentinck, chairman of the JIC, leapt to Maclean's defence, asserting that he was 'a former member of this office, shrewd, hard headed and rather cynical'. In the light of this the COS stated their intent to make recommendations to the cabinet based on the blockbuster.[51] On 25 November the COS set out their thoughts on Mediterranean strategy: while remaining committed to Overlord in spring-summer 1944, they felt the surest and fastest way to victory was to stretch the Germans as far as possible by threatening their vital interests in the area. In Italy the offensive would be pushed as far as the Pisa-Rimini line, while in Yugoslavia, Albania and Greece, Allied policy should be placed on a regular military basis with intensification of measures to nourish Partisans and irregular forces in these countries. This in turn meant that SOE would take on a more regular military aspect and become greatly enlarged by forces drawn from bodies such as the commandos.

At the 'Big Three Conference' in Teheran, Stalin appeared unmoved by Churchill's enthusiasm for the partisans. The possible entry of Turkey on the Allied side, the support of Yugoslavia and the capture of Rome were all viewed as 'relatively unimportant': what Stalin was interested in was Overlord. Nevertheless, at the end of the conference the first of the five 'military conclusions' was that the Yugoslav partisans should receive the greatest possible support in order to mystify and mislead the enemy.[52] One reason for Stalin not sharing Churchill's optimistic view of the partisans, was that the Soviets were highly sceptical about British figures for German divisions being contained in the Balkans. Another reason might have been that on the day the Teheran conference opened, Tito held a meeting of AVNOJ at Jajce, which essentially took the form of a new government in Yugoslavia, and at which he incidentally appointed himself Marshal. Tito had informed Dimitrov of his plans for AVNOJ while the Foreign Ministers Conference was in progress in Moscow. Stalin was more concerned about the conduct of the war than spreading social revolution and had dissolved the Comintern in May 1943 as a conciliatory gesture to his Western Allies. He feared that Tito's action had counteracted that gesture and Stalin was expecting some adverse reaction, but none was forthcoming.[53] This was partly due to the British and Americans being unaware of the full ramifications of the AVNOJ declarations: although some of the BLOs with the Partisans had attended the meeting, they probably did not fully understand what was being said. PWE provided a text, but—apparently due to some problems with monitoring or translating—managed to miss out the parts that might have aroused the suspicion or antagonism of the British, particularly the one that forbade King Peter to return to Yugoslavia until the people themselves had decided.[54]

While the Teheran conference was in progress, Maclean managed to fly back into Yugoslavia after a number of failed attempts. Meanwhile, the partisan delegation awaiting his return and growing impatient, had attempted to fly out of Glamoč in Bosnia in a captured aircraft. This ended in disaster when they were bombed from the air by a German reconnaissance 'plane and Lolar Ribar, a member of the partisan supreme staff and an important figure in the CPY, was killed, along with two other Partisans and two British officers. Maclean finally arrived on 3 December and extricated Deakin, Vlatko Velebit and Miloje Milojević just in time for Maclean and Deakin to meet Churchill in Cairo.[55]

The FO had asked for Armstrong and Bailey to be brought to Egypt at the same time as Maclean, so that they would be on hand for consultation and to provide details on the situation in Serbia.[56] The FO was acutely aware that the 'information' on Serbia in Maclean's blockbuster was total bunkum, and now that the communism of the Partisans was fully in the open, the FO was also worried about imposing a communist state upon Serbia, where loyalty to the king and his representative Mihailović was undeniable. The Russians had been reluctant to discuss the Balkans at all in the Moscow Conference and Douglas Howard suspected that this was because they were expecting the whole peninsula to drop into their lap after the war: he saw no reason to aid them in this, which was what Maclean's advice appeared to be leading to.

The Special Operations Committee in Cairo agreed that it was a good idea to bring out Armstrong and Bailey when it was first mooted in early November, but managed to find vast numbers of dangers and complications in implementing the proposal. It was impossible to bring them out by air, which left three options: to bring them out through Partisan territory, through collaborationist chetnik territory or through Albania. Mihailović would not care for the first and MO4 did not care for the second option. The SO committee favoured the Albanian route but it would take two or three months to extract the BLOs. One argument against bringing them out at all was that the committee felt that the presence of Armstrong and Bailey in Cairo at the same time as the partisans 'would lead to suspicion and misunderstanding on both sides.'[57] In the event, the partisan delegation, on FO instructions, had to remain in Alexandria—which offended them anyway because they thought this was to appease the YGE. Weeks went by while the possibility of bringing Bailey out—SOE had decided that Armstrong's place was with his mission—was discussed, but no action taken. Finally SOE stated that it was an impractical suggestion and simply could not be done, and in any case it was unlikely that Bailey would be 'able to add very much to our knowledge regarding the situation in Serbia, about which we have recently received such voluminous telegraphic reports.'[58] Thus in December 1943, while the policy of supporting both resistance movements in Yugoslavia was still technically in existence, it was only the Partisans' case which was represented in Cairo.

10

DITCHING MIHAILOVIĆ, OR THROWING OUT THE BABY WITH THE BATHWATER

Churchill's Cairo meeting with Maclean and Deakin, at which the latter presented what he describes as a 'hostile brief' on Mihailović, set the seal on the fate of the Yugoslav minister of war. On 10 December 1943, Churchill declared that he wanted Mihailović removed by the end of the year.[1] General Wilson suggested the simple expedient of letting him 'rot and drop off the branch'. This, however, did not answer the case: while Churchill was keen to capitalize on the Partisans' more aggressive approach to warfare, regardless of their political colouring, there was still the matter of King Peter and his throne to be resolved.

In the spring of 1943 the YGE had once again been plunged into crisis: an ongoing dispute between the Yugoslav ministers in London and Ivan Šubašić, former Ban of Croatia, in the United States, was preventing the formulation of a declaration of policy on support for a united Yugoslavia. A further complication had been added by King Peter's desire to marry. Slovene opinion was favourable, that of the Croats indifferent, but some of the Serb ministers regarded the celebration of the monarch's nuptials in wartime as being totally out of keeping with Serb tradition. The FO was inclined to agree with the Serbs, fearing that his marrying outside the country, while his people suffered occupation, might lose him support. In addition, the king's future mother-in-law, Princess Aspasia of Greece, was perceived as potentially an even more baleful influence than his own mother. Rendel suspected that she was manipulating King Peter and influencing his cabinet reshuffle. Jovanović finally resigned on 17 June and Trifunović took over, although his premiership was short-lived as he too failed to resolve the problems.

By this time the FO was heartily sick of the YGE, a feeling not entirely unreciprocated. Eden felt that the YGE was in total disarray and that its stock, which had never been high, had plunged to zero. He feared that the discredit threatened to extend to the king and the concept of Yugoslavia as a whole, which had long-term implications for a post-war 'satisfactory reorganization of the Balkans'. Eden had given some thought to how the British might use their influence 'to save young King Peter, who is now our only hope, from the bog in which his present government will land both himself and his country'.[2] Eden's solution was to get Peter to move to Cairo with a small group of ministers. The general idea was that they would thus be closer to their homeland as new developments took place there: it would also get the YGE out of the FO's hair. The king, his new premier Božidar Purić and the mini-cabinet arrived in Cairo in September 1943, where Ralph Skrine Stevenson had replaced Rendel as the British Ambassador to the Yugoslav government. This was not a fortunate change for the YGE. Rendel had become rather fed up with the exiles' wranglings, and had made the departure for Cairo his excuse to give up his post. Nevertheless, however fed up he became, Rendel had always attempted to be fair and had done his best to put the Yugoslav case to the FO. He had also witnessed the emergence of Mihailović as resistance leader, and was keenly aware of the British role in getting the YGE to recognize him, a fact which often led Rendel to argue for patience and fair play for Mihailović. Stevenson shared none of this history, and in the absence of it relied heavily on Cairo SOE and, subsequently, on the advice of Deakin and Maclean.

When the new Allied missions were established in Yugoslavia in September, it was hoped that not only would they be able to reconcile the internal divisions, but also pave the way for the return of Peter as a constitutional monarch. A new propaganda line was proposed, which would play down the old parties and affiliations associated with the exiled politicians, portraying King Peter as quite separate and independent, and representing him as a unifying force with modern democratic ideas. Eden and the FO had given up on the exiled politicians: while not a little weary of the king's own contributions to the problems, they still regarded him as the best hope of reconstituting Yugoslavia after hostilities had ceased. Churchill's own fondness for royalty and conviction that it was essential that Peter regain his throne, combined with his rose-tinted view of Tito, led the PM to conceive of a post-war Yugoslavia ruled jointly by the king and the communist guerrilla leader.

The FO did not share Churchill's insouciance regarding the partisans' political colouring, and sounded out SOE on rescuing Maček from Croatia. It was felt that Maček would provide an 'invaluable counterpoise to the pan-Serb element on the one hand and the communist element among the partisans on the other'.[3] The news that the Partisans viewed Maček as a traitor, despite his steadfast refusal to collaborate with Pavelić, led the FO to conclude that the communists were determined to suppress all political competitors, and this made him even more valuable in their eyes as a possible rival to Tito in Croatia. PWE disagreed, arguing that Maček would do little to solve the YGE divisions and, since the Partisans suspected him of being an *attentiste*, he would be more hindrance than help in reconciling Peter and the partisans.[4] Quite how he could have been other than *attentiste* while under house arrest is another question. SOE Cairo settled the matter by stating that the rescue was impossible: the Partisans suspected Maček of opposing their movement, and without their connivance and help nothing could be done.[5] There does not appear to be any evidence of SOE broaching the subject with the Partisans, presumably for fear of offending them.

The FO's cautious reception of Fitzroy Maclean's 'blockbuster' was revealed in the minutes on his report, particularly those concerning his assessments of Serbia which were obviously from Partisan sources. E.M. Rose argued that to maintain Yugoslavia as a single state, it was necessary to obtain an agreement between the Partisans and the king, who would bring Serbia with him, but pointed out that this was incompatible with Maclean's recommendation that the British drop Mihailović. Such a course of action would either also mean a break between the British and King Peter or, if he accepted it, his own rejection by the Serbs. Howard agreed with Rose: the liaison officers had reported that Mihailović represented the majority of Serbs so to abandon him was tantamount to handing them over to communism. It was one thing to increase supplies to the Partisans, quite another to break with Mihailović.

Eden and Orme Sargent were rather less convinced, fearing that it might eventually be unavoidable to come down in favour of Maclean's proposal on Mihailović 'even though this will mean sacrificing our long-term political objectives to short-term military necessities'.

Only a few days after the lengthy FO minutes on Maclean's report had been written up, three telegrams arrived from Stevenson in Cairo. The first relayed a message from Armstrong, showing Mihailović's position in Serbia to be paramount: Howard was just about to submit a minute to the COS saying that in view of this the British could not throw him over and support only the Partisans, but the second two telegrams completely changed the position.

They suggest that Mihailović's fear of communism has driven him into active collaboration with Nedić and therefore indirectly with the Germans. If the case is proved against him it will mean a radical alteration to our whole policy.[6]

This dramatic new development was the result of messages from Lieut.-Colonel Cope, a BLO with the Neronian mission at Djurić's headquarters, and concerned an order issued by Mihailović.[7] Following the Venezia Division incident, the disastrous BBC broadcasts and the failure of the British at his HQ to prevent the partisans encroaching on his territory, Mihailović had decided to go back on his promise to avoid fighting the Partisans. The latter had attacked his own men from the rear while they were fighting Germans, and he instructed his commanders to use the same tactic—and any others necessary to drive the Partisans out of the area. He went on to refer to Nedić's recent mobilization order for young men: as the Yugoslav Home Army was in such desperate need of clothing, arms and ammunition this seemed a golden opportunity to obtain them from Nedić, by allowing some of its members to answer the call-up, with the proviso that only the most reliable men were to go. Each one was to return to the Mihailović forces when he got the word and under no circumstances to fight against them. Thus Nedić would only 'obtain apparent hold of our men'.[8]

The interpretation of this in Cairo as an order to collaborate seems to have stemmed from a garbled version radioed to SOE by

Cope. It was either the result of Cope, who did not read Serbo-Croatian, misunderstanding the order or, more likely, Djurić deliberately misleading his BLOs: given his past history, any information emanating from Djurić should have been treated with caution. He had been the subject of a number of complaints, the most recent in late October when Stevenson relayed to Premier Purić the grievances of the British military authorities, who deemed Djurić to be incapable of initiating action against the enemy, or even of protecting the stores supplied by SOE for sabotage operations. He was also, although operating in Serbia itself and therefore ostensibly under direct command of Mihailović, apparently not obeying Mihailović's orders and not co-operating with the BLOs in his area.[9] His clashes with the Partisans, during which he had not impressed the BLOs with his military prowess, and SOE Cairo's inept attempt at mediation, had indirectly led to the capture and subsequent death of Neil Selby. Another cause for suspecting Djurić's reliability had been provided in October in the form of his relationship with Vera Pešić, ex-mistress of the German General Bader, and allegedly a Gestapo agent. She had come into the hands of Djurić as a prisoner, but he had subsequently refused to allow the British officers with him to interrogate her, and had instead struck up a sexual liaison with her and apparently come under her influence. Vera Pešić was only the latest in a long line of Djurić's mistresses and had been preceded in July by 'a Russian lady doctor who had been suspected of being a German spy'.[10]

The confusion over the Cope telegram highlights the problems inherent in the communications system of the British missions who did not have direct radio contact with each other, which meant in this case that Armstrong and Bailey could not obtain first-hand information from Cope and Major Raw at Djurić's HQ. Raw had persuaded Djurić to come to some sort of agreement with the Partisans in his area, which had earned him a severe reprimand from Mihailović. This, Bailey thought, might have aroused in Djurić an anxiety that could have caused him to be 'a little careless in his allegations', which at the very least were exaggerated and in Bailey's opinion it would be ill-advised to take any action on the strength of them, especially as he did not rule out the possibility that Djurić might be intriguing against Mihailović.[11] Mihailović felt that the

British mission had been dilatory in securing Tito's co-operation in keeping the partisans out of the Sandjak, and until they demonstrated their good faith in representing his interests to Tito he was not inclined to make concessions to the partisans in Serbia.[12] He also considered Djurić's conciliatory attitude to the Partisans to be the root of the trouble in his area; in other areas of Serbia where local commanders had been more vigorous in dealing with them the Partisans had left. At the time the territory under Djurić's command was being reduced and it was possible that he might lose his command altogether. Probably as a result of this, Djurić *had* been intriguing, telling Cope and Raw, that Mihailović was 'swaying over to the Axis', and suggesting that Radović should replace Mihailović, although he wanted the BLOs to keep this quiet.

Djurić muddied the water further by telling Cope that Mihailović had issued another order forbidding his commanders to have any dealings with the Nedić government without his express orders, and to have *no* dealings with the Germans. Djurić claimed to be unable to understand this 'reversal of policy'.[13] The reason that Djurić could not understand the 'reversal' was that it was no such thing, but exactly what Mihailović had ordered in the first place. It appears that Djurić was trying to cover himself before he handed the original order to Cope.

Even when the full text of Mihailović's order reached Cairo, Stevenson was still under the impression that there was a separate one on collaborating with Nedić. On 26 November Bailey gave a detailed explanation of the situation which completely rebutted the allegations, but this seems to have had little impact. The damage had been done, the concept of Mihailović as a collaborator had been established, and the debate had turned from whether to make a break with him, to how and when. On 2 December Cairo SOE advocated an immediate break,[14] they had already prepared for this: Major Dugmore's Monkeywrench mission with the Partisans in eastern Serbia had been sent in on 28 November, in readiness for a break with Mihailović.

Neither the original text of Mihailović's order nor Armstrong and Bailey's comments on the situation were made widely or swiftly available: for example Armstrong's report took almost a month to reach the FO. This is presumably another example of Bailey's and

Armstrong's communications going through very slow channels of transmission. Despite Armstrong and Bailey's explanations, on 7 January 1944, Stevenson was still quoting Mihailović's order as 'coming close to collaboration with the enemy'.[15]

It was hardly surprising that the combination of this 'new evidence' and Maclean's and Deakin's personal opinions led Churchill to the conclusion that Mihailović should be dropped by the end of the year. In addition, he was perceived as a major obstacle to King Peter reaching an agreement with Tito. So the suggestion that he be left to drop off the branch just would not do; the king had to repudiate his minister of war and openly embrace Tito if he stood any chance of regaining his throne. While King Peter was quite amenable to dealing with Tito, he was rather more reluctant to disavow someone who had upheld his cause so loyally throughout the war.

Even before Churchill's declaration, there had been considerable pressure on the king and the YGE to dismiss Mihailović from his post. On 8 November 1943 Eden met King Peter and Purić and pressed the matter by telling them that, at the Moscow conference, it had become obvious that the Soviet government had a very low opinion of Mihailović's attitude. Molotov, the Soviet foreign minister, had apparently shown considerable interest when Eden mentioned that the British intended to ask the general to carry out certain specific military operations in the near future, and that a failure to accede to this request would lead the British to revise their policy of helping him. Had Purić seen some of the reports from Armstrong and Bailey, and pleas for sorties from other BLOs in Serbia, he might have been tempted to ask: 'what help?'. As it was, he protested that it was in both British and Yugoslav interests that Mihailović should be able to deploy sufficient forces around Belgrade at the time of liberation to hold the country for the king.[16]

The 'specific military operations' Eden mentioned were not only to test Mihailović's willingness to act, but also to convince Peter that he should dismiss him. Stevenson thought that if this should provoke the whole of the YGE to resign, British advice to the king would be to accept the resignations and—by implication—make him more amenable to British advice in future. The Special Operations Committee met on 2 December and decided to set up the test operations because they said that most of the evidence regarding his collaboration could not be published; they were convinced that Mihailović could not, or would not, carry out the tests, and this would provide the justification they wanted for making a break. Mihailović's forces were required to destroy railway bridges in the Ibar and Morava valleys; he was asked to confirm his agreement before 29 December.[17]

Cairo had underestimated both Mihailović's forces and the BLOs with them. Although Mihailović had been reluctant initially, some of the younger officers at his HQ had prevailed upon him to agree. An affirmative reply was given with a request for supplies of explosives and arms and for an extension of the deadline until mid-January, which was the earliest the operations could be accomplished because of the scale of planning needed. Cairo replied that they already had enough explosives in the country, no extra sorties would be flown in connection with the operations, and nor would matériel used be replaced afterwards.[18] Mihailović's agreement caused consternation at the FO. A successful completion of the 'test' would be a potential source of embarrassment and the excuse for dropping Mihailović would be void: therefore it had to be cancelled. Withdrawing support after the event would leave the British open to the charge of bad faith. Stevenson thought this could be explained away by telling Mihailović that the operations had been essential on military grounds and that the withdrawal was due to his long-term non-co-operation and to the collaboration of some of his commanders. He argued that the situation in occupied Yugoslavia was such that it was not always possible to act with 'strict punctilio'. The FO was not happy with this and Orme Sargent noted that he had 'always thought the test operation a silly device which was bound to land us in difficulties'.[19] By early January Cadogan and Eden agreed with him and felt it was safer to call off the whole thing.

Although the FO decision was communicated to Stevenson on 5 January it was not passed on to Armstrong and plans went ahead, with the night of 5–6 February chosen as the optimum date because the moon set at 0407 hours. Cairo's signal to Armstrong on 4 February telling him not to proceed with the operations, apparently on the grounds that it would be British and not Yugoslav people who would blow the bridges, brought forth an explosive response. Armstrong berated Cairo for the dreadful position he and his officers had been placed in, and for a total lack of understanding of the time and effort involved in planning the operations, which were to include wide-scale attacks by Mihailović commanders on a variety of enemy strongholds.[20] All the BLOs involved realized that this was a test, and were certain that Mihailović knew too. Armstrong had been told at the outset that it was and that a final decision on future policy depended upon Mihailović's response. Armstrong and his BLOs were, therefore, under the impression that some gain might be made by complying with the request. They had pulled out all the stops, made plans and reconnoitres in fearful winter conditions, not without danger to themselves, while intelligence on rail traffic had been laboriously collected by Serbs. Now they were ordered to cancel everything. The BLOs also knew that it was not even the best time to carry out these particular acts of sabotage, which would have been much more useful when the Germans were withdrawing from Greece along the Ibar and Morava valleys.[21] It can only be assumed that the BLOs, whatever their individual views of Mihailović, thought highly enough of the forces they were with to try their utmost to pass the test.

Archie Jack and Armstrong were organizing the destruction of the Ibar bridges while Jasper Rootham and Pavlović were in charge of the Morava bridge, where the plan entailed hijacking a train. Pavlović's local commanders also had a back-up plan for cutting the rail in case the main one did not succeed. On 10 February, six days after Cairo told Armstrong not to proceed, Rootham received a wire from Cairo asking if he could carry out the Morava scheme on the night of 20–21 February.[22] Altogether, the whole story of the test operations was a shambles to say the least, and took no account of the position of the BLOs in Serbia.

On 13 December, just a few days after Armstrong was asked to put the test proposal to Mihailović, and long before any reply was received, Cairo SOE sent a signal to all sub-missions, but not to Armstrong, in Mihailović territory—'at their discretion'—to leave the commanders they were with and join the nearest partisan group. Presumably this was Cairo SOE jumping the gun and reacting to Churchill's 10 December pronouncement about making an immediate break. It was an absurd signal, not least because for most of the BLOs concerned there were no Partisans in their vicinity to join:

even if there had been, some assessed this line of action as 'the quickest way to get a knife in the back we could think of'.[23] Subsequent signals confused the issue further, eventually leaving the BLOs with no idea of what was going on and unsure of whether they were to go or stay. A couple of BLOs took the signal seriously and left for the partisans. Bailey left Mihailović's HQ in January, not to join the Partisans, but in a last-ditch attempt to get to Cairo and see what was actually going on: his party travelled via Mihailović sympathisers to the coast and was evacuated on 14/15 February to Bari and then on to Cairo.

The plan for an immediate break with Mihailović and withdrawal of the BLOs in Serbia had been cancelled by the FO when they finally caught up with the full implications of the AVNOJ declarations of 29 November at Jajce. Having thought that simply disowning Mihailović would enable King Peter to be recognized by Tito, the FO was now presented with the fact that the Partisans had forbidden the king to return until allowed to do so by the people of Yugoslavia. Orme Sargent wondered what had happened since Maclean had left Yugoslavia, having received reassurances that Tito was resolved not to raise the question of the monarchy at this juncture. He also wondered whether Tito's change of heart was due to Russian pressure; or the discussions with the Partisan delegation at Alexandria leading Tito to conclude he was in such a strong position militarily that he could make political terms; or possibly that he was involved in some intrigue with the Greek communists.[24] It might simply have been that Tito knew the British were ditching Mihailović, regardless of the negotiations over the monarchy. The message to the BLOs to desert to the Partisans was sent on 13 December. At about the same time, Deakin took over as head of the Yugoslav desk in Cairo, and SOE had arranged with the Partisans that any such BLOs coming their way would be given safe conduct. On the very next day, 14 December, Partisan HQ instructed Velebit, head of the delegation in Alexandria, to pass on to the Allies the full text of the AVNOJ declarations, drawing their attention particularly to the part relating to the YGE and King Peter.[25]

FO dismay increased when Maclean took the view that no useful purpose would be served by raising the question of the monarchy with the Partisans, and he felt that to do so might seriously damage his mission.[26] Maclean also pointed out that the plan to send Peter to join Tito would be viewed as coming two years too late. The idea of sending King Peter to join the Partisans is perhaps an indication of the desperation setting in as regards obtaining an agreement between him and Tito, before the latter was in such a strong position that he would be able to 'snap his fingers' at the British. The FO thought that if Peter could be returned to Yugoslavia the Partisans would find it difficult to oppose him, given that many of their followers were still monarchists at heart.

The clarification of the AVNOJ declaration and Maclean's opinions gave the FO pause for thought. They began to question the wisdom of abandoning Mihailović with the speed recommended by Stevenson and Maclean, especially as in the interim Mihailović had offered to come to an arrangement with Tito to end the civil war if the British would act as intermediaries. This had been dismissed by Stevenson as a delaying tactic, and by Eden as a death-bed repentance, both believing that even bringing up the question with Tito would undermine his confidence in the British and scupper the plan to bring him together with the king. All suggestions for trying to bring pressure on Tito by, for example, threatening to withhold supplies, had been vetoed in Cairo as counterproductive.[27] The British were left with only one bargaining counter— Mihailović—and, by extension, the BLOs with his forces. Leaving them where they were, even if their position was hazardous, was part of the plan to persuade Tito to come to an agreement. If King Peter would give all-out support to the Partisans, the FO reasoned, then many of his Serbian subjects would follow his example, and the BLOs in Serbia would be able to facilitate this change. Conversely, if Tito would not make an agreement, then the whole policy regarding Mihailović might need to be reconsidered, so the BLOs should remain where they were. The men themselves eventually came to feel that they were being treated as expendable and that they had been abandoned by Cairo. Whether Cairo SOE cared about their welfare or not, and there were elements who did not, the suggestion that their safety was worth the gamble was first voiced at the FO.[28] The BLOs were left in a state of limbo, kicking their heels in Serbia, receiving no sorties except for occasional drops of personal items, and with nothing to do, except for a few adventurous spirits who went in for some freelance sabotage.

Meanwhile, attempts to reach an agreement over King Peter's throne continued with an appeal to the Soviets to use their good offices to persuade the partisans to accept the king. In return, the FO would advise the king to dismiss Mihailović and get his forces to co-operate with the partisans. The Soviets, as usual, claimed that they did not know enough about the Yugoslav situation to interfere, and would prefer to wait until their own mission arrived there.[29] Their official mission that is, as SOE had intelligence that—without consulting or informing them—the Soviets had infiltrated three men and one woman in October 1943. SOE's opinion was that this must be a mission of considerable importance for the Soviets to undertake such a long and hazardous flight to get it into Yugoslavia. Colonel Hill, SOE's man in Moscow, thought it a pity that he was not fully informed of details of SOE operations in Yugoslavia as this limited his ability to co-operate closely with the NKVD.[30] It was later suggested that Hill co-operated all too closely with the NKVD and that he was possibly a double agent.[31]

As December wore on Maclean's advice offered no comfort to the FO, until eventually Armin Dew of the Southern Department wondered if he and Stevenson were simply following a policy of total appeasement towards the partisans. Maclean was certain that getting rid of Mihailović was essential, but equally positive that this would not sway Tito towards the king. However, once Mihailović had been dropped he thought there *might* be some chance of an agreement. This opinion was seconded by Deakin and Stevenson; Randolph Churchill, who was about to join Maclean's mission, also concurred. Their combined opinions convinced Churchill that this was the course to follow. (The PM, with fond fatherly affection, thought that Randolph was *always* right—an opinion not universally shared.) Churchill now perceived Mihailović not as a bargaining counter but as 'a millstone round the neck of the little king'— he had to go.[32] Eden was not so taken with the advice the PM was receiving from Cairo, he commented: 'Naturally to Maclean Tito is all white and Mihailović all black. I have a suspicion that grey is a more common Balkan colour.'[33] The Foreign Secretary urged caution until an agreement had been reached with Tito, and the British had something concrete to offer the king in return for dismissing Mihailović. But Churchill also saw the question only in black and white, and was adamant that the solution lay with King Peter dismissing Mihailović immediately, rather than in the British simply disowning him. Eden had warned that before any spectacular break was made with Mihailović, the 'case against him for treachery must be unanswerable'; to fail to make this case would be a gift to German propaganda.[34]

SOE Cairo produced the 'evidence', which was thin to say the least, resting mainly on contacts between Axis forces and various commanders Mihailović admitted to be 'part of his military organization', and the fact that he had taken part in operations against the partisans. Stevenson rounded it all off by re-running the Cope telegrams affair. The 'evidence' did not convince the FO, or change Eden's view of the question, but the initiative had moved to the authorities in Cairo who had Churchill behind them. Accordingly, the Commander-in-Chief Middle East decided that the BLOs with Mihailović were serving no useful military purpose, 'but their presence with his forces reacts unfavourably on our military relations with the partisans.'[35]

At a meeting of the Special Operations Committee on 24 February the military representative put the case for retaining a small intelligence-gathering mission, otherwise there would be little or no information emanating from central Serbia. Stevenson argued against this, on the grounds that it would have a detrimental effect on relations with Tito, and that Mihailović would use it as positive propaganda for himself. The information gained would anyway, Stevenson asserted, have little value since Mihailović would simply feed the mission what he wanted them to hear: therefore the disadvantages outweighed the advantages. There was, however, time to consider the matter as Armstrong was cut off from Mihailović's HQ by bad weather and German troops, which gave Cairo a week's grace to consult Maclean on Tito's probable reaction.[36] This seems more than a little fatuous: Tito was hardly likely to think it a reasonable idea for the British to keep *any* sort of mission with his great rival in view of his plans to move into Serbia.

The British were also very concerned about American intentions, fearing that they would insist on keeping an intelligence mission, which would not only embarrass the British, but give Mihailović scope for playing off the allies against each other. It was known that Mihailović had a wireless link to Fotić, the Yugoslav ambassador in Washington, and that Mansfield, who had come out of Yugoslavia with Bailey, had messages for Eisenhower and Roosevelt, in which Mihailović probably appealed for American aid. Bailey had just reached Cairo and said he thought his exodus from Yugoslavia had been deliberately delayed so that Todorović, Lukačević and Bačević, Mihailović's 'emissaries', could leave the country first. In the event they all left at the same time. Even so, SOE was concerned that Mansfield and Todorović would join forces to whip up sympathy for Mihailović, especially in the United States.[37] SOE and OSS in Cairo had discussed the possibility that Mihailović was receiving encouragement from Washington, and both appreciated the inherent danger of a rift between them. Only Muselin of the OSS now remained at Mihailović's HQ and Donovan had told him to stay put in the event of a British evacuation. Donovan was very much in favour of retaining an American presence with Mihailović, and the State Department had strong views on the necessity of securing intelligence from his territory. After much discussion, dispute and diplomatic pressure, the British prevailed and the Americans agreed to withdraw the last OSS officer along with the British missions.[38]

Supporting Tito, who had plenty of admirers in OSS, was not at issue. The main difference between the British and Americans was the question of abandoning Mihailović. Just before the Teheran Conference, Donovan had proposed to Roosevelt that both resistance movements should receive all possible aid. The President agreed, but did little to push the idea at Teheran in the face of Churchill's determination to obtain a declaration of full Allied support for the partisans.

Once Mansfield arrived in Cairo he produced a long and detailed report, which, although not uncritical of Mihailović's leadership, presented a very positive image of his movement's potential. On the strength of this, Donovan decided to send a larger OSS team to Serbia, but at the last moment the missions were stood down after Churchill had appealed to Roosevelt to fall in with British policy for the sake of Allied unity.[39] Even so, SOE's suspicion that Donovan would attempt to send a mission of some sort to Serbia turned out to be correct. On 26 August 1944 Lieut.-Colonel

Robert Macdowell arrived in Serbia, ostensibly on the purely human-itarian mission of arranging the evacuation of downed USAAF air-crew, but with the main function of intelligence-gathering. The resulting report, dated 23 November 1944, was very much at odds with British conclusions regarding the Serbian nationalist move-ment and Mihailović.[40]

The final order to the BLOs in Serbia to leave was a total debâcle, largely due to Churchill and his efforts to save King Peter's throne. On 25 February 1944 Churchill, ignoring Eden's advice, sent a message to Tito through Maclean, informing him that the British missions were being withdrawn from Mihailović and pleading the case for King Peter.[41] Philip Broad, who was now attached to Stevenson's embassy as an adviser, wrote to Deakin to say that OSS were not to see the PM's message. In a post-script he mentioned a delayed FO signal instructing SOE to inform Mihailović first of the withdrawal of the BLOs, and if it was not too late, Maclean should delay passing Churchill's letter to Tito until Armstrong's mission had received the order to withdraw. Although Maclean received the warning in time, on 1 March he was told to deliver the letter to Tito anyway, but to emphasize its secrecy. On the same day, the order for the BLOs to leave arrived at Mihailović's HQ; as both he and Armstrong were absent, Lieut.-Colonel Howard, Armstrong's second in command, handed the message to one of Mihailović's senior officers.

By 7 March it had still not been possible to communicate the message to Mihailović. Nevertheless, Stevenson could 'see no harm' in agreeing to Maclean's request for Tito to repeat the PM's mes-sage to his committee, 'providing secrecy will be observed'.[42] This was an unlikely proposition—the withdrawal of the British from Mihailović was too good a piece of propaganda for the Partisans to pass up. It had, anyway, been in the air since mid December, and had undoubtedly strengthened the Partisans' negotiating hand. If Tito was telling the truth when he informed Moscow that Maclean had said that the British would not insist on reinstating the king, then the partisans held *all* the cards.[43] It was little wonder that the British were making no headway in gaining any concessions over King Peter's throne.

Before Armstrong or Mihailović returned to HQ the message Howard had delivered produced a reaction from a group of Serb officers there. They told Howard that they opposed Mihailović's go-slow policy and, claiming a strong following both inside and outside Serbia, asserted that their main aim was to fight the occupiers while avoiding civil war with the partisans. They felt the only way to achieve this was to replace Mihailović and suggested Colonel Radović or Colonel Putnik as suitable candidates, emphasizing that for any replacement to enjoy sufficient authority in Serbia, he would have to be appointed by the king himself.

The idea of replacing Mihailović had first been mooted in November 1943, when some of the British sub-missions had been asked to assess the reaction of local commanders if Mihailović were to be removed. The mission in eastern Serbia—once they had recovered from the initial shock—replied that they thought things would fall apart unless the king himself took over and-or a great deal more support was forthcoming.[44] Bailey and Armstrong had made detailed plans for Radović to return to Yugoslavia, possibly to set up a separate command in southern Serbia: they were uncertain as to what his attitude to the Partisans might be—possibly, they thought, not entirely different to that of Mihailović. The whole scheme, however, rested on Mihailović being removed from his post as minister of war and becoming simply a commander in Serbia, a suggestion which Purić was not inclined to go along with, arguing that it was utterly impossible to contemplate, since Mihailović was the symbol of Serbia. Armstrong and Bailey's plans had become submerged in the Cope-Djurić affair, following which just getting rid of Mihailović became the main issue, rather than what would happen afterwards. The suggestion by some of the sub-missions that the king should come in to take command got overtaken by Churchill's plan to engineer a partnership between Tito and King Peter.

The officers who had approached Howard made it plain that Serbia and the Serbian people would never accept a government headed by Tito. They did not support the YGE, but were universally loyal to the monarchy. These ideas had been expressed at the recent National Congress at Ba—organized by Mihailović in January 1944, in answer to the establishment of AVNOJ as an alternative government—at which a number of prominent political figures had met to discuss the future political orientation of the country. In addition, the officers were convinced that Maček, who was

anti-communist and pro-monarchy, still enjoyed great support in
Croatia. In view of this General Wilson concluded:

It is not possible to bring about a united anti-German Yugoslavian resistance movement. This does not mean however that it is impossible to
develop matters in such a way that Serbs on the one hand, and the Partisans
on the other, act independently to produce the maximum resistance
against the Germans.[45]

Wilson favoured the idea of replacing Mihailović with someone
who was more active—provided the successor and Tito could reach
an agreement—as it would be of enormous benefit in stretching the
Germans to the limit.

In Cairo Bailey produced an appreciation on the possibility of
the dissidents at Mihailović's HQ taking command. In this he
asserted that while Tito was supreme in both a political and military
sense in the greater part of the country, his writ did not—and
would not—run in Serbia. Mihailović was unshakeable in his determination to fight partisans rather than Germans: once the Allied
missions withdrew, Mihailović would concentrate on this, while
Tito would endeavour to fight his way into Serbia. The ensuing pro-
tracted and indecisive fight would cancel out any military advantages the Allies might have from Yugoslav resistance. Bailey's solution
was that, before the Allied missions departed, they should encourage the dissidents to take the law into their own hands by removing
Mihailović and his immediate entourage. The dissidents should
then reach a territorial agreement with Tito and initiate action
against the Germans, while abstaining from politics and concentrating on purely military activity. Meanwhile Tito should be advised
to discontinue his efforts to fight his way back into Serbia. Arrangements should be made for the dissidents to maintain contact with
the British in North Africa, and Bailey suggested that he should
return himself to liaise with them.[46] This was turned down by the
Special Operations Committee, despite the fact that if the plan to
replace Mihailović had been carried out, it would have obviated the
need to withdraw the British missions.

The fact that Bailey wanted to return indicated that he felt he
could work with Mihailović's successors to achieve something positive. In London on 14 March, Bailey attended a meeting with

Churchill, Eden and high-ranking officials of the FO. Before receiving Bailey's appreciation the FO had produced its own brief for the PM, advising that King Peter should form a new government acceptable to Tito, including among others Simović and Mirković. Orme Sargent was amazed to hear from Bailey that these two were not at all popular in Serbia where Simović was blamed for the capitulation in April 1941, while Mirković was out of favour for opposing Jovanović's government in 1942. For his part Bailey was astonished by the ignorance at the FO and not a little miffed to discover that his report 'of course had not been read in its entirety by anyone present'. (This paragraph in the SOE Diary is headed 'Diplomats seek to Evade Responsibility. Nobody had fully read Bailey's Report.') He felt he had made some progress with the PM though, whom he had met on 7 March, and who now appreciated the important forces controlled by Mihailović. At the meeting it was recognized that while Mihailović's position was strong in Serbia, as long as he remained in control there was little chance of using his forces to further British interests. Therefore it was proposed that King Peter should be persuaded to dismiss his entire government, including Mihailović, and to send in a new commander-in-chief to take over. Bailey felt this plan was unlikely to succeed: he argued that Mihailović would probably refuse to obey the king's orders on the grounds that he was being seriously misinformed regarding the true situation within the country. Orme Sargent was alarmed at the drastic measures Bailey proposed for the elimination of Mihailović: the 'PM was anxious to avoid this [murder] if possible' but it was obvious that the PM's main sympathy lay with Tito. The meeting concluded with Churchill instructing SOE to sound out the BLOs, in the utmost secrecy, on the possibility of the dissidents deposing Mihailović themselves, and of the BLOs own safety if the palace coup should fail.[47]

One of the dissidents was in London at the time, as Mihailović's representative at King Peter's wedding. Lukačević suggested to Bailey the organization of a mobile force of about 3,000 men who would wear British uniform and come under the direct control of the Commander-in-Chief Middle East. He asserted that he could get this force off the ground within one month of his return to Yugoslavia and double its size within three months. It would need a

British mission to provide technical expertise and liaison with the C-in-C Middle East to carry out specific operations, such as the Ibar and Morava bridges scheme suggested in December. Lukačević had been one of the group of officers who had persuaded Mihailović to agree to that particular proposal and to make the offer of negotiations with Tito. At the time, Lukačević had been against any suggestion of replacing or dismissing Mihailović for fear of fragmenting the movement in Serbia. The dissenting officers' grievances against Mihailović stemmed from his inactivity and his pursuit of the civil war: they were willing to make non-aggression pacts with the Partisans to facilitate actions against the Germans, but were not willing to join forces with the communists. The new force that Lukačević proposed would not fight the Partisans, and would disregard any adverse orders it received from Mihailović. Bailey felt that Lukačević's standing with Mihailović's staff, commanders and troops would mean that the plan stood a reasonable chance of success, and appears to have been in favour of giving it a try. However, at the FO, the plan was deemed to contain too many difficulties and political complications: these included the opinion that as the British were at the time withdrawing their missions from Serbia it would be difficult to explain it to Tito.[48] Another reason, although not stated, was that while Lukačević had been interrogated in Cairo about collaboration and cleared, SIS still harboured doubts about him because they knew that he had previously been involved in some sort of negotiations with the Germans.

In Cairo SOE there was already an established preference for supplying and building up the Partisans in Serbia, rather than trying to salvage what they could of Mihailović's organization.[49] General W.A.M. Stawell, who had replaced Keble in November 1943, co-ordinated the BLO's opinions, which indicated that the dissidents were not capable of deposing Mihailović, and added his own, concluding that the Partisans in Serbia should be supported, while W/T sets were to be left with the more dissatisfied commanders such as Djurić, Marković and Pavlović.[50] Stawell must have been basing his judgement on the same exaggerated figures for Partisan numbers in Serbia as Keble had used in his earlier reports.[51] The BLOs on the ground could have told him that the Partisans were very much in the minority there, so either Stawell was not receiving all their information or he was ignoring it. When they finally left Yugo-slavia, some of the BLOs found areas they knew to be under Mihailović's control were classed as Partisan-held territory. Bailey had earlier stated that, even with British help, the Partisans would not be able to stage effective action against the Germans in Serbia proper. Given Stawell's opinion that the dissidents—in common with the rest of the Yugoslav Home Army—owed their first loyalty to the king, but their second to Mihailović, his recommendation could only lead to the civil war spreading throughout Serbia just as Bailey had warned. Stevenson had previously asserted that the Brit-ish should not interfere with internal Yugoslav politics: but to sup-ply aid to the Partisans in an area where they barely existed could only increase their chances of gaining influence there. Even if the British had given up on Mihailović himself, to give the Partisans an entrée into Serbia—where all informed reports indicated that they enjoyed little popular support—was blatant interference and can only be interpreted as taking sides in the civil war.

After the British missions had left Serbia, the dissidents tried in vain to contact SOE on the transmitters that had been left with them. They eventually concluded that 'the broadcasts may not have been listened for at the correct time'. In August 1944 Lukačević and four others wrote to Maclean asking him to arrange communi-cations for them with the commander of the Allied forces in the Mediterranean and the Royal Yugoslav government. The officers also asked for Maclean's help in concluding a non-aggression pact between their forces and the Partisans, so that both could concen-trate on fighting the Germans and their allies.[52] This approach, apparently without the knowledge of Mihailović, was welcomed by Harold Macmillan, by then resident minister for the Mediterranean, and the Chiefs of Staff as a step towards unity and away from the threat of civil war. However, MO4 was anxious to know what Tito's reaction would be before the British took any action on the pro-posal. Maclean discussed it with Tito, who said that the 'Chetniks must come under his operational control as part of his forces'.[53] As Lukačević and the others had made it plain, both in their letter to Maclean and on previous occasions, that they had no intention of joining the Partisans, this was obviously an unsatisfactory reply for them. The opportunity to use these officers—along with the

15,000 men they claimed to have at their disposal—to carry out the types of operation Lukačević had suggested to Bailey in London, was missed.

Bailey's analysis, which had been greeted as sensible by both Selborne and the British military authorities, contained the old problem of separate resistance forces in particular areas: official British policy now favoured a federal Yugoslavia, which coincided with Tito's long-term plan for organizing the country after the war. Discussions were underway with Tito about the composition of his Yugoslav government; having already established AVNOJ as an alternative government, Tito had indicated that additional members might possibly be allowed to join, as long as they were not tainted by any association with Mihailović or the YGE.[54] Churchill had already accepted the advice of Maclean, Stevenson and Randolph that Tito would be the dominant factor in post-war Yugoslavia, and was conducting negotiations on that premise.

General Stawell had judged that Mihailović would not endanger the lives of the BLOs: this was unusual, since most of Cairo SOE and various other organizations there were buzzing with the rumour that they were about to have their throats cut.[55] In fact, nothing could have been further from the truth. After an initial frisson of fear when Cairo SOE was sending messages about fleeing to the partisans, the BLOs were relieved—and somewhat humbled—to find that their hosts treated them with kindness and consideration for their well-being. An atmosphere more sorrowful than angry seems to have pervaded the last days of the Allied missions with Mihailović's forces. After news from the Teheran Conference, one Serb officer remarked to Archie Jack that he hoped the British had got a good price for selling out Mihailović's forces and that it would prove to be worthwhile. 'This was said politely and without rancour', but Jack got the message and felt perplexed and ashamed himself.[56] Many BLOs were reluctant to leave the people they had worked with for the past year and whom, in some cases, despite frustrations, they had come to regard as friends. In addition, some felt that they were just beginning to make some headway in persuading their local commanders to become more active and that they were being pulled out at precisely the wrong time. Rootham and Greenwood resorted to sending urgent signals to Cairo SOE in the hope of making them aware of the true situation, bypassing Armstrong, who they felt no longer knew nor cared about what was going on.[57] These signals seem to have fallen on deaf ears.

The BLOs who had taken Cairo's advice to flee to the partisans in December did not fare any better in their radio dealings with MO4. Captain Robert Wade had left the Kopaonik area, commanded by Keserović, and headed west. En route he met up with Hudson and Seitz and proceeded to Berane in Montenegro, which was now under Peko Dapčević's command with Major Anthony Hunter as his BLO. In Berane they were joined by Major Peter Kemp, who had just left Kosovo after Cairo had informed him that the irridentist aims of the Albanian resistance forces with whom he had contacts there were 'causing an unfavourable impression among Tito's partisans'. This little group spent the best part of three months just hanging about in Berane, getting fed up of the Partisan propaganda that was constantly fed to the local population, while the locals themselves told the group that stories of large scale fighting in the countryside *was* simply propaganda. Wade still had his W/T set, and when reporting this to Cairo, gave his opinion that the Germans could enter Berane at any time they pleased. While Dapčević was courteous and friendly, the Partisan commissars were not so happy to entertain liaison officers who had served with their opponents. The crunch came when the Partisans demanded that Wade hand over his radio, and Cairo appeared to agree that he should comply to avoid misunderstandings with the Partisans in Montenegro. This brought forth an explosive response from Hudson, berating MO4 for their broken promises to him over two and a half years. He concluded: 'At least refrain from treachery to your officers in the field. Such conduct is unworthy of prostitutes, let alone SOE staff officers.' Three days later, on 28 March, they were finally evacuated on an old Italian 'plane, to Cairo via Brindisi and Bari.[58]

Mihailović accepted the withdrawal, on condition that the missions should not go out through partisan territory. Despite the urgent messages that flew back and forth on the withdrawal of the BLOs, and the precipitate delivery of the final order, they were not evacuated until the end of May. The original plan had been sent to Armstrong on 19 February, but when the final order to withdraw reached him on 6 March he was told that flying would be delayed as bad weather was forecast for the next five weeks. This seems to have been a very long-range weather forecast, and the prevailing conditions did not appear to be delaying the 'planes ferrying partisan wounded from Montenegro to Italy, one of which finally evacuated Hudson and his companions. The mission, which had been joined by a large number of downed American aircrew, was eventually told that the RAF was coming in to get them, and to prepare a landing strip of 1,200 yards. Archie Jack was in charge of this, but unable to find a long enough strip laid out the correct number of landing lights, but at shorter intervals on an 850-yard field. The first 'plane took off with fifteen passengers, disappeared over the edge of the mountain, dropped, then gained height, clipped the top of a cherry orchard on the other side of the valley, taking half a tree in its undercarriage, which remained down, and finally crossed the Adriatic. The next pilot, forewarned, took only ten passengers. After these two RAF 'planes the American air force took over the operation. By this time many of the BLOs had entirely lost faith in MO4, so when Jack was refused permission to bring Mueller out with him, Jack just ignored the order and boarded him on one of the outward bound flights anyway.[59]

When agreeing to the evacuation, Mihailović had stipulated that Lukačević and Bačević should be returned. The Special Operations Committee agreed to this, but were in no hurry to send them back, preferring to wait and see if Mihailović would live up to his side of the bargain. However, the FO did not want to give him an excuse for 'running out' on his undertaking to evacuate the missions, and told Cairo to return the two officers.[60] The only setback in the final exodus was caused by the British themselves who relieved Lukačević and Bačević of some documents they were carrying to Mihailović, who when he learned of this, detained Armstrong and a few other officers until the documents were sent in on the following day.[61]

When the BLOs arrived in Bari, southern Italy, where SOE had established its new base, they found that their troubles were not over. Far from being welcomed by the organization they had been attempting to serve in the field—often in the face of total incompetence on the part of that organization to say the least—they found themselves treated as pariahs for having been with the 'wrong side'.

On a mundane level they were not issued with fresh kit for some days; on a much more serious level, some were not properly debriefed.[62] Deakin later said that he was aware that the BLOs from Serbia had been shabbily treated; he had personally debriefed Hudson, putting him up at his own flat in early April, but had been away sick when the others came out.[63] Attempts to discover some explanation for what they regarded as 'the whole mess', produced lame excuses. Jack, who had been at school with 'Kluggers'—as Klugmann was known to his school-fellows—persuaded him to meet a group of the BLOs to explain what had gone wrong. Kluggers agreed reluctantly and made some unconvincing apologies and explanations which left them none the wiser at the end. When they tried to correct information they knew to be erroneous they met with downright hostility. Rootham and Jack visited the map room in Bari and found the areas they had just left and knew to be Yugoslav Home Army territory were depicted on maps as under Partisan control. No-one would listen to their first hand information, until Rootham became so furious that he swept all the flags from the map. After this all BLOs who had been with Mihailović's forces were banned from the map room.[64] When some of the more hardy—or perhaps naïve—souls volunteered to go to the Partisans, where they felt their experience might be put to good use, they were informed that Tito had forbidden the return to Yugoslavia of anyone who had served with Mihailović's forces.[65] They were surprised by the very pro-partisan atmosphere which pervaded the SOE office in Bari, and taken aback to be told that they had been brainwashed whenever they put forward a different opinion. The only friendly greeting they received came from a group of young women in the signals department, who implied that their messages from the field had been tampered with.

The BLOs who tried to correct what they perceived as a misguided view, first by sending desperate messages from the field and then by trying to put their case in Bari, essentially had been flogging a dead horse for some time. Once Mihailović had ceased to be a bargaining counter in the negotiations with Tito, his abandonment by the British was certain. The only remaining loose end was the question of King Peter's throne and, to some degree, the justification for leaving to his fate the leader who had been portrayed as the hero of European resistance not so very long before. Thus, in an attempt to convince King Peter that he must repudiate Mihailović, and to reassure the FO, the Americans and public opinion that the British were doing the right thing, the old chestnut of collaboration was brought into play in a big way.

When the Soviets had first started their campaign against Mihailović in the summer of 1942, the FO had defended him against the allegation that links with the Nedić forces indicated treachery: infiltration of Nedić's forces had been deemed to be a useful ploy. Mihailović viewed Nedić as a traitor, and also as a personal enemy from pre-war days, but regarded the majority of Nedić's 'official chetniks' as ordinary Serbs who were, in general, loyal to the exiled king and to Orthodox Christianity. Although he would have preferred not to, Mihailović was not averse to disguising his own followers as Nedićists when it proved beneficial, as in November–December 1941 when he had to go underground, or in order to obtain the arms that were not forthcoming from the British when Nedić issued the mass call-up. It was also a policy approved of by the YGE, and in November 1943 Bailey had refuted the idea of co-operation between Mihailović and Nedić, adding that the presence of agents in Nedić's forces and spies with Ljotić's men, were 'no more proof of collaboration than the presence of British agents in Germany prove collaboration between us and Hitler'.[66] As well as supplying information and intelligence Nedićists provided useful cover and disguise for the BLOs. Rootham reported that they facilitated travel through enemy-controlled areas, and on a number of occasions Archie Jack was taken by a Nedić sergeant to reconnoitre bridges for demolition. The sergeant provided a horse and cart for Jack to travel in, got him past German sentries on the bridges and arranged a safe house for him in the German garrison town of Sabac. Greenwood was convinced that had the time for the *Ustanak* arrived, that all the Nedić forces 'would have joined us with their arms'. On Christmas Day 1943 he accepted an invitation from the local commanding officer of the Nedićists for a Christmas drink, which was a pleasant social occasion. The fact that the BLOs were 'collaborating' with these forces seems to indicate that the bulk of them, as Mihailović had judged, were loyal to himself, the king and the Allies. While the BLOs were often young and adventurous—

even occasionally foolhardy—they were not stupid enough to risk their lives for a Christmas drink with people who were enemies.

Attempts to exploit Nedić forces did hold dangers other than the accusation of collaboration however. Dimitrije Djordjević was arrested in autumn 1943 for belonging to the Serbian Culture Club which, amongst other things, collected intelligence for Mihailović's organization in Belgrade. He found Banjica prison full of Mihailović's men whom the Germans had spotted were not genuine recruits to the Nedić militia. Hundreds were caught and either executed or sent to Mauthausen concentration camp.[67]

Great play had been also made of collaboration with the Italians. This was a trifle duplicitous of the British, who had supplied gold to Mihailović for the express purpose of buying weapons from the Italians at a time when SOE had not been able to supply matériel themselves.[68] However, Mihailović was always careful to make a distinction between useful contacts and getting too close to the Italians, and broke with Trifunović Birčanin when he felt the Dalmatian leader had done just that. Rendel had warned the FO that BBC broadcasts denouncing Slovene village guards for 'collaboration' with the Italians ran the risk of falling into a pit of communist propaganda, not least because Bailey himself had resorted 'to various ruses to keep the Italians quiet'.[69] Peter Wilkinson, on meeting Tito on 6 December 1943, suggested that as large-scale airborne supplies from Italy were not yet up and running then SOE could supply gold, which it had in unlimited amounts, so that as a stopgap the Partisans could buy weapons from the Germans. This, he assured Tito, was a tried and tested means of getting arms for the Polish Home Army.[70]

Deakin, who had been on the receiving end of Velebit's lessons on Mihailović's collaboration, noted that the Partisan forces with which he left Split in September 1943, and a local Ustasha garrison, diplomatically ignoring each other's presence.[71] A sensible arrangement, since neither wanted a fight at that point: a pragmatic accommodation to survive. The Partisans also had agents in the Ustasha organization, but this continued to be portrayed as a sensible and clever means of gleaning information, while similar tactics by Mihailović were used in evidence against him. The case against Mihailović and his followers was summed up in a slim pamphlet,

The Chetniks: a Survey, penned in the Bari office of ISLD by Stephen Clissold and Pamela Bisdee.[72]

There appears to have been no hard evidence available to prove any collaboration between Mihailović and the Germans in Serbia. Greenwood was adamant that collaboration with either German or Bulgarian occupation forces was out of the question in his area of eastern Serbia. Rootham reported that one brigade commander had been shot for writing to the Germans to suggest a non-aggression pact, but suspected that another local commander might have made some such accommodation. Cairo SOE had talked of there being enough evidence to justify withdrawing support without the test operation, but although this was constantly promised to the FO, it never seems to have been forthcoming.[73] Interestingly, the one positive contact Mihailović had with the Germans before 1944, when he tried to obtain arms from them to fight the partisans in November 1941, seems to have passed by the British. Subsequent attempts by the Germans and by Nedić to make some sort of deal with Mihailović were rebuffed. Hitler regarded Mihailović as an enemy: a price was put on his head on numerous occasions, although when the same price was put on Tito's head this was given much more publicity in the Allied media. Some of the commanders in Montenegro and Dalmatia, who nominally came under Mihailović's command, and who had been the main instigators of co-operation with the Italians, made agreements with the German forces who replaced the Italians after September 1943, for much the same reasons that they had contacts with the Italians—namely fear of the communists.[74] None of the British officers attached to the commanders in Serbia witnessed any collaboration between the forces they were with and the Germans.

At the end of October 1943 'most secret sources' intercepted a message to Mihailović commanders in north-eastern Bosnia and Herzegovina which gave them permission to have contact with the Germans. But in this case he was acting on the orders of the YGE who, also according to 'most secret sources' had just communicated with their minister of war 'by clandestine W/T in its insecure code'.[75] The timing of this is critical, since it came after the Partisan takeover of the Lim valley following the Italian armistice, the deterioration of relations with the British caused by the BBC broadcasts, and the fear that the Partisans were about to push their way into Serbia without the British mission lifting a finger to stop them. If accommodations were made with the German occupiers then it was a short term policy to save Serbia from the communists and, although a desperate action, was not out of keeping with the fragmentation, mistrust and betrayal that characterized the whole Yugoslav situation.

The appellation 'collaborator' was allowed to be attached to his name, not necessarily out of conviction but for convenience. Mihailović could not be goaded into the sort of actions that would avoid embarrassment for the diplomats with the Soviets, or which would satisfy the immediate military aims of the Chiefs of Staff. Churchill's attempts to reconcile Tito and the king further undermined Mihailović's position. That he could not be left to rot and drop off the branch was a combination of saving King Peter's throne and saving British face. It could not be admitted that support was being withdrawn from him and his movement simply because they were not as active as the Partisans, and Tito had made it clear from the outset that the British could not have Draža Mihailović *and* the Partisans. The British chose the Partisans.

11

BACKING THE PARTISANS: FROM ILLUSION TO REALITY

Following the Chiefs of Staff decision, at the Sextant Conference in Cairo at the end of 1943, to increase supplies to the Partisans and to carry out limited operations across the Adriatic, SOE underwent another transformation. The North African and Middle East Commands were unified as Allied Forces HQ with Jumbo Wilson in charge of strategy for the whole Mediterranean theatre of war. Harold Macmillan, as Minister Resident in North Africa, became responsible for British policy in the area, and Philip Broad joined his staff to advise him on Yugoslavia. With the opening up of southern Italy, Bari became the headquarters of Special Operations Mediterranean (SOM) on 12 April 1944; its purpose was to co-ordinate all special operations organizations in the area. As part of the new unified command, MO4 became Force 133, jointly responsible to London SOE and to Allied Forces HQ. ISLD also moved to Bari to become part of SOM. In early June the Balkan Air Force (BAF) was established under the command of Air Vice-Marshal William Elliot. Gubbins was not so enthusiastic about the creation of the BAF, foreseeing a potential for friction between Stawell and Elliot.[1] In July Maclean's mission became No. 37 Military Mission. The Special Operations Committee, chaired by General Stawell, despite the FO preference for Philip Broad occupying that position, was responsible for allocating resources to the various missions in the Balkans.

At the meetings in Alexandria between the COS and the partisan delegation, Vladimir Velebit and his companions had set out their requirements, under the impression that the British had an infinite supply of matériel available. While the Allies were discussing the arming of a guerrilla force, the Partisan delegation was in the process of attempting to establish a regular modern army, and form an air force. Velebit later admitted that at that stage the partisans would have been unable to service heavy equipment, even if the British had been able to supply it; there was also a problem in taking delivery, as the Partisans were not capable of holding a line against the Germans on the mainland.[2] Even so, the COS were obviously impressed by the discussions, and decreed that from January 1944 the Yugoslav Partisans should receive 80 % of all supplies destined for the Balkans.[3] Doing their best to comply with Velebit's requests virtually cleared out all SOE's matériel in the Middle East, but the move to Bari meant that Italian equipment became available. Supplies were sent by sea and air to the Partisans at a rate which astonished the BLOs returning from the Mihailović forces.

The Germans had soon taken control on the mainland following the Italian defection, and Tito's HQ had had to move from Jajce to Drvar in western Bosnia. While the Germans held all the major ports, the Dalmatian islands were still in Partisan hands and two flotillas of British naval MTBs, operating out of Brindisi, supplied them on their islands and harassed German sea traffic. Eventually the island of Vis was selected as a major Allied/Partisan base, with No. 2 Commando, led by Jack Churchill, made available for its defence and for raiding parties on the Germans. Jack's brother was Brigadier Tom Churchill, who was introduced to Fitzroy Maclean at Christmas 1943 by Randolph Churchill, one of the many old chums that composed Maclean's mission. Tom Churchill was head of four different Commandos, and at different times three of them— No. 40 and No. 43 Royal Marine Commandos, as well as No. 2— operated with Force 133 in Yugoslavia. By May 1944 an infantry battalion had taken over responsibility for security on Vis, freeing the commandos to concentrate on raiding; later that month, after Anzio, more craft became available for sea transport, and by summer a small airstrip was established on Vis.

Less successful than the British commandos was Yugoslav Troop No. 10, commanded by Lieutenant Tripović and drawn from the Yugoslav troops in the Middle East who had opted to join the British forces at the settlement of the military crisis in July 1942. Initially welcomed as returning heroes, Tripović and his men were soon accused of being King Peter's spies by the Partisans. Tripović was faced with the dilemma of a desire to fight for his country's freedom with the Partisans on the one hand and loyalty to the king on the other. The balance proved impossible and Tripović and Troop No. 10 were sent back to Italy.[4]

Both SOE and ISLD Yugoslav offices were largely staffed by people who had long been enthusiastic in their support for the Partisans. Deakin moved to Bari as head of the Yugoslav desk, but left in May and joined Philip Broad on Macmillan's staff in June. After Deakin left, the back-up for Maclean's mission (Macmis) was run by Gordon Fraser, who freely admitted his communist sympathies,[5] and he was aided by James Klugmann. The new recruits from the regular military bodies, who did not share the history of SOE dealings with Yugoslavia, were often inclined to cast a colder eye on the Partisans. Not all were convinced of the military prowess of the forces they were with. Captain Brian Parker, one of the marines who saw much action on the islands including a pitched battle with the Germans on Brač, found the Partisans unreliable. He never could be sure if they would show up to take part in planned operations or not, and they often had an inclination to be unpredictably trigger-happy in situations, such as intelligence gathering reconnoitres, where rather more discrete conduct was called for. Parker met Tito a number of times and assessed him as a very strong and reliable character, although the men around him were not so impressive, displaying as they did 'a mixture of swagger and kidology'. Like many of the other members of the British military, Parker found that while the rank and file partisans—and local populations—were friendly and welcoming, the political commissars were often suspicious and distant, if not downright hostile.[6] It was also apparent that the politically-minded Partisans much preferred the presence of General Korneyev's Soviet military mission, which had finally arrived on 23 February, to that of the British. There were blatant attempts to convince the local population that the supplies they received came from the USSR rather than the Western Allies.[7] The Soviets were not really in a position to furnish a great deal of help since they were hard pressed themselves. When Korneyev went to Yugoslavia two Soviet Dakotas were stationed in Italy to support his mission. Later Bogomolov, now a member of the Allied Advisory Council for Italy, requested facilities for a Russian air base in Italy;

this was agreed in June 1944 and thereafter the Soviets made a useful contribution to supplying the Partisans.[8] It was however, nowhere near the scale of American and British air operations and the actual material was mostly American. Macmillan was half-amused, half-indignant at Bogomolov's attempts to further the impression in Yugoslavia that it was really Soviet aid reaching the partisans: a request on 7 July for three ships to send 'Russian' aid to the partisans was turned down on the grounds that the ships and air cover they would need were British and the stores American. On 25 July Macmillan noted in his diary: 'Russians want to give Tito two of the Dakotas we allowed them to put at Bari. This seems rather an impertinence, considering the Dakotas are lend-lease articles which the Russians obtained from America.'[9]

The newcomers also noted—and resented—the fact that they were constantly kept under surveillance by the Partisans, and their movements circumscribed 'for their own protection'. One reason for keeping a close watch on the members of the British mission was a general mistrust of their motivation, particularly in view of previous British support of Mihailović. Milovan Djilas felt that the British had made a choice between carrying out a landing and fighting the Partisans or coming to an agreement with them on a mutually profitable basis. 'They chose the latter, cautiously and without enthusiasm, while our own dogmatic ideological distrust kept us from understanding them, though it also preserved us from any hasty enthusiasm.' Djilas went on to say that Allied bombing of Yugoslav cities, especially Belgrade which was bombed on Orthodox Easter Sunday 1944, and again in September, aroused the suspicion that the British were aiming to make post-war reconstruction more difficult for the Partisans.[10] The first occasion was accidental but devastating. American bombers, unable to bomb the Ploesti oilfields in Romania, had headed for their back-up target of the Belgrade marshalling yards: unfortunately, their bomb-aiming equipment was not as accurate as it was supposed to be and they hit central Belgrade just as the Orthodox population was leaving church.[11] The September bombing was part of 'Operation Ratweek', the object of which was to halt all enemy traffic through and within Yugoslavia.

Another reason for limiting the movements of the Allied liaison officers was the Partisans' desire to disguise the fact that the civil war was continuing. While it had been understood by the British that Mihailović's main intention was to fight the Partisans rather than the occupying forces, it took them longer to recognize that it was also Tito's first concern to win the civil war. In April 1944, Tito had issued a reminder to all his commanders that Serbia, and partisan strength there, was of primary importance to the entire National Liberation Movement in Yugoslavia.[12] The Americans were concerned about SOE expanding its missions with the Partisans in Serbia, lest it should lead to the Allies becoming embroiled in Yugoslav internal troubles: OSS relayed to Macmillan's office the State Department's view that the complete elimination of Mihailović was undesirable. Philip Broad reassured the OSS representative that Partisans in Serbia would only receive supplies as long as they used them against the occupiers: liaison officers had been instructed to halt supplies at the first hint of them being utilized in purely internal conflict.[13] As SOE was just pulling out the BLOs with Mihailović, and those with the Partisans were not allowed freedom of movement to make independent observations, this reassurance was somewhat meaningless.

Differences were beginning to become increasingly apparent between Britain and America on the future of the Balkans, fuelled by American suspicions of Britain's imperialistic ambitions in the area. While Washington was trying not to get too involved in Yugoslavia, Churchill's pro-partisan policy did not entirely suit the Americans. 'Slim' Farish, the OSS officer with Macmis, produced another report on 28 June; this was very different in tone and content to the one he wrote in November 1943, which bore striking similarities to Maclean's blockbuster and had been written without setting foot outside Partisan HQ.[14] Although Roosevelt had been impressed by Farish's first report, which had reached him on his way to Teheran, he was not entirely convinced of Mihailović's collaboration. The President accordingly attached a Serbo-Croatian-speaking OSS officer to Farish before he returned to the Partisans in January 1944. With the help of Lieutenant Eli Popovich, Farish, who spoke no Serbo-Croatian himself, developed a much clearer picture of the complexities of the Yugoslav situation. By June 1944, after two months in Serbia, Farish had become aware of the tragedy befalling the ordinary people, and the fact that American-supplied guns were being used for the civil war rather than against the occupiers. In the meantime Seitz and Mansfield had also emerged from Serbia with their reports of what they had seen and heard on their grand tour. Donovan sent Colonel Robert McDowell into Serbia on 26 August 1944 to contact Mihailović's forces. When Churchill protested to Roosevelt that McDowell could scupper the last chance of saving the king, the President made conciliatory noises about withdrawing him; nevertheless, McDowell remained in Yugoslavia until 1 November. Speaking to some captured Partisans, he discovered that while all had been engaged against 'Nationalist' forces, none of them had fought against Germans or Ustashas: nor had any of them seen any Allied liaison officers in the vicinity of engagements, although some were known to be at Partisan rear HQ. McDowell asserted that some BLOs and USLOs had reported that they had not been allowed to witness Partisan actions, and suspected that rather than attacking the Germans, the Partisans were hoarding arms supplied by the Allies for use in the civil war. On leaving Yugoslavia McDowell produced a forty-page report which confirmed those suspicions.[15]

Having made no headway with his personal appeals to Tito on the question of the monarchy, Churchill decided to try another tack. On 17 May the PM informed Tito that, on British advice, King Peter had dismissed Purić's government—including Mihailović—and was about to form a new administration under Ivan Šubašić, a Croat Peasant Party politician and former Ban of Croatia. King Peter had agreed on 18 March to dismiss Purić, but asked for a month to select a new government.[16] Eden cautioned that any hiatus in the YGE carried the risk of Tito declaring AVNOJ to be the legitimate government, and perhaps even being recognized as such by the Soviets. The latter might excuse themselves on the grounds that they had not been given prior warning of Purić's dismissal, and the result would be to leave the king in a worse position than ever.[17] His position was already dismal: he had remained in London after his nuptials, rather than return to Cairo, as SIS had warned that his life might be in danger from elements there who had opposed the wedding. Meanwhile, within Yugoslavia the communist propaganda machine had made great play of his wedding being a betrayal of the

Yugoslavs suffering occupation and persecution. What Churchill planned was that, on dismissing Purić, King Peter could form a small administration composed of 'people not particularly obnoxious to Tito'.[18] Ivan Šubašić was selected as someone who would potentially build non-controversial bridges and he was also one of the people Tito had named as possibly an acceptable candidate to join AVNOJ, since he was untainted by any association with the YGE or Mihailović.[19] It was hoped that Šubašić would be able to negotiate the king's return to Yugoslavia.

On 25 May, before a meeting could be arranged between Tito and Šubašić, the Germans launched an airborne attack using gliders and paratroops, on Tito's HQ at Drvar. Martin Gilbert states that Enigma decrypts had indicated the German intention, but, for security reasons, no warning was sent to the British mission. However, both Ralph Bennett and Hilary King—who was in charge of communications at Macmis—say that the implications of the Enigma decrypts were not fully understood in time to give a warning, even if it had been desirable.[20] Everyone at Drvar—British, Partisans *et al.*—had noticed a great deal of air reconnaissance and had assumed an attack was imminent, although they thought that it would be a bombing raid rather than an airborne landing. Tito and the BLOs evaded capture but were on the run, and the Germans were in hot pursuit, destroying villages and killing their inhabitants as they went, while the Partisans fought a rearguard action. The British responded with bombing raids and launched a massive attack on the island of Brač in an attempt to distract the Germans and take the heat off Tito. The action on Brač by nearly 3,000 partisans and over 1,000 British commandos did divert the Germans from the 'Tito hunt', but at a cost. McConville described it: 'In terms of British manpower it was the largest [operation] undertaken in Yugoslavia during the Second World War, and in terms of blood and talent lost was the most expensive.'[21] Although it had provided a diversion, Tito had lost contact with most of his forces and was unable to control or direct operations. In early June Tito and Vivian Street, who headed Macmis in Maclean's absence, decided it was sensible to fly out of Yugoslavia to get a proper picture of what was happening and re-impose control. An airstrip was hastily constructed and arrangements made for the RAF to come in to collect them. In the event, Tito did not leave with the British but, much to their surprise, hopped on to the Soviet-piloted Dakota which came to collect General Korneyev and his people. After a brief stay in Italy, Tito was moved to the island of Vis, which had been secured by British commandos and Partisans, so that he would be on Yugoslav soil, with a new HQ in a cave on the highest point of the island.

Macmillan, pondering the psychological effect this new location might have on Tito, noted in his diary on 4 June: 'In some ways it may be helpful because it should increase our hold over him.' Churchill had spotted this too: 'Tito as a mountain chieftain in the fastness of Yugoslavia, and Tito as our guest on an island protected by British armies are two totally different things.'[22] This was a godsent opportunity for King Peter and Šubašić to go at once to Vis and make an agreement for unifying all the forces within Yugoslavia. On 10 June the PM sent Wilson a telegram suggesting that King Peter should land at Vis and take possession of his kingdom. Wilson and Macmillan concluded that the PM was not entirely cognisant of the complications of this, and in the event Šubašić went to Vis as 'John the Baptist', as Eden described him,[23] while the king waited in Malta to be wheeled on if Tito were agreeable. Tito, it seemed, was not anxious to meet the king 'at present'; in fact, he was not anxious to meet the king at all, and was constantly on his guard lest the British should engineer a surprise encounter.

Tito's new location, combined with the fact that the long-awaited second front had been opened in Western Europe, which should have removed some of the British *angst* regarding Stalin, did not increase the British hold over Tito at all. The Tito-Šubašić Agreement was reached on 16 June 1944, and Maclean described the meeting between the two men as a great success, at which some real progress had been made:[24] since *no* progress had been made hitherto in gaining anything in the way of a political agreement from Tito, *any* progress looked good. The main advance appeared to be that Tito had assured Šubašić that he did not intend to impose communism on post-war Yugoslavia, and had agreed to the formation of a united Yugoslav government which might include elements of the YGE (now a very small body). In return, Šubašić had recognized AVNOJ; he had also agreed to support the Partisans and appeal to the people of Yugoslavia to do the same, and that he would not include anyone hostile to the Partisans in his administration. The Partisan interpretation of this of course was 'anyone connected with Mihailović'.

This put Zhivko Topalović out of the running for a place in the new government, because of his position as political adviser to Mihailović. Topalović, leader of the Socialist Party, had left Serbia with the BLOs on 1 June in order to put forward the ideas of the National Congress which he had chaired the previous January. The purpose of the Congress, which met at Ba, was to promote a non-communist democratic political programme to counter the claims of AVNOJ. Before going to Vis, Šubašić had a long discussion with him in Bari, during the course of which Topalović had explained ideas and proposals for ending the internal strife and for the future of a democratic federal Yugoslavia. Topalović had offered to support and co-operate with Šubašić's government. One of the proposals was that King Peter should establish himself at a neutral point in Yugoslavia and co-ordinate action between the forces there by acting as commander in chief.[25] However, Šubašić had agreed to Tito's proposal that the question of the monarchy should be left until after the war, which precluded this as a solution to the divisions. The British began to see that Šubašić, selected for his ability to negotiate with Tito, had done that all too well: the two were getting along far too nicely.[34] When Churchill eventually met Tito and Šubašić together in Naples, it was apparent that the former had 'swallowed' the latter.[26]

The FO was not enthusiastic about the meeting between Tito and Šubašić on Vis, particularly because Tito had managed to slide away from meeting the king. Nor had their agreement come any closer to bringing about a *modus vivendi* between the Partisans and the non-Partisan Serbs: more ominous still was Tito's confidence that the Partisans were already so strong in Serbia that they could shortly obliterate the Chetnik movement.[27] This was not what was wanted at all. Eden and the FO had gone along with supporting Tito *only* for pragmatic reasons with the constant idea that somehow all the potential resisters in Yugoslavia could be made to work together. Mihailović's failure to achieve this, combined with the policy-makers constantly looking over their shoulders at the Soviets,

had led the FO to look to Tito to form a united *military* organization. The results of the meeting on Vis made them finally wake up
to the fact that Tito did not fulfil their desires either, and they
began again their lament of long-term interests being sacrificed to
short-term military ones.

The FO continued to question Maclean's handling of the partisans, particularly with regard to their aims in Serbia. Eden was not
happy to hear that Maclean

...lost no opportunity of reminding Tito that His Majesty's Government
are most anxious both on military and political grounds to see him extend
scope of his movement into Serbia and further increase his activities here. I
have pointed out that apart from immediate strategic importance of Serbia, civil war there would be to the advantage of no-one.[28]

Nor was Eden pleased with Tito's plan to send Lieut.-General
Ranković, his head of Intelligence and secret police, and Dr Ribnikar, vice-president of AVNOJ, to join Popović in Serbia. All three
were Serbs, and it was their task to establish a state council for Serbia, with Ribnikar as president. Maclean was sharply informed by
Eden that, while increasing supplies to Tito's forces in Serbia had
been considered as a way of getting Serbs to fight alongside the
partisans,

We are not concerned to help Tito impose himself and his regime on the
Serb people, which might produce bitter resentment and lasting ill feeling.
Our policy is to build by agreement between Tito and the Government a
system of co-operation between the Partisans and those Serbs who are
willing to fight the enemy.[29]

Maclean was, therefore, instructed to ask Tito to postpone the despatch of Ranković and Ribnikar until the question of Serbia had
been discussed by Tito and Šubašić, at their meeting with General
Wilson in Caserta, scheduled for 12 July. The agenda for this meeting was that Wilson would make it plain that the British regarded
the Partisans as a purely military organization, while Šubašić would
come to an understanding on the future of the various peoples in
Yugoslavia. Particularly important was persuading Tito to agree not
to impose communism, which was regarded as an essential reassurance for the population of Serbia. Probably responding to Topalović's
proposals, the FO had revived the idea of sending a Yugoslav officer

to replace Mihailović in Serbia: Stevenson hoped that once Tito had given such an assurance, it would strengthen the hand of that officer. Tito turned down the invitation to meet General Wilson in July—according to the Yugoslav historian Kljaković, because he was tipped off that the British intended to spring King Peter on him there.[30] If Tito did get a tip-off it was more likely to be that the British were contemplating the despatch of a replacement for Mihailović in Serbia, and this was not something to which Tito would have wished to agree. A few days after the meeting should have taken place, he apparently relented, but by that time Šubašić had returned to Britain, and it was decided that it would do Tito no harm to cool his heels for a while.[31] The meetings were eventually rescheduled for the middle of August, and Churchill was to take part himself.

While the FO had never taken a rosy view of Tito, Churchill certainly had. The warm and friendly letters the PM sent to the partisan leader through Maclean indicate that Churchill thought that here was someone he could do business with. It is difficult to ascertain the precise moment at which Churchill began to wake up to reality. Possibly the process began when Bailey and Hudson finally came out of Yugoslavia and began to present a much more complex view of the situation there—particularly with relation to Serbia—than that to which Churchill had previously been exposed. Hudson, although somewhat overawed to find himself lunching at Chequers with the PM, South African Premier Jan Smuts, Alan Brooke the CIGS, and Cunningham the First Sea Lord, stated quite categorically that Mihailović was no traitor. When Churchill asked what Hudson would do in Yugoslavia, he said that he would back Tito, but was too tongue-tied to add that he would do so with discretion and the utmost care, not bald-headed. He did, however, include these caveats in his written report which was circulated by Eden to the War Cabinet.[32] Bailey's comments on the Vis meeting were that Tito had allowed Šubašić to be at the helm outside the country in order to consolidate his own position within it, while the strength and solidarity of Mihailović's movement had either been ignored or underrated. Since his emergence from Yugoslavia, Bailey had also been highly critical of some of the opinions expressed in SOE appraisals of the situation there and of the relative efficacy of the opposing movements. He was furious when he read a couple of reports by Anthony Webb in Baker Street, both full of mistakes and misinformation; Bailey commented on the second 'this is a highly tendentious, ill-informed and illiterate paper' and, as it had been penned just before Christmas 1943, 'I cannot help thinking that the spirit of Christmas imminent has spread its wings before'.[33]

By the time Churchill met Tito in Naples on 12 August, the PM was aware that the Partisans were using the bulk of Allied supplies to fight Serbs rather than Germans, and took a fairly tough line on the question with the marshal. However, at the lunch following the meeting, Churchill made a laudatory speech, welcoming Tito as an ally; Pierson Dixon, who attended as the FO representative, felt this to be a tactical mistake, which undid the good of the sermon at the conference.[34] Tito assured Churchill that he had no desire to introduce communism to Yugoslavia, but when asked for affirmation of this in a public statement, Tito demurred, claiming that to do so at this particular moment would create the impression that he was acting under duress. Eden was very uneasy, feeling that Šubašić, as a Croat, underestimated the Serb problem, which led him in turn to underestimate the long-term potential for civil war.[35]

By 31 August Churchill finally seemed to have fallen into step with Eden when he sent the foreign secretary a memorandum, which stated:

It would be well to remember how great a responsibility will rest upon us after the war ends, with Tito having all the arms and being able to subjugate the rest of the country by weapons supplied by us. During the war we can put pressure on him to fight the Germans instead of his fellow-countrymen by the threat of stopping supplies, but this will have gone when the war is over. He will have the arms and the country at his mercy.[36]

Eden felt that the FO hardly needed reminding of this and his exasperation is almost palpable in his handwritten note in the margin: 'It is PM who has persistently pushed Tito despite our warnings.' The foreign secretary duly sent the PM a reminder of the dire warnings he had issued regarding the question of persuading King Peter to drop Mihailović without first having a reciprocal concession from Tito. Eden was also becoming anxious that Tito might be planning to unite Yugoslavia and Bulgaria. The FO had objected to the idea that Mihailović might be planning a Slav federation of

Serbia and Bulgaria, so Tito's possible plans for the *whole* of Yugoslavia were even worse in terms of giving the USSR access to the
Adriatic and isolating Greece.[37] While Eden was to a certain extent
justified in taking this 'I-told-you-so' attitude to the PM, he was
also being rather 'holier-than-thou' in regard to the FO position.
He was quite right in saying that Churchill had pushed for the
abandonment of Mihailović without any *quid pro quo*, but in turn
London SOE's advice regarding long-term interests had been
ignored by the FO, because they were so nervous of being at cross-
purposes with the Soviets.

Now that everyone was sharing doubts about Tito and the future
of Yugoslavia, Eden felt that much depended on the attitude of the
'Russians', as the Red Army was so close to the Yugoslav borders,
he decided some straight talking with Stalin was in order.[38] He was
right to be concerned about the proximity of the Red Army, but a
little late as regards the straight talking with Stalin. A few days later
Tito 'levanted'—as Churchill put it—from Vis, courtesy of the
Russian air group at Bari, to make arrangements for the Red Army
to come over the borders to help him liberate Serbia. It took some
time to discover exactly where he had gone, but this was the final
straw for the PM.

Churchill's reservations regarding Serbian support for the Partisans had made the question of establishing the NLA in Serbia—
always uppermost in Tito's mind—more pressing. Alive to the fact
that his long-term plans were not in accord with those of the Allies,
Tito's solution was to present them with a *fait accompli*. Even before
he returned to Vis after his meetings in Italy, Partisan operations to
get back into Serbia were under way, and once back on his island he
took personal control. At the end of August 1944, with the Soviet
army on the eastern border of Romania, and the likelihood of a
Bulgarian withdrawal from Serbia, Tito issued a directive to his
commanders to be ready for new developments and rapid troop
deployment in Serbia.[39] The Partisans were aided in their plans by
'Operation Ratweek', in which the BAF, US 15th Army Airforce
and the NLA combined to hinder the withdrawal northwards of
German Army Group E and prevent them fighting on other fronts.
There were four main targets for the Allied bombers: the Zagreb-
Brod-Belgrade railway; the Danube bridges in the vicinity of

Belgrade; the Belgrade-Nis-Skopje-Athens railway; and rail links between the river Sava and the Adriatic. Maclean went to Serbia for the first time to take part in Ratweek, which commenced on 1 September 1944, while BLOs with various NLA commanders directed the heavy bombers to targets specified by the Partisans. The destruction, a great deal of which was in Serbia, was massive. Maclean had been surprised at Tito's ready agreement to the plan, but it gave the Partisans the ideal opportunity to carry the civil war into Serbia under cover of the confusion of Ratweek. The scale of the Allied bombing raids in support of partisan action also proved to be a useful recruiting sergeant for the NLA, as did King Peter's broadcast of 12 September, in which he described the partisans as 'our National Army' and urged all Yugoslavs to support Tito.[40] Despite reservations that both the FO and PM harboured about Tito, the king had been prevailed upon to make this broadcast. It was not favourably received by Serbs in London: Dr Milan Grol— by no means a 'pan-Serb', and not an adherent of Mihailović— informed Stevenson that he could not possibly support a government whose policy was to impose the NLA on Serbia by force of arms. He favoured compromise, based on the ideas that Topalović had brought from the Congress of Ba.[41]

The Soviets obligingly made a swift detour into Yugoslavia to help the Partisans gain control of Belgrade before sweeping on to Hungary. Maclean was pleased, as he felt this precluded the onset of a lengthy civil war—Mihailović would be 'on the run', and Tito, with the Red Army at his side and the arms supplied by the Western Allies, would be in an unchallengeable position. To capitalize on the goodwill they had been building up with Tito and to save him from the arms of the Russian bear, all that the British had to do was forego any 'humming and hawing', and drop the king and Šubašić. Macmillan noted Maclean's opinion in his diary on 25 September, and agreed with his thesis, although he was afraid that the FO would 'shilly-shally' and miss the bus.

Maclean and the 'Tito fans', as Macmillan termed them, had seriously misread the signs: far from fearing the embrace of the Russian bear, the Partisans had always looked to the Soviets as their most desirable ally; they had simply been making do with the Western Allies until they could come into the open. Tito had kept in touch with Moscow throughout his various dealings with the British, and sought Stalin's opinion on questions such as the monarchy and the negotiations with Šubašić. The Soviets had constantly advised caution—not to upset the British on the one hand, but not to give away too much on the other. They had also advised Tito in the aftermath of the Schwarz and Weiss offensives to conserve his forces for a future decisive battle. This was in July 1943, just at the time that SOE was establishing missions with the partisans, while Churchill and the COS were looking to the Partisans to be more active against the Axis occupiers than the Yugoslav Home Army.[42] In addition to helping the NLA take Belgrade, Tito used the Red Army as a counterbalance to the Western Allies. He had turned his appeal for aid upon its head to become a Soviet request for permission to pass through Yugoslav territory, a precedent which meant that the Western Allies would also be obliged to seek permission for the entry of any of their forces.[43] This gave Tito a very strong hand, and once he was established in Belgrade, his relationship with the British was not so important. By December Churchill realized that he had been nurturing a viper in his bosom.[44]

Tito was always careful to be diplomatic and conciliatory in his dealing with Maclean: for example, he was quick to smooth the ruffled feathers caused by Bakić's peremptory demand for the withdrawal of Floydforce in January 1945.[45] Floydforce was made up of Tom Churchill's commandos, under Brigadier O'Brian Twohig, and had been sent in late October in response to Tito's request for British artillery to hamper the German withdrawal through Montenegro. During the three months that Floydforce served there it became obvious that while their military aid was welcome, the Partisans mistrusted them as capitalist agents to a point that was sometimes detrimental to co-ordinated operations against the Germans. By the end of 1944 it was clear that the Germans were on the run, and this is what precipitated Bakić's note to Maclean. The incident illustrates that while Tito and the Partisans had achieved a good deal of what they were aiming for, they were still fearful of having it snatched away by Allied military intervention. Some minor concessions were made to the Western Allies by the establishment of a regency and a Popular Front provisional government in March 1945, but it was quite clear that Tito was in charge. After Maclean

left, by his own admission while the going was good,[46] the relationship between the provisional government and the British became
much more formal. Stevenson and Deakin went to Belgrade to
reopen the British Embassy, and Air Vice-Marshal Lee replaced
Maclean in March. The special relationship was over, and problems
and disputes began to develop; the situation was not helped by
Tito's speeches on his visit to Moscow in April, which praised the
USSR while belittling the help he had received from Britain.[47]

The deteriorating relationship became increasingly apparent to
the BLOs: aggressive and confrontational incidents became more
frequent as the Partisan movement grew increasingly wary of Allied
personnel on Yugoslav soil. To some degree this was understand-
able, since by late 1944 virtually every British 'undercover' organization had at least one mission in the country. In addition to the
SOE missions, there was 'A Force', ostensibly in Yugoslavia to help
extricate people escaping Nazi persecution, but in reality engaged
on deception operations; the SAS, SBS and MI9—the rescue service for escaped prisoners of war—were also operating there. ISLD
had five missions active in Partisan territory, none of which knew
what the other was up to.[48] Despite the establishment of SOM,
many of these organizations were operating independently of—and
sometimes in competition with—each other, which often led to
open hostility when they came into contact. The only thing any of
them appear to have agreed on was that there were too many missions and that the others should not be there.

As the war neared its final phase Slovenia became an increasingly
important factor in both Yugoslav and Allied thinking. The British
had always been alive to the fact that it was a crucial area: during the
first two years of the war SIS had handled all dealings with Slovenia.
It was now particularly sensitive in view of Tito's expansionist plans
in the north-west, where he wanted to add to Yugoslavia the 'Slav'
regions of Italy and of Austria. In Naples Churchill had told Tito
that all such questions would be left for the peace conference, but it
eventually became clear that Tito did not want to wait for that.

After contact had been made with the partisans, Major William
Jones became SOE's representative in Slovenia from the summer of
1943. Peter Wilkinson's long-term plan, which he started to organize in July 1943, was to use the area and the Partisan organization

as his back door into central Europe. With the agreement of Fitzroy Maclean, Wilkinson and Major Alfgar Hesketh-Pritchard, the spearhead of the Clowder mission, flew into Glamoč and met Tito at Jajce on 6 December 1943 to discuss the possibility of making contact with anti-Nazi groups in central Europe. Tito gave his permission for them to proceed to Slovenia.

On the journey Wilkinson wrote to Gubbins on 16 December giving his impressions of the situation in Yugoslavia. He was very critical of Cairo SOE and its lack of support for the officers in the field that he had encountered on the way. He was also critical of OSS, who seemed to be overlapping with SOE while trying to run independent operations 'rather selfishly and not v. skilfully'. The Partisans had been charming, but he cautioned Gubbins not to overrate the Yugoslavs who he described as having 'grave limitations and much resemble the Poles in character and capacity'. Wilkinson thought the Soviet mission was pretty influential, but that they did not entirely understand the partisans. He was being careful not to cross Maclean who Wilkinson felt had 'done well and would have done better if he had taken on one or two of our officers. As it is there is no, repeat no, sabotage work being done though the possibilities are enormous.'[49]

Wilkinson had reached Major Jones by Christmas and reported that the Partisans regarded him as 'mad but holy'. More importantly, on 8 January Wilkinson met Boris Kidrić, Secretary of the Slovene Communist Party and a member of the Slovene Liberation Government—the most powerful man in the Slovene CP. He was amenable to helping the Clowder mission, but pointed out that German-annexed Slovenia was very tightly controlled and that Partisan IX Corps, operating in Slovene speaking regions of north-eastern Italy, were the best bet for establishing contact with the substantial Slovene minority living in southern Austria. This area, south of the river Drau and including the towns of Villach and Klagenfurt, had been incorporated into Carinthia after the First World War, and it was a partisan war aim to reunite it with Slovenia. Wilkinson realized that to accept help from the partisans for Clowder implied recognition of these territorial claims, but felt it was too good a chance to miss, although he did tell Kidrić that he was not empowered to make any post-war commitments. From mid-February supply drops of arms and ammunition started to arrive for the Clowder mission and its allies.

Clowder was controlled directly from Baker Street as Wilkinson had no confidence in Cairo, and operated as part of No. 1 Special Forces, which was the advanced detachment of 'Massingham', SOE HQ with AFHQ Algiers, headed by Douglas Dodds-Parker. The Clowder mission was based at Monopoli, just south of Bari, and was reinforced by members of the Austrian Section from Baker Street. While Wilkinson returned to London to report on the establishment of Clowder and its future plans, Major Charles Villiers flew to Monopoli en route to Slovenia to take charge of the mission in May 1944. It was soon discovered that SIS had a mission in the region with a very similar task to Clowder: in this case, rather unusually, the two organizations seem to have co-operated with each other, with SIS providing agents—primarily Austrians—who were meant to supply leadership and guidance for an independent Austrian resistance. These agents were not a great success with the Partisans, especially after one of the Austrians was captured by the Germans and talked under duress. Villiers returned to his base to find the village destroyed, the local people taken away, and his own bunker empty with 'most valuable, secret and compromising material' missing. After this the partisans stated that they did not want any non-British agents attached to them. The Partisans had not been enthusiastic anyway about the idea of these agents assuming control, they preferred to use their communication lines to Austria for their own or Soviet purposes. This led Villiers to conclude that it was desirable for British penetration of Austria to become independent of the partisans as soon as possible.[50]

When SOM was established at Bari, Wilkinson was determined not to come within its realm and to 'avoid the embraces of Maj General Stawell … so far as Clowder was concerned, I was convinced this embrace would be the kiss of death.' Gubbins entirely agreed and on 30 July 1944 sent a personal telegram to Wilkinson, now back in Monopoli, to ditch his plans to rejoin Villiers and Hesketh-Pritchard in Slovenia. The 20 July bomb attempt on Hitler's life, although it had failed, had given rise to optimism in some quarters that the collapse of the Nazi state might have been closer than anticipated. If Germany looked close to collapse then it seemed reasonable that some Austrian resistance might be stimulated. Gubbins felt that Wilkinson would be better placed to encourage and supply this expected resistance from an area outside the control of the Slovenian Partisans. This was why he insisted that Wilkinson stick firmly within 'Massingham' and not get mixed up with either SOM or the BAF. It was essential to be separate from, and quite independent of, both the Partisans and the British missions supporting them.[51] Presumably this was because the resistance Wilkinson was to organize in Austria was not simply to hasten the end of the Third Reich, but also to prevent Tito and the Yugoslav Partisans achieving their territorial ambitions in the north-west.

By 10 November, however, the Clowder mission had concluded that no organized resistance existed in Austria: the Gestapo—also aware of the sensitivity of the area—had done a thorough job in eliminating any potential elements of oposition. The policy of Germanification had made people change their names, moved populations away from border areas, and witnessed the deportation of around thirty percent of Slovenes to concentration camps or industrial centres as forced labour. Almost 90 per cent of those deported were drawn from the intellectual and professional classes and the combination of Nazi law and its enforcement by the Gestapo made life dreadful for the remaining Slovenes. The only active resistance was the Slovene minority in the 'Trigger' area, with its HQ north-west of Klagenfurt: it was these people that Hesketh-Pritchard was operating with. It was also clear by then that the German collapse was not as close as had been hoped.

In June 1943 in Naples, Churchill and Alexander had discussed the possibility of an advance through the Ljubljana Gap to Vienna as an alternative to 'Anvil', the Allied landings in southern France. The independent force that the Clowder mission was trying to establish would have been useful to the Allies if they had decided to act on Alexander's plan. It was never really a starter, especially as the Americans had preferred Anvil, but the idea stuck in Tito's mind as something to beware of. Both the Ljubljana Gap plan and the idea of a force not directly under Yugoslav partisan control were obstacles to Tito's ambitions for expansion, a factor which probably ultimately cost Hesketh-Pritchard his life. In mid October, as the British–partisan relationship cooled, he had persuaded the partisans he was with to accompany him across the Drau river. It was a last ditch attempt to recruit an independent force in Austria, not to aid the Ljublijana Gap scheme which was long dead, but in order to have available a force which might counter Tito's push into Carinthia. His crossing coincided with the onset of bad winter weather: the resultant impossibility of providing supplies by air, coupled with their dangerous situation inside the Reich being pursued by the enemy, apparently led to a rapid deterioration in relations with the Partisans. Hesketh-Pritchard's last signal, on 3 December, was addressed to Wilkinson and read 'Give my love to all at White's. This is no life for a gentleman.' Then there was silence: the Partisans he was with swore he fell in battle, but investigators concluded that he had been assassinated by his companions, probably on orders from a higher political quarter.[52] Hesketh-Pritchard's attempts to recruit non-Slovenes, coupled with the deteriorating relations by the end of 1944, demonstrated to Tito that allowing SOE to operate in Carinthia had not gained him any advantage in persuading the British to recognize his projected frontiers.

The ever-increasing danger of Tito's expansionism caused great concern to the British in the early months of 1945, and eventually led to what has been described as the race for Trieste and Venezia Giulia. The Western Allies were advancing up the western side of the Adriatic as fast as they could while the Partisan raced along the eastern side: both were hampered by the Germans, who, despite everything, still had a great deal of fight left in them. In Yugoslavia, the retreating Germans had a shorter front which was easier to defend, and their withdrawal from the Balkans was continuing in a fairly orderly manner. For the Partisans the situation was complicated in that the Germans were not their only enemies; the NLA was still carrying on the civil war, while at the same time trying to secure the Adriatic coastline against any possible landing from the west.

As the Red Army entered Serbia, Mihailović had ordered the *Ustanak*: he sent a number of messages to Wilson, asking for guidance to co-ordinate his forces' actions with Allied plans. In his appeals to Wilson, Mihailović had included the Muslim and Croat Domobrans and the Slovene home guards in the forces ready to act under Wilson's orders—these were, loosely, civil defence forces who had been organized and armed by the Italians and by the Germans. Although they had displayed collaborationist behaviour, he said, they were patriotic forces who had simply been biding their time: this had now come.[53] These messages were studiously ignored in Italy, as to get involved with Mihailović again would undermine the agreement Churchill had reached with Stalin concerning Yugoslavia, and the Tito-Šubašić agreement, even though by that time the latter was generally perceived by the British as hardly worth the paper it covered. Churchill's agreement with Stalin was written on the now notorious scrap of paper that the PM had pushed across the table to the Soviet leader at the Moscow conference in October 1944, which carved up eastern Europe into spheres of influence, with Yugoslavia being defined as '50–50' between the Soviets and the West. Hungary was also 50–50; Romania was 90–10 and Bulgaria 75–25, both in favour of the USSR; Greece was 90–10 in favour of Britain and the USA. Macmillan noted in his diary on 24 October, in the wake of a message sent by Topalović on Mihailović's behalf: 'We managed to kill the Mihailović business, although the Americans hanker after him still.'

As neither Mihailović nor other organizations such as the Domobrans received any word of encouragement, some began to move to the north-west to meet up with the Western Allies, to offer their services in person. This was both an embarrassment and a disappointment to the FO, as it had hoped that these forces would fight independently against the Partisans and prevent them crossing over into Venezia Giulia and Carinthia.[54] This would have been the ideal solution for the British, who could derive benefit from the opposition to the partisans while disclaiming any responsibility. It was decided that they could not be handed back to Tito's people or overtly made use of, and, therefore, the only other alternative was to disarm and intern them as surrendering combatants in the Yugoslav civil war. On 17 April, SOE had reported to the FO that the Domobrans were stronger than the Partisans in Slovenia, but in the event of reinforcements from Croatia for the latter, there was likely to be a blood-bath. It therefore made sense for the Domobrans to head for the British, rather than wait. Orme Sargent did not think that there were any of Mihailović's forces among those heading for the north, as they were last heard of bottled up in southern Bosnia, where Mihailović had gone after leaving Serbia in September 1944. But in the following April, General Damjanović, who had been Nedić's *chef de cabinet* while covertly retaining loyalty to Mihailović, and had subsequently been made commander of the Yugoslav Home Army units in Slovenia, also began to move west.[55] This was probably more in hope of linking up with the Americans than the British, an idea proposed by McDowell before he left. At a meeting with Major Radovan Milinkovich, a Chicago-born Yugoslav who was Wartime Intelligence Chief on Mihailović's Staff, McDowell suggested, after hearing of the westward moves of the Red Army, that the Mihailović forces might yet win the political victory although they had lost the civil war. This could be achieved with American backing if they concentrated on fighting the communists, whom the Americans now perceived as a major threat.[56] McDowell proposed that if Mihailović could establish a government at Banja Luka, the Americans would recognize this as the legitimate government of Yugoslavia, as opposed to Tito's AVNOJ, and provide support as their troops moved in from the west.[57] These proposals were at odds with British and official American policy: it is unlikely that McDowell was acting independently, in which case the proposal probably originated with the anti-communist Donovan. In the event, it came to nothing as Mihailović was unable to reach Banja Luka, and the Americans never came anywhere near the town either. While in Serbia, McDowell held joint talks with Mihailović and Starker, chief adviser to Neubacher, German special envoy to south-eastern Europe, with a view to securing the surrender of the Germans in Yugoslavia through a special Anglo-US mission—presumably so that the 'Nationalist' forces McDowell supported could forget about the Germans and concentrate upon the communists. This apparently bore no fruit because the Germans did not care for the terms, but would have failed in any case because it was not in line with Allied policy towards German capitulation.

The Germans in Italy surrendered on 29 April: it was a purely military affair—Macmillan had kept out of the way in case the Soviets should suspect that political deals were being made. Himmler's offer of German surrender to the Western Allies only had already been refused. The remnants of the German forces in the east, fearful of falling into Soviet hands, all made their way west to surrender to the Americans and British. In addition to the 100,000 prisoners in Italy, the Western Allies were attempting to cope with almost 400,000 German troops trying to surrender in southern Austria.[58]

The Allies lost the race for Venezia Giulia: Tito's troops arrived in the centre of Trieste on 1 May, one day ahead of the New Zealand Second Division, and on 3 May the Partisans took Fiume. While negotiations over Venezia Giulia were being conducted with Tito, he was attempting another *fait accompli* by moving his forces into southern Carinthia, in a bid to add that province to Yugoslavia too. This time the Western Allies won the race, arriving at Klagenfurt a matter of hours before the partisans; nevertheless, the latter continued to pour into the area in an attempt to gain control. Everyone seemed to be converging on the same corner of southern Europe: the Western Allies, the Partisans, the surrendering Germans—along with Russians and Cossacks who had been fighting with them— Domobrans, chetniks, Ustashas, and straightforward refugees who, for various reasons, feared the communist takeover in Yugoslavia. Added to these were the Soviets and Bulgarians, the latter having switched sides after the Red Army arrived in Bulgaria in early September 1944. To complicate the situation further, the British commanders were now contemplating the possibility of having to fight against the partisans to make them leave. This was not an appealing prospect with the Soviets so close, the Americans hanging back, and their own forces believing first that the war was ended, and second that Tito's partisans were such wonderful allies. Although both political and military leaders had become increasingly disillusioned with—and wary of—Tito, the fact had not been made public, and propaganda had continued to portray the Yugoslav Partisans as brave brothers-in-arms. The majority of the military who had fought their way up the western side of the Adriatic were unaware that they had been engaged in a race with the Partisans. After VE Day on 8 May 1945, there was a general expectation that the European war was all but at an end, and no one had an appetite for a fresh round of conflict in Europe. There was also the recent experience in Greece to be borne in mind: the conflict there between British forces and the communist resistance had caused much controversy in Britain.

There had been various, largely inconclusive discussions during 1944 on what the future might hold for SOE. As the war came to an end and the prelude to the cold war began to look just as dangerous, SOE's final role was transformed into one of damage-limitation and tidying up. One of the earliest arrivals in Klagenfurt was Peter Wilkinson, head of SOE's 'Sixth Force', which Barker describes as a "platoon-sized private army",[59] the members of which were people recruited for the Clowder mission. These 'politically aware and polylingual' officers Wilkinson felt would be ideal for sorting out the complexities and confusion he foresaw that British corps commanders would be faced with in southern Austria. In the longer term Wilkinson conceived No 6 Special Force as SOE's post-war incarnation, he envisaged 'a sort of political reconnaissance unit and action group for special operations in the British Zone of Occupation' in the immediate aftermath of hostilities.[60] Wilkinson left Klagenfurt after five days, leaving his 'private army' to do the tidying up, which included organizing the repatriation of large numbers of the Yugoslavs who had come over the border to seek British protection. Many of the disarmed forces were sent back across the Yugoslav borders in closed trains, under the impression that they were bound for Italy, only to find the Partisans waiting at the journey's end. The fate of those returnees—who were shot and flung into mass graves—was well publicized during the Aldington-Tolstoy libel case in 1989. The SOE officers who provided liaison between the British army and the Partisans in May 1945 testified that they had no idea that they were sending these people to their death; they thought those accused of war crimes would have a proper trial and that the others would be 're-educated' by the Partisans.[61] Perhaps they really did believe this at the time, but others on the spot were not quite so optimistic. Arthur Marlow of ISLD says that what awaited those being sent back was certainly common knowledge among the secret organizations, and Wilkinson himself later implied this in his *Foreign Fields*.

One aspect of the whole shabby episode has never properly been explained: this is *why* the British returned the Yugoslavs when most did not come within the terms of the Yalta agreement. Nicolai Tolstoy, who did much original and far-reaching research for his *The Minister and the Massacres*, is certain that it was the product of a conspiracy, although it is difficult to understand what would be the motivation of those he accuses of masterminding this. Darko Bekić has also done much research into the topic, and disagrees with Tolstoy's conspiracy theory.[62] There was certainly more than enough confusion in the area in May 1945 for the tragic episode to have been yet another blunder. Whichever it was, the Partisans saw the makings of a conspiracy. They apparently murdered the repatriated people—estimated at 24,000—not simply for revenge, but also out of suspicion that the British had sent them back as a fifth column, to undermine the fledgling communist state. Perhaps that was the intention of Wilkinson's private army: the displaced persons could not be used to fight directly against Tito, but they might at least have been seen as potentially useful for causing confusion and chaos in north-western Yugoslavia when returned in such large numbers. Although this seems unlikely, if that was the plan, why disarm them?

The British did not have to fight their erstwhile Yugoslav allies. Tito's forces withdrew from Carinthia a few weeks later, probably due to lack of support for their claims to the province from the Soviets. King Peter never returned to Yugoslavia. Šubašić's participation in the Yugoslav government was short-lived; he resigned in October 1945. In the Yugoslav election on 11 November 1945 the 'Popular Front' swept to victory, thanks to the fact that the CPY controlled the army, secret police and militia. The resultant Constituent Assembly proclaimed the Federal People's Republic of Yugoslavia, made up of six republics: Croatia, Slovenia, Serbia, Bosnia-Herzegovina, Macedonia and Montenegro, and within Serbia Vojvodina and Kosovo became autonomous territories. In 1946 Mihailović was captured, put on trial in Belgrade, and executed. The question of Venezia Giulia was finally settled in 1954. SOE was wrapped up shortly after the end of the war, its functions—and records—reabsorbed by SIS.

CONCLUSION

SOE was created when British ability to act decisively against the Axis was limited by both physical and psychological factors. It might have seemed a good idea at the time, although there were many who doubted it from the start, but the whole concept was deeply flawed. The idea of creating secret armies was all very well in theory, but considering that the British were hard pressed to supply their own forces at that stage of the war, it was over-optimistic to say the least. The idea of fomenting chaos and revolution to disturb the Axis occupation totally disregarded the consequences for the people in Europe who were supposed to stir up this chaos. Finally the concept of the whole anti-Axis population in Europe being directed and guided by SOE to dovetail their activity with British war-aims totally ignored the fact that those people might have their own ideas of how to resist—or survive—occupation and of how they wanted to organize their political systems after the war. All of these shortcomings are apparent in SOE's involvement with wartime Yugoslavia.

SOE's whole *raison d'être*, and justification for its existence, was constantly to be 'doing something'. After a rather fallow period following the overrunning of most of Europe by the Axis, when the majority of SOE agents had to make a rather ignominious retreat, the Yugoslav uprisings in the summer of 1941 provided them with an opportunity to 'do something' there. Unfortunately, due to lack of resources—particularly aeroplanes—and, to a certain degree, lack of personnel, the 'something they could do' was very limited. The first tentative missions into Yugoslavia reflect the lack of experience and organization in the initial stages of SOE's active existence.

In the early days of the war Yugoslavia played no part in British strategic thinking: there was a brief flurry of interest at the time of the coup d'état, and again at the time of the uprisings. Other than that, the legend of Mihailović and his brave resistance movement was Yugoslavia's main contribution to the waging of the war as far as the British military were concerned. It was due to the image that had been created for Mihailović—which was one he never wanted—that the FO encouraged, or even pressed, the YGE to make him their minister of war. At the time the one SOE officer in Yugoslavia was incommunicado, and SOE was still trying to make contact with other elements of resistance. British recognition of Mihailović was based entirely on political, not military, grounds.

In late 1941 and during the first half of 1942, Mihailović admirably suited British needs. Regardless of the reality in Yugoslavia, he provided useful propaganda to encourage the British public and those inside 'Fortress Europe'. His policy of building a secret organization that could be called upon when needed was sensible. Although immediately following the summer uprisings London SOE had been keen to encourage active resistance, the repressive German response had knocked the revolt on the head, and SOE's attitude to Yugoslav resistance reverted to encouraging sabotage rather than armed rebellion, especially after Selborne took over from Dalton in February 1942. Mihailović was also viewed as a bastion of order and continuity compared with the perceived threat of chaos posed by the communist movement.

Mihailović and his 'secret army' could have been left quietly alone to do small acts of untraceable sabotage and keep up the spirits of their own people and those of the rest of occupied Europe if it had not been for the developing paranoia of the British about the Soviets. In response to the Soviet propaganda campaign against Mihailović and his followers in the summer of 1942, the FO appeared to expect the Yugoslav minister of war actually to live up to the image that had been created, and were sadly disappointed to discover it was a false one. Mihailović was not a super-hero, ready to throw himself and his followers against the might of the Axis regardless of the cost. The YGE and its minister of war had their own conception of how opposition to the Axis should be carried out; it was essentially a defensive policy, to spare the civilians—particularly the Serbs—from unnecessary loss so that they would still be there and still have the strength to oppose the occupiers when it was sensible to make a major move. Some of the BLOs who went into Serbia in 1943 agreed with this policy; they felt that the scale of reprisals carried out by the Germans in retaliation for acts of sabotage that had little long-lasting effect held the danger of totally demoralizing the population.

The increased action that the FO wanted Mihailović's people to carry out held no long-term benefit for Yugoslavia; in fact, although portrayed as being of use to the Allies in North Africa, its main purpose was to mollify the Soviets. By the time Bailey arrived to pull the chestnuts out of the fire, it was almost too late to do so: the quarrel with Hudson, the failure to provide any reasonable amount of military supplies, and the arrival of the totally unsuitable and disruptive Robertson-Radojević, had already led Mihailović to question the wisdom of getting involved with SOE. Bailey *might* have been able to save the situation if SOE had the capacity to provide adequate—or even just more—aid after his arrival. As it was, Bailey was left trying to obtain more from Mihailović than the latter thought reasonable to give, without being able to produce the level of support that might have overcome the detrimental effect of reprisals. By the time that SOE had increased manpower and resources available, it was turning away from Mihailović and towards the Partisans.

Tito and the Partisans, despite attempts to contact them, had the good fortune during the early part of the war *not* to have an SOE mission attached to them. Although they later complained that they had been ignored and received no help from any quarter while they continued their struggle alone, they were able to make their mistakes out of sight of SOE. While Hudson and Bailey sent long and sometimes conflicting reports about Mihailović and company, which veered from the totally positive to the totally negative, the partisans went about achieving their own particular aims unreported. When SOE eventually made contact with the partisan movement it had toned down its extreme revolutionary character—with a few sharp prods from Moscow—and had transformed itself into a national liberation movement. As a result, Cairo SOE was able to describe it as a predominantly military organization which, although headed by communists, was mainly composed of people who were essentially politically moderate. The idea that SOE missions with the Partisans would enable the British to capitalize on their military prowess, while possibly guiding the rank and file towards a more democratic future, entirely missed the basic nature of Partisan resistance. The very reason that they were more active than Mihailović's forces was that they were engaged in a revolution.

From the middle of 1942, British policy towards Yugoslav resistance was increasingly governed by the relationship with the USSR. The continuing postponement of the second front in western Europe left the Western Allies vulnerable to charges of bad faith from the hard-pressed Soviets who felt they were bearing the brunt of the war in the bloody battles on the eastern front. This factor raised the spectre of a separate peace if the Allies could not provide some relief for the Soviets. With the continuing Soviet propaganda campaign against Mihailović, the FO and the British military also became increasingly worried about being at odds with the USSR over Yugoslavia. What the British were unaware of was that the Soviets were also prey to the same fears of a separate peace and, certainly in the early stages of the war, of Tito fomenting social revolution in Yugoslavia, which they felt would put them at odds with the west. That was one of the reasons why Tito was instructed to co-operate with the nationalist resistance and concentrate on fighting the common enemy rather than play politics. The Soviets, however, had a better poker-face than the British, constantly denying any contact with, or control over the Yugoslav partisans. Everyone knew that this was not true, but seemed unable to do anything about it in the face of denial or silence. However, the British might have paused to wonder why it was that the Soviets made no attempts to send an official mission to the Partisans until long after SOE had contacted them, established missions and commenced large-scale supply of military aid. The Soviet mission only arrived once the British had decided—and declared—that they were abandoning Mihailović. It is also rather ironic that at the very moment that SOE was establishing its early missions with the Partisans the Soviets were advising Tito to conserve his forces for future 'decisive action'—the self-same policy that the British were so bitterly critical of when espoused by the YGE and Mihailović.

The idea that switching support from Mihailović to Tito was the result of a communist plot in Cairo SOE has been extensively dealt with by both David Martin's *Web of Disinformation* and Michael Lees' *Rape of Serbia*. James Klugmann, a communist and apparently a long-time Soviet agent, has long been suspected of being the master-mind of these machinations. In addition to Klugmann, there were plenty of fellow-travellers who were inclined to support the com-munist resistance rather than that recognized by the royalist gov-ernment. This was also the case in other organizations where the pro-Tito climate was as strong as—or even stronger than—that in Cairo SOE: MO4 could not have put over the idea of supporting the Partisans without the complicity of ISLD, PWE and the BBC.

In addition, as the war progressed, it became not only a fight *against* fascism, but a fight *for* a brave new world, particularly for the younger people involved. In the process the USSR had ceased to be portrayed as the great eastern menace of the 1920s and 1930s and had become a heroic ally: Stalin moved from being the orchestrator of show trials, purges and persecution and became instead 'Uncle Joe'. It is perhaps not surprising that Mihailović was perceived as representing the old order while Tito appeared to be surging for-ward to this brave new world. By a combination of plotting and prejudice a situation developed in which all the cards were stacked in favour of Tito and the Partisans.

Nevertheless, all the plotting and colouring of opinion in Cairo would have come to nothing without the massed conservative forces of the FO, Churchill and Fitzroy Maclean. While Basil Davidson claims the credit for the 'Children of Light' moving the immovable by setting in motion the plan to contact the Partisans, he misses the point that the FO—because of its nervousness about the Soviets—had been preparing to override London SOE's objections on this point for some considerable time. The FO had begun to contemplate this before Davidson arrived at Cairo SOE. Davidson, and others, have also overestimated the power of SOE to influence Churchill: the information in Keble's memo in early 1943 was *not* a major revelation for the PM, he already had far more information than MO4 from the Enigma material with which he was supplied on a daily basis. What the memo did was to set out neatly the case for utilizing the Partisans at a time when he badly needed extra action in the Balkans which could be linked to the British contri-bution to the war effort in communications with the Soviets. Per-haps the main achievement of MO4 in this case was selecting Deakin as the first official link with Partisan headquarters in order to ensure the continuation of Churchill's attention. In the long-term Deakin was much more influential than Klugmann or any of the other fellow travellers. His reports not only confirmed the idea of the Partisans as a mighty guerrilla force, but also set in train the thought that it was not worthwhile to back both resistance forces and the one to choose was Tito's.

Deakin set the scene, and the tone, which led to Churchill appointing and briefing Fitzroy Maclean as leader of the mission to the Partisans. Although Eden later queried Maclean's judgement and at times wondered what course he was charting with the Partisans—certainly not the one favoured by the FO—in the summer of 1943 the foreign secretary was as eager for Maclean's appointment as the PM, backing him up in overruling Selborne's objections. Maclean was the most unexpected factor of all. Who, in their wildest imaginings, would have foreseen an ex-member of the FO and Conservative MP going all-out to aid the establishment of a communist regime? Certainly the 'Children of Light', whatever else they managed to achieve in terms of cooking the books and slanting the evidence, could not have had any influence in Maclean's appointment. Maclean's instant judgement—that the Partisans were destined to be the future rulers of Yugoslavia—turned into a self-fulfilling prophesy. The ambassador-leader outshone the 'Children of Light' and relegated them to a back-up organization for his mission.

When the idea of backing both sides was first raised, Baker Street had cautioned that this would mean falling between two stools and, inevitably, a choice would have to be made: on political grounds they claimed that this could *only* be Mihailović. They were overruled on the first count by arguments of military necessity, which, in turn had been born out of the relationship with the USSR. They were overruled on the second by the advent of Maclean.

The British military—which also tends to be a rather conservative body—claiming no interest in matters political, pushed for short-term military advantage. In response to the Chiefs of Staff's March 1943 directive, SOE had managed to co-ordinate opposing guerrilla forces in Greece, where the National Bands agreement produced considerable military benefit; the Chiefs of Staff thought that SOE could do the same in Yugoslavia. Although the National Bands agreement was short-lived, it demonstrated that it was possible to make use of both resistance movements: since they could not be united they could at least be run in tandem. This was the thinking behind the telegram they prevailed upon Glenconner to send to Mihailović instructing him to move to the east of the Ibar. It was also why the Chiefs of Staff were in favour of Mihailović being deposed and continuing support of his organization under another leader.

However, the situation in Greece was quite different from that in both Yugoslavia and Albania. The SOE missions in Greece operated as a single unit under the command first of Eddie Myers and then of C.M. Woodhouse, and were not attached to particular rival guerrilla groups. This gave them the advantage of being able to move between groups at will, and of having a single finger on the pulse. Because Woodhouse had an all-round picture of what was going on, he was able to rebut allegations that Zervas was collaborating and, later, that he was refraining from harassing the Germans in the summer of 1944. In the latter case, Woodhouse discovered, Zervas was doing so because he had been instructed by the staff at SOE to conserve his forces for the final push.[1] In addition, Greece was strategically more important to Britain than Yugoslavia, and ultimately short-term military advantage was not allowed to take precedence over long-term political interests.

In contrast to Greece, there were two distinct missions in Yugoslavia, operating independently and employing two distinct styles of liaison. Maclean, supported by SOE Cairo/Bari, at times seems to have functioned as the Partisans' ambassador to Churchill rather than the other way about. He appears to have been ready to offer total support to the Partisans without making any serious attempt to gain anything in return for aid and political recognition. At the other end of the scale was Armstrong's mission, which was more or less disastrous from the outset, not least due to the failure of back-up and the sometimes bizarre activity of Cairo SOE and the BBC. The differences between the two missions was compounded by the fact that there was no liaison or communication between them; the original plan when the two high-level missions were being organized, which envisaged close co-operation and co-ordination between the two, went out of the window as soon as Maclean arrived in Yugoslavia.

By the time that the Chiefs of Staff wanted to continue to make use of Mihailović's putative successor, Maclean's opinions on the future of Yugoslavia had superseded the policy of backing both sides. Having asserted that the communists would be the dominant factor in Yugoslavia, he advised that the only possible course for the British government was to be with them not against them. The fund of goodwill built up by giving Tito all-out support, he argued, would assure a continuation of British influence in post-war Yugoslavia. He also painted a picture of a reconstituted federal Yugoslavia, in which the divisions between the various groups would be healed because of the multi-ethnic composition of the partisan movement.

The FO had never fluctuated in its aim of reconstituting Yugoslavia after the war; otherwise, it was felt, the small states that would emerge would not be strong enough to survive on their own. By 1943 it was obvious that Mihailović could not deliver this: the accusations of narrow Pan-Serbism were not justified on a personal level, but the actions of some of his commanders and advisers left him open to this. Serbia was perceived by the FO—and by Tito— to be the lynch-pin of Yugoslavia. This was the terrible dilemma: Tito had the military potential, while Mihailović held Serbia. The FO agonized over the question: despite Maclean's exaggerated claims for Partisan strength in Serbia, and attempts by SOE to build them up there, the Partisans had only a limited constituency in Serbia. By the time that Eden and Churchill began to become seriously concerned about communism being imposed on Serbia, it was rather late in the day. The combination of Ratweek and the Red Army settled the question.

Being minister of war was a major drawback for Mihailović: the post had been thrust upon him largely because of the early propaganda campaign. He was certainly not a politician, by contrast with Tito whose greatest asset was his political skill and ability to see— and take—the clearest path to achieving his political ends. Nevertheless Mihailović took his role as minister of war seriously, and felt, probably in an exaggerated way, that he was actually in command of the various local leaders who remained loyal to the king. His dealings with his SOE liaison officers was also coloured by the fact that he was the official representative of his own government in his own country, and therefore entitled to follow his own path. This did not make the relationship any easier; the BLOs noted that because of his position Mihailović felt that he could do what he wanted, assuming that all would be forgiven and his reputation redeemed by the *Ustanak*. If the Allies had planned an invasion of Yugoslavia, this might have been the case: as it was, Mihailović—in conjunction with the YGE—was still following a policy that had long ceased to be considered useful.

For their part the commanders, particularly those outside Serbia, while willing to acknowledge Mihailović as the representative of the king, did not necessarily come under his direct control—some because they were at too great a distance, others because they wanted to run their own show. The arrangements, some of them made with the Axis forces, left Mihailović open to accusations of collaboration. Whether he approved of their actions or not, he was constrained to retain their loyalty so that he would have them available to secure the country for the king at the time of the *Ustanak*. He could not afford to follow the advice proffered by SOE and denounce them to save his own reputation. In cases where he *did* approve their actions, it was at the behest of the YGE and *after* he had lost faith in the British following the debâcle in the aftermath of the Italian armistice.

When the time came for the parting of the ways, this proved to be extremely useful. The British abandoned Mihailović because he would not fall in with their plans to fight the occupiers, but it could not be admitted that he was being thrown over simply because he was not as active as the Partisans. While Cairo SOE claimed to have evidence of Mihailović's collaboration, the FO was never convinced of it. Nevertheless, when support was switched to Tito the publicly stated reason was that some of his commanders had been in collaboration with the enemy. This was probably enough to establish the idea of guilt by association in the mind of the British public to justify the transformation from super-hero to has-been. The British, who were fortunate enough not to have to live under occupation, were probably unable to distinguish between collaboration and accommodation. The publicly projected image of occupied people fell neatly into two divisions: collaborators, who were shabby misfits often motivated by monetary gain, and—the majority—

brave, self-sacrificing and displaying all the traits of the English conception of fair play. A good example of this is the 1943 film *The Hangman Also Dies*, a fictionalized account of the assassination of Heydrich (and the only screenplay by Bertold Brecht), in which the citizens of Czechoslovakia—from well-heeled intelligentsia to peasant vegetable vendor—were portrayed as enormously good and brave. It was a good film to fortify the resolve people on the home front, but a million miles from the reality of occupied Europe.

Had Britain been occupied there would have been no shortage of Pétains or Nedićs, but no-one was willing to acknowledge that at the time. The only British who did come under occupation were the Channel Islanders; instances of their collaboration were later swept under the carpet as unsuitable for public consumption. White-hall documents released on 1 December 1992 revealed the extent of collaboration between the administrations of Jersey and Guernsey and the occupiers, and the fact that no action had been taken against those involved.

Glenconner's warning in late 1942 that to attempt to back both sides would merely serve to fan the flames of civil war proved to be totally accurate. By the time that SOE was operating with the two resistance movements in Yugoslavia, both Mihailović and Tito were well aware that the Germans were ultimately heading for defeat, and accordingly both set about winning the civil war. Mihailović was determined to ensure that the communists would not take over when the occupation ended, while Tito was equally determined to complete the revolution and be in a position to establish a commu-nist state. For all the debate over long-term political interests being sacrificed to short-term military ones, the British did not in fact obtain very much in terms of the latter. The main beneficiary was the German occupier. The deception plan did little in the way of drawing German troops away from the Russian front, and the Ger-mans who were in Yugoslavia could almost sit back and allow their opponents to do their job for them. When either side actually did engage them, the Germans stood a fair chance of the opposing side attacking the attackers in the rear. The Germans were able to take advantage of the civil war right to the end, when they facilitated the movement of Mihailović's forces and the rag-bag of other anti-communists to the north-western borders; the conflict this pro-duced allowed them to continue their orderly retreat.

Once Tito had been recognized and began to receive material aid, he concentrated most of his energy on his domestic rivals, particularly on the drive to get back into Serbia. By the time Churchill woke up to what Tito was really about, it was too late to make another about-turn. Apart from the problem of getting the public to swallow such a move for the second time, there was also the proximity of the Red Army. To challenge Tito at that late stage would have been tantamount to throwing down the gauntlet to Stalin, whose true colours had also become more visible at the time of the Warsaw uprising. In addition, Churchill was more concerned about the future of Greece, in which British interests were much stronger than Yugoslavia; he needed Stalin to stick by the 90 per cent–10 per cent agreement there, and as Tito's new state was independent—after all, it was Churchill who had laid the foundations for the Tito-Šubašić agreement—he could not claim that Yugoslavia had turned out to be other than '50–50'. It was all very well for Churchill to say that SOE had cooked the books and that he had been misled,[18] but his own misplaced faith in Tito and his personal involvement in trying to establish a hybrid monarchist-communist system in Yugoslavia could hardly be laid at the door of SOE.

The same pattern of high expectation—particularly that inherent in the original concept of SOE, that they could organize and deliver the required outcome from resistance movements—is visible in the relationship with both Mihailović and Tito. Having failed to bend Mihailović to their will, SOE in Cairo put forward the idea that a few British officers on the spot could solve all the problems and maximize the potential of the communist resistance. Laying aside the implications of conspiracy, the fact that this idea found credence is indicative of the echoes of imperialism that are to be found in the whole philosophy of SOE. Decisions were taken by all British bodies concerned which would affect the future of the people of Yugoslavia without any reference to the aspirations of those people themselves.

At the end of the war most of the British who had helped turn a collection of hardy and hunted guerrillas into a government went home, leaving the people of Yugoslavia to make what they could of Tito's concept of democracy. They were all rather quiet until 1948, when the Tito-Stalin break allowed them to claim that their judgement had been vindicated. Tito was a good chap after all; they had been right in thinking that he was his own man and not Moscow's. Over the succeeding years the 'Tito fans' found their way into print, and established what Mike Lees termed 'the received wisdom'. Tito, always the consummate politician, came back into the fold.

NOTES

Chapter 1   Swashbucklers and Secret Agents

1. Christopher, Andrews, *Secret Service*, Heineman, London 1985, pp. 379–421.
2. Kim Philby, *My Silent War*, MacGibbon & Kee, London 1968, p. 4.
3. Bickham Sweet-Escott *Baker Street Irregular*, Methuen, London 1965. p. 17.
4. Peter Wilkinson, *Foreign Fields*, I.B. Tauris, London 1997, pp. 56–7.
5. Andrews, *Secret Service*, pp. 445–7.
6. WP(49)168, CAB 66/7 discussed at WM(40)141 of 27 May 1940, CAB 65/13.
7. Ben Pimlott, ed., *The Second World War Diary of Hugh Dalton, 1941–45*, Cape, London 1986, p. 52.
8. Ben Pimlott, *Hugh Dalton*, Cape, London 1985, pp. 281–98.
9. Sweet-Escott, *Baker Street Irregular*, pp. 40–1.
10. Peter Wilkinson and Joan Bright Astley, *Gubbins and SOE*, Leo Cooper, London 1993, p. 76.
11. *The Memoirs of Lord Gladwyn*, Weidenfeld and Nicolson, London 1972, p. 101.
12. Ivor Porter, *Operation Autonomous*, Chatto & Windus, London 1989, p. 67.
13. Interview with Archie Jack, Haute-Savoie, June 1988.
14. George Taylor Papers, King's College London.
15. Churchill to Ismay, 10 Feb. 1944, PREM 3 185/1.
16. Interview with Pamela Bisdee, member of SIS in Cairo and Bari, Midhurst 9 Sep. 1986.
17. 'SOE Activities in Yugoslavia', 31 Dec. 1940, FO371/30212.
18. Pimlott, *Hugh Dalton*, pp. 320–45.
19. *Memoirs of Lord Gladwyn*, p. 102.
20. Wilkinson, *Foreign Fields*, p. 186.

Chapter 2   Doing something in the Balkans

1. Porter, *Operation Autonomous*, p. 32.
2. Maurice Pearton, *Oil and the Romanian State*, Clarendon Press, Oxford 1971, p. 249.
3. Frank G. Weber *The Evasive Neutral*, University of Missouri, Columbia 1979, pp. 5–6.
4. David Dilks, ed. *The Diaries of Sir Alexander Cadogan*, Cassell, London 1971, p. 166, note.

5. Terence Shone, Memorandum on Yugoslav Foreign Policy, 4 Nov. 1939, FO371/23885.

6. Charles Richardson, *Flashback*, William Kimber, London 1985, p. 93.

7. *Ciano's Diary*, Heineman, London 1947.

8. Campbell to Halifax, 10 April 1939, FO371/238830.

9. Shone to Halifax, 11 Aug. 1939, FO371/23885.

10. Bailey to Maxwell, 24 Nov. 1941 HS5/875.

11. Campbell to FO, 10 Aug. 1940, HS5/928.

12. Jebb to Cadogan, 16 Aug. 1940, HS5/928.

13. Campbell-FO correspondence, 25 July–3 Aug. 1940, HS5/928.

14. P. Dixon, Activities in Yugoslavia, 23 Aug. 1940, HS5/928.

15. Nelson to Jebb, 1 April 1940, HS5/928.

16. Basil Davidson, *Special Operations Europe*, Gollancz, London 1980, pp. 78–9.

17. Campbell to Hopkinson and Cadogan, 18 Oct. 1940, HS5/928.

18. Sweet-Escott, *Baker Street Irregular*, p. 24.

19. P. Dixon, minute on 'Yugoslavia and the War', 20 Nov. 1940, FO371/25034.

20. Sargent to Jebb. 15 Nov. 1940, HS5/928.

21. Pimlott, *The Diary of Hugh Dalton*, p. 139.

22. Taylor 'Certain Activities in Yugoslavia', 24 June 1941, gives a complete account of all his activities in Belgrade, George Taylor's Papers.

23. Louis Hagan, ed, *The Schellenberg Memoirs*, André Deutsch, London 1956, pp. 190–7.

24. Philip Nichols, memo, 8 Nov. 1940, FO371/25034.

25. Ilija Jukić, *The Fall of Yugoslavia*, Harcourt Brace Jovanovich, New York 1974, p. 57.

26. Nelson to Jebb, 6 Jan. 1941, HS5/928.

27. Dilks, *Diaries of Sir Alexander Cadogan*, p. 365.

28. Interview with Tom Mapplebeck, London, Sep. 1988.

29. Pimlott, *Diary of Hugh Dalton*, p. 178.

30. Dilks, *Diaries of Sir Alexander Cadogan*, p. 336.

31. Nichols to Jebb, 29 Mar. 1941, HS5/928.

32. Cadogan to Churchill, 'Kazan', 21 Feb. 1941, FO371/30212.

33. 'Interference with German Oil Supplies', SOE memo, 8 Jan. 1941, COS(41) 3(0) in CAB 80/56.

34. Campbell to FO, 19 Feb. 1941, FO371/30212.

35. Churchill to Prince Paul, and FO to Campbell, 22 Feb. 1941, FO371/30212.

36. Pimlott, *Diary of Hugh Dalton*, p. 185.

37. Noel-Baker to Eden, 14 Feb. 1941, HS5/928.

38. Davidson, DMI, to Jebb, 31 March 1941, HS5/928.

39. Pimlott, *Diary of Hugh Dalton*, pp. 192–227.

40. Alexander Glen, *Footholds against a Whirlwind*, Hutchinson, London 1975, p. 61.

41. Nelson to Jebb, I July 1941, HS5/928.

42. Bob Dixon to Philip Broad, 3 May 1941, HS5/928.

43. Broad to Nelson, 25 April, HS5/928.

Chapter 3 Return to Occupied Yugoslavia

1. Stevan K. Pavlowitch, *A History of the Balkans*, Longman 1999, p. 314.
2. Orme Sargent minute, 14 Oct. 1941, FO371/30220.
3. George Rendel to Doulas Howard, 29 April 1942, FO371/33455.
4. Howard minute on 'Resistance in Yugoslavia', 6 Oct. 1941, FO371/30220.
5. P. Dixon minute on 'The Yugoslav Government', 14 Sep. 1941, FO371/30292.
6. Sargent, minute, 14 Oct. 1941, FO371/30220.
7. Ralph Murray to P. Dixon, 6 Dec. 1941, FO371/30221.
8. Seton Watson, report 3–10 Nov. 1941, HS5/875.
9. Milan Deroc, *British Special Operations Explored*, Columbia University Press, New York 1988, pp. 35–52, gives a detailed analysis of the revolts and their various causes.
10. Sir R. Campbell, Lisbon, to FO, 25 July 1941, FO371/30214.
11. Dixon to Kirkpatrick, 4 Sep. 1941, FO371/30215.
12. Micheal Stenton, *Radio London and Resistance in Occupied Europe*, Oxford University Press 2000, pp. 323–4.
13. Glenconner to Brooks, 13 Nov. 1941, FO898/157.
14. Jebb to Howard, 2 Dec. 1941, FO371/30221.
15. Julian Amery, *Approach March*, Hutchinson, London 1973, p. 239.
16. Stevan K. Pavlowitch, *Unconventional Perceptions*, pp. 67–105.
17. Deroc, *British Special Operations*, pp. 58–60.
18. Bailey to London SOE, 20 Aug. 1941, HS5/874.
19. SOE Notes for Simović, 8 Sep. 1941, HS5/874.
20. *The Memoirs of Lord Chandos*, Bodley Head, London 1962, p. 239.
21. Pimlott, *Diary of Hugh Dalton*, p. 251.
22. Sweet-Escott, *Baker Street Irregular*, pp. 74–5.
23. Countess of Ranfurly, *To War with Whitaker*, Mandarin paperback, London 1995, pp. 64–100.
24. Artemis Cooper, *Cairo in the War, 1939–1945*, Penguin Books 1995, p. 96.
25. Michael Lees, *The Rape of Serbia*, HBJ, p. 14.
26. Interview with Archie Jack.
27. Sweet-Escott, *Baker Street Irregular*, pp. 75–80.
28. Amery, *Approach March*, p. 246.
29. Interview with Jasper Rootham, Wimborne.
30. Simović to Churchill, 14 Aug. 1941, PREM 3 510/12.
31. Information from Dominic Flessati, Hudson's biographer.
32. Deroc, *British Special Operations*, pp. 200–2.
33. Notes on the two meetings and Ilić's letter, 11 Sep. 1941, HS5/874.
34. SOE notes, 16, 17 and 18 Sep. 1941, HS5/874.
35. D/H70 to D/HV (Pearson) 22 Dec. 1941, HS5/875.
36. Rendel to Eden, 13 Sep. 1941, FO371/30292; 'King Peter of Jugoslavia and General Simović', 19 Sep. 1941, FO371/30265.
37. Amery, *Approach March*, p. 244.
38. Hudson to Cairo, 26 Sep. 1941, WO202/128.

39. Information from Flessati, and Jebb, 'The Rebellion in Yugoslavia', 14 Oct. 1941, HS5/939.
40. Amery, *Approach March*, p. 253.
41. Deroc thesis, chapter 9, p. 11.
42. Hugh Dalton, 'Memorandum on Propaganda', 6 Dec. 1941, FO898/11.

Chapter 4 Backing Mihailović

1. Information from Flessati.
2. Simon Trew, *Britain, Mihailović and the Chetniks, 1941–42*, Macmillan, London, 1998, pp. 62–4.
3. Pavlowitch, *The Balkans*, p. 314.
4. BBC transcript of 'The Sword and the Shield', broadcast 4 Sep. 1984.
5. Hudson 'Series B' Telegrams, April 1943, FO536/31.
6. Christie Lawrence, *Irregular Adventure*, Faber & Faber, London 1947, pp. 227–8.
7. Glenconner to Dixon, 15 Nov. 1941, FO371/30220 and Glenconner to Brig. Brooks, 13 Nov. 1941, FO898/157.
8. Mihailović telegram no. 36, 22 Nov. 1941, WO202/128.
9. 'The Yugoslav Revolt', 26 Nov. 1941, FO371/30221.
10. Deroc, *British Special Operations*, pp. 187–93.
11. Mihailović telegram no. 39, 2 Dec. 1941, WO202/128.
12. Stevan K. Pavlowitch Interview with Hudson, 25 Nov. 1983.
13. 'Message from HMG to Colonel M, to be sent via SOE, 26 Nov. 1941, FO371/30221.
14. Pavlowitch, *Unconventional Perceptions*, p. 74.
15. Mišo Leković, 'Cinjenice o Misiji Majora Terenza Atertona', serialized in *Poltika*, Belgrade 21 May-5 June 1986.
16. C–in–C, Middle East to War Office, 1 Dec. 1941, FO371/30221.
17. Mišo Leković, 'Boravak Britanske Vojne Misije na Oslobobjenoj Teritoriji Crne Gora I Jugoistocne Bosne', *Istoriijski Zapisi*, vol. XXVIII, no. 1–2, Titograd 1971, pp. 301–28.
18. Vladimir Dedijer, *With Tito through the War: Partisan Diary 1941–45*, Hamish Hamilton, London 1951, pp. 71–75.
19. Leković, 'Boravak Britanske'.
20. Ibid.
21. Mihailović telegram no. 197, 24 May 1942, WO202/128.
22. Pavlowitch Papers, information from David Martin 4 Dec. 1976.
23. Leković, 'Boravak Britanske'.
24. Pavlowitch, *Unconventional Perceptions*, pp. 67–105.
25. Correspondence with C.M. Woods, SOE Adviser, FCO, 20 Feb. 1985.
26. SOE War Diary, HS7/266.
27. Pearson to Taylor, 25 July 1942, HS7/266.
28. 'Diary of Events in the Early Stages of the Dispute Concerning the Yugoslav Forces in the Middle East, 11 Jan.–15 Sept. 1942', gives a potted history of the affair, FO371/33461.
29. 'Yugoslav Army Crisis', Sargent minute, 12 March 1942, FO371/33452.

30. Campbell-Sargent correspondence 1 and 16 July 1942, FO371/33490.
31. Rendel to Sargent, 18 July 1942, FO371/33458.
32. Leković, 'Boravak Britanske'.
33. Leković, 'Cinjenice o Misiji'.
34. Rendel to FO, 12 May and Rendel to Howard 27 May 1942, FO371/33455.
35. Jovanović to Rendel, 26 June and Rendel's reply 1 July 1942, FO371/33458.
36. AD to CEO (Jebb), 3 Jan. 1942, HS5/939.
37. Rendel-Howard correspondence, 28 May and 11 June, FO371/33456 and Rendel to Dixon 15 June, Howard to Rendel 24 June 1942, FO371/33457.
38. Report by Col. T Thompson, 28 April 1942, WO208/2014.
39. Pavlowitch, *Unconventional Perceptions*, pp. 103–4.
40. MO4 [Cairo SOE] to Philip Broad, 26 Oct. 1943, WO202/144.
41. Rendel to Howard, 18 and 23 July 1942, FO371/33458.
42. Philby, *My Silent War*, p. 38.
43. Pavlowitch, *Unconventional Perceptions*, pp. 19–21.
44. Eden memo, FO371/33465, and Eden to Churchill 7 Dec. 1941, PREM 3 510/1.
45. Martin Gilbert, *Road to Victory*, Heinemann, London 1986, p. 75.
46. Report by Maj. D. Talbot Rice, MI3b, 15 Mar. 1942, WO208/2014.
47. Report by Col. B.L. Deeds, 18 April 1942, WO208/2014.
48. 'Transmission of Help to General Mihailović', 11 May 1942, FO371/33493.
49. Rendel to Dixon, 28 May and 3 June 1942, FO371/33456.
50. David Stafford, *Camp X*, Viking, London 1987, p. 136.
51. Bailey, 'American Intentions in Europe', 8 Aug. 1942, HS5/939.
52. Dixon to Murray, 18 June 1942, FO898/157.
53. Murray to Kirkpatrick, 21 June 1942, FO898/157.
54. SOE War Diary p. 47, HS7/266.

Chapter 5 Propaganda Wars

1. Geoffrey Swain, 'Tito and the twilight of the Comintern' in *International Communism and the Communist International, 1919–43*, ed. T. Rees and A. Thorpe, Manchester University Press 1998, pp. 205–221.
2. Maj D. Talbot Rice, MI3b, 15 Mar and Capt B L Deeds, 18 Mar 1942, WO208/2014.
3. FO to Kuibyshev, 7 Aug 1942, FO371/33468.
4. Gilbert, *Road to Victory*, pp. 111–20.
5. W.S. Churchill, *The Second World War*, Cassell, London 1948–54, vol. 4, p. 428.
6. Copy of the memo and Eden minute, 7 Aug. 1942, FO371/33490.
7. Aide-Memoire, 3 Aug. 1942 and FO minutes, FO371/33469.
8. Murray to Dixon, 29 Aug. 1942, FO898/157.
9. Eden to Southern Department, 7 Aug. 1942, FO371/33490.
10. 'The Situation in Yugoslavia', 2 June 1942, PREM 3/510/12.
11. A summary of the meeting is given in 'Relations between Gen Mihailović and HMG', Hugh K. Grey, 27 July 1944, FO 371/44276.
12. Pearson to Howard, 20 and 23 Aug. 1942, FO371/33469.

13. Howard's notes, 23 Aug. 1942, FO371/33469.
14. DMI Report & map, 23 Aug. 1942, WO208/2014.
15. Notes on the Partisan-Mihailović Issue, R. Murray, 19 Aug. 1942, FO878/157.
16. J. Costello, *Mask of Treachery*, William Morrow, New York 1985, p. 411.
17. P. Calvocoressi, *Top Secret Ultra*, Cassell, London 1980, pp. 94–5.
18. Pearson to Murray, 'Use of the word Partisans in broadcasts', 23 Sep 1942, FO898/157.
19. For a full account of these misions, see Simon Trew, *Tito, Mihailovic and the Chetniks, 1941–42*, Macmillan, London 1998, chapter 6.
20. Dixon to Pearson, 9 Oct. 1942, FO371/33470.
21. Hambro to Selborne, 22 Dec. 1942, HS5/923.
22. SOE Diary, Sep.–Dec. 1942, HS7/267.
23. SOE Diary, July–Aug. 1942, HS7/266.
24. Pearson Memo on Bailey's mission, 26 Aug. 1942, HS5/939.
25. SOE Diary, p. 2000, HS7/267.
26. Mihailović telegram, 11 Sep. 1942, WO202/128.
27. SOE Diary, pp. 186–7, HS7/267.
28. Sargent, June 1942, FO371/33134.
29. 'Situation in Yugoslavia', 26 March 1942, FO371/33466.
30. Glenconner Report, 18 Nov. 1942, WO202/132A.
31. Dixon to Pearson, 9 Oct. 1942, FO371/33470.
32. Eden to Churchill, 15 Sep. 1944, FO371/33503.
33. Martin van Creveld, *Supplying War*, Weidenfeld & Nicolson, London 1977, pp. 181–201.
34. FO to Moscow, 24 Feb. 1943, FO371/37579.
35. Eg., Mihailović Villa Resta no. 651, 16 Sep. and no. 636, 14 Sep. 1942, WO202/128.
36. Hudson, GESH 229, 230 and 251, 8 Dec 1942, WO202/356.
37. Dixon to Murray, 18 Jun and Murray to Kirkpatrick, 21 Jun 1942, FO898/157.
38. Mihailović, Villa Resta no. 209, 26 May 1942, WO202/128.
39. Eden to Rendel, 11 Dec. 1942, FO371/33503.
40. Rendel, 'General Mihailović, HMG Attitude', 31 Dec. 1942, FO371/37578.
41. St K Pavlowich interview with Boughey, 29 Oct. 1976, Pavlowitch Papers.
42. Brig. C.S. Vale to Gen. M. Radovitch, 1 Dec. 1942, FO371/33474.
43. Eden to Churchill, 17 Dec. 1942, FO371/33474.
44. 'Mihailović-Partisan Dispute', Eden minute 3 Jan., Cadogan minute 4 Jan. 1943, FO371/37578.
45. 'Function of Radio Karageorge', 20 Jan. 1943, FO371/37602.
46. Cairo SOE to Baker Street, 31 Oct. 1942, HS5/929.
47. Selborne—Eden correspondence, 22 Jan. and 2 Feb. 1943, FO371/57578.
48. Bailey to Cairo, 21 Jan. 1943, HS5/923.
49. St K. Pavlowitch, *Tito: Yugoslavia's Great Dictator*, Hurst, London 1992, pp. 35–9.
50. Bailey's reports to Cairo, repeated to London, 21–26 Jan. 1943, HS5/923.
51. Pearson to Hambro, 26 Jan. 1943, HS5/923.

52. Pearson to Dixon, 16 Nov. 1942, FO371/33472.
53. Sargent to W.J. Keswick, 29 Jan. 1943, FO371/37578.
54. Bailey report, 2 Feb. 1943, FO371/37579.

Chapter 6   Yugoslavia, from Side-Show to Centre Stage

1. 'The Balkans', 20 March 1943, COS (43) 142 (0) in CAB 80/68.
2. Klaus Jurgen Muller, 'A German Perspective on Allied Deception Plans in the Second World War', *Intelligence and National Security,* vol. 2, no. 3, July 1987.
3. Jovanović to Rendel, 16 Feb., and FO to Pearson 4 Mar 1943, FO371/37580.
4. Milovan Djilas, *Wartime,* Secker and Warburg, London 1977, pp. 232–44.
5. W.R. Roberts, *Tito, Mihailovic & the Allies,* Rutgers University Press, New Brunswick, NJ 1973, p. 111.
6. Pearson to Howard, 12 Feb. 1943 enclosing Bailey's Review of the Partisans, FO898/157.
7. Glenconner to FO, 28 Feb. 1943, FO371/37580.
8. Pearson to Hambro, 15 Nov. 1942, HS5/929.
9. 'A Short History of the Revolt in Yugoslavia', MI3b, 27 April 1943, WO201/1599.
10. Pearson to Hambro, 13 and 23 Feb. 1943, HS5/923.
11. Pearson to Howard 9 April 1943, enclosing Hudson's Series A and B telegrams, FO536/31.
12. Rendel to Howard, 6 May 1943, FO371/37585.
13. DMI MI3b report, 27 April 1943, WO201/1599.
14. Rendel to Eden, 30 March 1943, FO371/37582.
15. Mihailović to Jovanović, 19 Dec. 1942, FO371/37578.
16. Bailey to Cairo 29 Feb. 1943, HS5/923.
17. HS5/929.
18. DHV to A/DS 23 March 1943, HS5/923 MO4 to Baker Street, 25 March 1943, HS5/923.
19. Interview with Archie Jack.
20. Bailey to Cairo, 16, 22 and 23 March 1943, demonstrate that confusion, FO371/37582.
21. Mihailović to Jonović, 2 and 10 March 1943, FO371/37583.
22. Bailey to Cairo and Hambro to Lockhart, 13 April 1943, FO371/37584.
23. Rendel to Howard, 22 May 1943, FO371/37586.
24. Rendel to Howard, 14 Dec. 1942, FO371/33472.
25. Pearson to Howard, 13 Jan. 1943, FO371/37607.
26. 'SOE Policy towards Yugoslavia', 15 Jan. 1943, FO371/37607.
27. Basil Davidson, *Special Operations Europe,* pp. 141–52.
28. Davidson, Imperial War Museum Sound Archives, 10505/3.
29. Stenton *Radio London,* p. 359.
30. Keble HS5/929.
31. 'Operations in Yugoslavia', 30 Jan. 1943, FO371/37579.
32. HS5/923.
33. Jean Howard, interview with HW; and correspondence 28 Jan. 1981, Pavlowitch Papers.

34. Gilbert, *Road to Victory*, pp. 312–13.
35. Hambro to Sargent, 22 Feb. 1943, FO371/37579.
36. L.C. Hollis 'Support of Operations in Yugoslavia', 11 Feb. 1943, FO371/37579.
37. C.R. Price to Sargent, 7 March 1943, FO371/37581.
38. Baker Street to MO4, 20 Feb. 1943, HS5/923.
39. Hambro to Sargent, 22 Feb., and Sargent to Hambro 23 Feb. 1943, FO371/37579.
40. Glenconner to Baker Street, 30 Jan. 1943, HS5/923.
41. Hambro-Selborne correspondence, 8 March 1943, HS5/923.
42. 'General Mihailović and the Partisans', 6 March and Howard minutes, 13 March 1943, FO371/37581.
43. Bailey's reply to the questionnaire, March 1943, FO371/37582.
44. Pearson to Howard, 12 March 1943, FO371/37581.
45. Keble to Murray, 9 Feb. 1943, WO202/132A.
46. Hambro to Lockhart, 12 April 1943, HS5/924.
47. Rendel to Sargent, 9 March and Rendel to Howard 13 March 1943, FO371/37581.
48. Sargent to Selborne, 7 April 1943, HS5/924.
49. FO, to Moscow, 24 Feb. 1943, FO371/37579.
50. 'General Mihailović and the Resistance in Yugoslavia', 8 March 1943, FO371/37581.
51. Howard to Clark-Kerr, 15 April 1943, FO371/37583.
52. H.L. Baggallay to Clark-Kerr, 17 March 1943, FO371/37583.
53. COS(43) 142(0) in CAB 80/68.
54. 'A Short History of the Revolt in Yugoslavia', MI3b, 27 April 1943, WO201/1599.
55. Selborne to Sargent, 9 April 1943, FO371/37583 and Selborne's comments on Sargent's letter, 7 April in HS5/924.
56. Hambro to Glenconner, 2 April 1943, George Taylor Papers.
57. Howard minute on 'Mihailović-Partisan Conflict', 29 April 1943, FO371/37584.
58. Bailey telegram, 6 April 1943, FO371/37584.

Chapter 7 Contacting the Partisans

1. Information from Flessati.
2. Bailey, 'Note on the Despatch of Captain Charles Robertson to Yugoslavia', 16 July 1946, FO371/59469.
3. SOE Diary, July–Aug. 1942, pp. 48–9, HS7/266.
4. Interview with M. Kolarević, London.
5. SOE Diary, Sep.–Dec. 1942, pp. 235–6 and 291–2, HS7/267.
6. Bailey telegram, 28 Aug. 1943, FO371/37590.
7. Interview with M. Kolarević.
8. Lees, *Rape of Serbia*, p. 49.
9. C.M. Woods, SOE adviser at the FCO, correspondence 5 May 1988.

10. David Stafford, *Camp* X, Viking 1987, pp. 167–201.
11. Lethbridge to St K.P., 2 Feb. 1975, Pavlowitch Papers.
12. Deakin, *The Embattled Mountain*, Oxford University Press, 1971, note p. 209.
13. Nikola Pasić, correspondence, Dec. 1986.
14. Lees, *Rape of Serbia*, p. 17
15. Stafford, *Camp* X, p. 176.
16. Alexander Simic-Stevens, 'Pathfinder Fungus', *Journal of the British-Yugoslav Society*, winter 1984 and spring 1985
17. Pasić correspondence
18. Dedijer *With Tito*, p. 302–3.
19. Dušan Biber, 'The CPY and its attitude to England', paper presented at the Imperial War Museum, Dec. 1982.
20. Deakin, *Embattled Mountain*, pp. 219–21.
21. Interview with Jasper Rootham, Wimborne, 2 Jun. 1988.
22. Deakin, *Embattled Mountain*, pp. 214–16.
23. ibid.
24. Morton to Sargent, 8 June 1943, FO371/39609.
25. Deakin, *Embattled Mountain*, p. 216.
26. Pearson to Howard, 25 May 1943, FO371/37586.
27. Yugoslavia: AH31 and the Partisans, 11 June 1943, HS5/924.
28. MO4 to Bailey, 24 May, FO371/37586.
29. AD1 to CD, 26 and 30 May 1943, HS5/924.
30. 'SOE Activities in Yugoslavia', 10 June 1943, FO371/37608 and 'General Mihailovic', 15 June 1943, FO371/37588.
31. Bailey to MO4, 29 May, and MO4 to Bailey, 31 May 1943, FO371/37586.
32. 'Yugoslav Directive to General Mihailovic', 11 May 1943, FO371/37585.
33. 'General Mihailović', Howard minute, 15 June 1943, FO371/37588.
34. Rendel to Dixon, 8 June 1943, FO371/37587.
35. Mihailović to Jovanović, 29 May 1943, FO371/37587.
36. Rendel to Sargent, 10 June 1943, FO371/37609.
37. Howard minute, on 'Situation in Yugoslavia', 10 June 1943, FO371/37609.
38. Richard Casey to Admiral Cunningham, enclosing the report, 1 June 1943, PREM 3/510/7.
39. Morton to Sargent, 8 June 1943, FO371/37609.
40. Morton to Rowan, 15 June 1943, PREM 3/510/7.
41. Selborne to Churchill, 18 June 1943, PREM 3/510/7.
42. Churchill to L.C. Hollis, 23 June 1943, PREM 3/510/7.
43. L.C. Hollis to Sargent, enclosing 'Extract from COC Meeting, 6 May 1943', FO371/37585.
44. Morton to Rendel, 8 June and Howard minute on 'Yugoslavia', 21 June 1943, FO371/37609.
45. Eden to Churchill, 24 June 1943, PREM 3/510/13.
46. COS to MEDC, 27 June 1943, PREM 3/510/13.
47. Biber, 'The CPY and England'.
48. Interview with Pamela Bisdee, Syers' former wife.
49. Dedijer, *With Tito*, 8 June, p. 328.

50. Deakin, *Embattled Mountain*, p. 62.
51. Dedijer, *With Tito*, p. 360.
52. Deakin to MO4, 12 Sep. 1943, HS5/960.
53. Interview with Sir William Deakin, London, 23 Sep. 1988.
54. Basil Davidson, *Partisan Picture*, Bedford Books, London 1946, p. 12.
55. Lees, *Rape of Serbia*, p. 217.

Chapter 8   Tuning up the Balkans

1. Sweet-Escott, *Baker Street Irregular*, pp. 164–5.
2. Interview with Archie Jack.
3. Interview with Arthur Marlow, Eastborne.
4. SOE Diary, Oct.–Dec. 1943, HS7/271.
5. Gubbins and 'C', notes of meeting, 23 June 1943, HS7/270.
6. D/HV to AD6, 4 April 1943, HS5/940.
7. SOE Diary, July–Aug. 1942, pp. 8–9, HS7/266.
8. SOE Diary, pp. 154–6, HS7/267.
9. SOE Diary, p. 839, HS7/270.
10. SOE Diary, p. 199, HS7/267.
11. Interview with Archie Jack.
12. Interview with Jasper Rootham.
13. Interview with M. Kolarević.
14. Lees, *Rape of Serbia*, pp. 135–45.
15. Greenwood, Imperial War Museum, Dept of Sound Archives, Tape 11374/4.
16. Wilkinson, *Foreign Fields*, p. 148.
17. Jasper Rootham Diary, Tonbridge School Library.
18. Fungus to Cairo, 17 Oct. 1943, WO202/140.
19. SOE Diary, July–Sep. 1943, pp. 766–8, HS7/270.
20. Simić-Stevens, 'Pathfinder Fungus'.
21. Selborne to Eden, 6 Aug. 1943, FO371/37589.
22. Bailey to Cairo, 6 July 1943, FO371/37589.
23. C.M. Woods, FCO, correspondence 5 Jan. 1988.
24. CD to Sargent, 6 Sep. 1943, enclosing telegrams between Bailey and Cairo, FO371/37590.
25. CD to VCD (Hambro to Sporborg), 21 June 1943, 'Directive to Deakin of 20 May 1943', HS5/924.
26. Howard to Pearson, 12 Aug. 1943, HS5/960.
27. Correspondence with S. Johnson.
28. Jasper Rootham Diary.
29. Wilkinson, *Foreign Fields*, p. 148.
30. Bailey to Cairo, 5 July 1943, HS7/270.
31. Rootham Diary.
32. Bailey, via Cairo to Baker Street, 16 July 1943, HS5/960.
33. Lees, *Rape of Serbia*, p. 169.
34. Lindsay Rogers, *Guerrilla Surgeon*, p. 180.
35. Turnpike via Pikestaff to Cairo, 20 Oct. 1943, WO202/140.

36. Mansfield and Seitz, In Op Log, 17 Nov. 1943, FO371/37618.
37. Angelica to Cairo, 30 Oct. 1943, In Op Log, WO202/148.
38. Sehmer War Diary, WO202/162.
39. Rootham Diary, 27 and 28 Aug. 1943.
40. Cairo to Bailey, 17 Aug. 1943, FO371/37611.
41. Interview with Archie Jack.
42. Porter, *Operation Autonomous*, pp. 85–6.
43. Sweet-Escott, *Baker Street Irregular*, pp. 194–5.
44. SOE Diary, 'Slovenia', Howard to Boughey, 16 June; Pearson to Hambro, 6 July; note on meeting 19 Jul. 1943, pp. 760–2, HS7/270.
45. Wilkinson, *Foreign Fields*, p. 135.
46. SOE Diary, July–Sep. 1943, HS7/270.
47. MO4 to Baker Street, 16 July 1943, HS5/960.
48. Deakin to Cairo, series of telgrams, late Aug. 1943, HS5/960.

Chapter 9   Backing Both Sides: Two Brigadiers and 'Equal Support'

1. Keble to Glenconner, 16 Jun. 1943, HS5/924.
2. Sargent to Sir F. Bovenschen, 27 Jun. 1943, FO371/37609.
3. 'Brief for Captain Fitzroy Maclean' (undated, Jul. 1943), FO371/37590; 'Brief for Colonel Maclean', 20 Jul. 1943, FO371/37610.
4. P. Auty and R. Clogg, eds, *British Policy towards Wartime Resistance in Yugoslavia and Greece*, Macmillan, London 1976, p. 222.
5. Nicholas Brashaw, a postgraduate research student in the History Department at Southampton University, argues that Maclean was a red herring, used by Churchill to ensure the safety of the Enigma secret.
6. Churchill to Eden, 28 July 1943, Eden to Selborne 2 Aug. 1943, FO371/37610.
7. SOE Diary, 31 July 1943, HS7/270.
8. Selborne to Eden, 5 Aug. and FO minute, 1 Aug. 1943, FO371/37610.
9. Hambro to Cairo, 3 July and Bailey to Cairo 6 July 1943, FO371/37589.
10. Selborne to Eden 6 Aug. 1943, FO371/37610.
11. FO to Minister of State Cairo, 31 July and FO to Pearson 1 Aug. 1943, FO371/37610.
12. Maclean to Sargent, 30 Aug. 1943, FO371/37611.
13. Sargent to Eden, 1 Sep. and Eden minute, 4 Sep. 1943, FO371/37611.
14. Mountbatten to Gubbins, 1 Oct. 1943, SC3/408/G, Mountbatten Papers, University of Southampton.
15. 'Communications with Gen. Mihailović', 15 June 1943, HS5/924.
16. CD to Sargent, 6 Sep. 1943, FO371/37590.
17. 'Mihailović', minutes by Eden, Howard, and Sargent, 9 Sep. 1943, FO371/37590.
18. Lees, *Rape of Serbia*, pp. 160–2, and Sehmer War Diary, WO202,162.
19. MEDC to COS, 21 July 1943, FO371/37321.
20. Deakin to Cairo, 14 Aug. 1943, FO371/32611.

21. Cairo to Fungus and other missions, 8 Sep. 1943, WO202/438.
22. Deakin, *Embattled Mountain*, pp. 114–16.
23. Armstrong to Cairo, 14 Oct. 1943, FO371/37615.
24. Armstrong to Cairo, 17 Oct. 1943, FO371/37613.
25. Albert Seitz, *Mihailović, Hoax or Hero?*, Leigh House, Columbus, OH 1953, p. 117.
26. Dedijer, *With Tito*, pp. 365–6.
27. Armstrong to Cairo, 3 and 4 Oct. FO371/37615.
28. Rootham Diary, 8 Dec. 1943.
29. Bari to Resident Minister, Caserta, 11 Jan. 1945, FO371/48805, and 'Seaborne Supplies to the Partisans', Nov. 1943, WO201/1581.
30. Sehmer War Diary, WO202/162.
31. Roughshod Report, Capt. Purvis, 1 June 1944, WO202/162.
32. Elizabeth Barker, 'Yugoslav-Bulgarian Relations through British Eyes, 1940–45', IWM Anglo-Yugoslav Colloquium, Dec. 1982.
33. Minister of State Cairo to FO, 8 Oct. 1943, FO371/37603.
34. Armstrong to Cairo, 12 and 14 Oct. 1943, FO371/37615.
35. Mansfield Report, reproduced in David Martin *The Web of Disinformation*, Harcourt Brace Jovanovich, New York 1990, pp. 378–411.
36. Rootham Diary, 22–24 April 1944.
37. Maclean to Cairo, 30 Oct and Stevenson to FO, 5 Nov. 1943, FO371/37616.
38. Stevenson to FO, 9 Oct. 1943, FO371/37616.
39. Rapier telegrams, MO4 to Baker Street, 26 Oct. 1943, HS5/960.
40. Cairo to Armstrong, 21 Nov. 1943, FO371/37616.
41. Maclean, 'The Partisan Movement in Yugoslavia', 6 Nov. 1943, FO371/37615.
42. 'The Partisan Movement in Yugoslavia', 6 Nov. 1943, FO371/37615.
43. Dugmore, 'Notes on Eastern and Central Serbia for period 29 Nov.' 43 to 20 Jun. '44', WO202/155.
44. Conversation with Vane Ivanović, Sandhurst, 14 Nov. 1994.
45. CD to Sargent, 6 Sep. 1943, enclosing SOE telegrams to and, from Bailey, FO371/37617.
46. Mansfield Report, in Martin, *The Web*, pp. 326–62.
47. Armstrong Report, dated 23 Nov. 1943, FO371/37617.
48. British Embassy to Yugoslavia to FO, 27 Nov. 1943, FO371/37612.
49. Interview with Archie Jack.
50. Gilbert, *Road to Victory*, pp. 556–79 covers all these conferences in detail.
51. V. Cavendish Bentink minute, 16 Nov. 1943, FO371/37615.
52. Document No. 132: Military conclusions of the Teheran Conference, 1 Dec. 1943, in Jacobson and Smith, *World War II: Policy and Strategy*, Santa Barbara 1979, p. 282.
53. Pavlowitch, *Tito*, pp. 43–4.
54. Auty and Clogg, *British Policy*, pp. 41–4.
55. Maclean, *Eastern Approaches*, pp. 310–5.
56. FO to Stevenson, 10 Nov. 1943, FO371/37616.
57. Stevenson to FO, 16 and 24 Nov. 1943, FO371/37616.
58. Stevenson to FO, 3 Dec. 1943, FO371/37617.

Chapter 10 Ditching Mihailović

1. Churchill to Stevenson, 10 Dec. 1943, WO201/1581.
2. Eden to Churchill, 'The Yugoslav Government' 13 Jun. 1943, FO371/37593.
3. E.M. Rose minute 2 Nov. 1943, on 'King Peter of Yugoslavia', FO371/37615.
4. Elizabeth Barker to E.M. Rose, 8 Nov. 1943, FO371/37615.
5. Stevenson to FO, 30 Nov. 1943, FO371/37617.
6. Howard minute, 22 Nov. 1943, on 'Yugoslavia—Brigadier Maclean's Report', FO371/37616.
7. Cope to Cairo, 11 and 17 Nov. 1943, FO371/37614.
8. Cope to Cairo (undated), full text of Mihailović's order, FO371/37616.
9. Stevenson to Purić, 22 Oct. 1943, FO371/37614.
10. Sehmer War Diary, 19 April–13 June 1943, WO202/162.
11. Bailey to Cairo, 26 Nov. 1943, FO371/37619.
12. British Mission to Mihailović, Oct. 1943, FO371/37616.
13. Cope to Cairo, 20 Nov. 1943, FO371/37616, and Stevenson to FO, 3 Dec. 1943, FO371/37617.
14. Stevenson to FO, 2 Dec. 1943, FO371/37617.
15. Stevenson to Eden, 7 Jan. 1944, FO371/44244.
16. Eden [in Cairo] to FO, 8 Nov. 1943, FO371/37591.
17. Stevenson to FO 3 Dec. 1943, FO371/37617 and MO4 to London 13 Dec, WO202/139.
18. Armstrong to Cairo, 26 Dec. WO202/136, Cairo to Armstrong 31 Dec. 143, FO371/44242.
19. Stevenson to FO, and Sargent minute 24 Dec. 1943, FO371/37619; FO to Stevenson 5 Jan. 1944, FO371/37620.
20. Cairo to Armstrong 4 Feb, WO202/145, Armstrong to Cairo, 7 Feb. 1944, WO202/143.
21. Interview with Archie Jack.
22. Rootham Diary.
23. Interview with Jasper Rootham.
24. 'Collaboration of Tito with King Peter', Sargent minute 22 Dec, and Sargent to Stevenson 24 Dec. 1943, FO371/37619.
25. Partisan HQ to Velebit, 14 Dec. 1943, FO371/37619.
26. Maclean to Sargent, 27 Dec. 1943, FO371/48810.
27. FO-Stevenson correspondence, 23–28 Dec. 1943, FO371/37620.
28. E.M. Rose minute, 24 Dec. 1943, FO371/37619.
29. Balfour (Moscow) to Cadogan, 31 Dec. 1943, FO371/37619.
30. SOE Diary, Oct.–Dec. 1943, p. 1024, HS7/271.
31. L.H. Manderstam with R. Heron, *From the Red Army to SOE*, William Kimber, London 1985, p. 147.
32. Churchill to Eden, 29, 30 Dec. 1943 and 2 Jan. 1944, FO371/44243.
33. Eden to Churchill, 19 Jan. 1944, FO371/44245.
34. 'The position in Yugoslavia', 10 Jan. 1944, FO371/44244.
35. Stevenson to FO, 14 Feb. 1944, WO201/1583.
36. Stevenson to FO, 23 and 24 Feb. 1944, WO201/1583.

37. SOE Diary, Jan.–Mar. 1944, p. 1148.
38. Washington to FO 25 Feb. and Stevenson to FO 1 Mar. 1944, WO201/1583.
39. Roberts, *Tito, Mihailović and the Allies*, pp. 148–256.
40. MacDowell Report, 23 Nov. 1944, reproduced in Martin, *Web of Disinformation*, pp. 378–41.
41. Churchill to Maclean, 25 Feb. 1944, WO201/1583.
42. Broad to Deakin, 25 Feb., and Stevensov-FO correspondence 1 and 7 Mar. 1944, WO201/1583.
43. Pavlowitch, *Tito*, p. 44.
44. Rootham Diary.
45. 'Situation in Yugoslavia', 12 Mar. 1944, WO201/1583.
46. Correspondence with Gervase Cowell, 14 Nov. 1988.
47. SOE Diary, 'Bailey at Downing Street', pp. 1145–7, HS7/272.
48. Bailey, draft telegram to Cairo, undated, and Howard minute, 29 March 1944, FO371/44252.
49. 'Appreciation regarding the military situation in Serbia', 19 Nov. 1943, WO201/1581.
50. Correspondence with Gervase Cowell, 14 Nov. 1988.
51. Keble, 'Balkan Politico/Military Situation', 28 Sep. 1943, WO201/1581.
52. Letter from Lukačević, Ostojić, Bačević, Novaković and Krivosić to Maclean, undated (14 Aug. 1944), FO371/44262.
53. Maclean to COS, 24 Aug. 1944, FO371/44262.
54. Stevenson to FO, 3 March 1944, WO201/1583.
55. Interview with Pamela Bisdee.
56. Interview with Archie Jack.
57. Rootham Diary, 6 April and 7 May 1944.
58. Peter Kemp, *No Colours or Crest*, Cassell, London 1947, pp. 240–2, and Wade interview, Pavlowitch Papers.
59. Interview with Archie Jack.
60. Stevenson-FO correspondence, 11 and 16 March 1944, WO201/1583.
61. Greenwood, IWM tape.
62. Interview with Jasper Rootham.
63. Interview with Sir William Deakin.
64. Interview with Archie Jack.
65. Interview with Mike Lees.
66. Bailey to MO4, 26 Nov. 1943, FO371/37619.
67. Dmitrije Djordjević, *Scars and Memories*, p. 47.
68. Dalton to Churchill, 11 Dec. 1941, PREM 3/510; Stevenson to Sargent, 26 Feb. 1944, FO371/44250.
69. Rendel to Dixon, 3 June 1943, FO371/37620.
70. Wilkinson, *Foreign Fields*, p. 145.
71. Deakin, *Embattled Mountain*, p. 239.
72. 'The Chetniks, a Survey', Sep. 1944, WO204/8109.
73. FO minute undated, Jan. 1944, FO371/59408.
74. Mansfield Report, 1 March 1944.
75. 'Most Secret Sources', Oct. 1944, WO201/1581.

Chapter 11   Backing the Partisans

1. Wilkinson, *Foreign Fields*, p. 187.
2. Vladimir Velebit, "The First Military Mission of the NLA to the British High Command", Anglo-Yugoslav Colloquium, IWM, Dec. 1982.
3. E.B. Haslam, "British Aid & Supplies to the NLA", IWM, Dec. 1982.
4. Michael McConville, *A Small War in the Balkans*, Macmillan, London 1986, pp. 106–14.
5. Vane Ivanović correspondence, Pavlowitch Papers.
6. Interview with Brian Parker, Poole.
7. Interview with Nigel Watson.
8. SOE History, 'The Russian Air Base in Italy', HS7/203.
9. Harold Macmillan, *War Diaries: The Mediterranean, 1943–1945*, Macmillan, London 1984, pp. 491–2.
10. Djilas, *Wartime*, pp. 348 and 399.
11. Information from Vane Ivanović, 14 Nov. 1984.
12. Vojmir Kljaković, 'Tito's Talks in Italy and Moscow, Aug. & Sep. 1944', Angl–Yugoslav Colloquium, IWM, Dec. 1982.
13. Broad to Algiers, 11 May 1944, FO371/44255.
14. Franklin Lindsay, *Beacons in the Night: With OSS and Tito's Partisans in Wartime Yugoslavia*, Stanford University Press, 1993, p. 25.
15. Farish Report and McDowell Report, both reproduced in Martin, *Web of Disinformation*, pp. 371–411.
16. Churchill to Eden, 19 Mar. 1944, FO371/44250.
17. Eden to Churchill, 21 Mar. 1944, FO371/44250.
18. Churchill to Broad, 12 Apr. 1944, FO371/44305.
19. Stevenson to FO, 3 Mar. 1944, WO201/1583.
20. Gilbert, *Road to Victory*, p. 779. Hilary King, 'The British Mission at Drvar', and Ralph Bennett, 'Ultra and Drvar', Anglo-Yugoslav Colloquium, IWM, Dec. 1982.
21. McConville, *A Small War*, p. 187.
22. FO minute, 12 Jun. 1944, FO371/44290.
23. Eden 7 Jun., note on Stevenson to Eden, 6 June 1944, FO371/44291.
24. Macmillan, *War Diaries*, p. 469.
25. Eden Memo, 'Yugoslav Affairs', 5 Apr. 1944, CAB 66/52.
26. Gilbert, *Road to Victory*, p. 893, and Churchill to Eden, 15 Aug. 1944, FO371/44315.
27. FO to Stevenson, 21 Jun. 1944, FO371/44312.
28. Resident Minister Bari to Resident Minister Algiers, 2 July 1944, Eden's handwritten comments, FO371/44259.
29. FO to Bari for Maclean, 5 July 1944, FO371/44259.
30. Kljaković, "Tito's Talks in Italy and Moscow".
31. Macmillan, *War Diaries*, p. 485.
32. 'Summary of Lt-Col. Hudson's Report and Recommendations', 21 April 1944, circulated by Eden 1 May, CAB 66/49, and information from Flessati.
33. SOE History, Bailey's handwritten comments on Webb's reports, HS7/203.

34. Gilbert, *Road to Victory*, p. 890.
35. Eden to Churchill, 15 Aug. 1944, FO371/44315.
36. Churchill to Eden, 31 Aug. 1944, FO371/44263.
37. Eden minute, 10 Aug. 1944, FO371/43589.
38. Eden to Churchill, 15 Aug. 1944, FO371/44263.
39. Kljaković, "Tito's Talks in Italy and Moscow".
40. 'Speech in Serbo-Croat by HM King Peter of Yugoslavia, broadcast on 12 December at 20.00 by the BBC', FO371/44306.
41. Stevenson to Sargent, 14 Sep. 1944, FO371/44317.
42. I am grateful to Nicholas Brashaw for pointing out this message; it is to be found in HW/17/51:ISCOT 1048.
43. Pavlowitch, *Tito*, p. 47.
44. Churchill to Eden, 19 Dec. 1944, FO371/48805.
45. Maclean to FO, 14 Jan. 1945, FO371/48808.
46. Maclean, *Eastern Approaches*, p. 407.
47. Arthur S. Gould Lee, *Special Duties*, Sampson Low Marston, London 1947, pp. 293–4.
48. Interview with Nigel Watson and Arthur Marlow.
49. Wilkinson, *Foreign Fields*, p. 148.
50. Clowder Mission Reports, HS6/17.
51. Wilkinson, *Foreign Fields*, p. 192–3.
52. T.M. Barker, *Social Revolutionaries and Secret Agents*, East European Monographs, Columbia University Press, 1990, p. 49.
53. Villa Resta, No. 5 of 10 Dec. 1944, FO371/48808.
54. Stevenson to Macmillan, 27 Apr., and Sargent to Churchill 29 Apr. 1945, FO371/48812.
55. Nicolai Tolstoy, *The Minister and the Massacres*, Century Hutchinson, London 1986, p. 5.
56. Unsigned account of conversation with Milinković, Nov. 13 1944, FO371/48810.
57. Interview with M. Kolarević, who attended the meeting.
58. Macmillan, *War Diaries*, pp. 746–57.
59. Barker, *Social Revolutionaries*, p. 61.
60. Wilkinson, *Foreign Fields*, p. 214.
61. Robert Lockhead and Charles Villiers testifying in the Aldington-Tolstoy case, reported respectively on 24 Oct. and 2 Nov. 1989, in *The Independent*.
62. Darko Bekić, interview in *Danas*, Zagreb, 18 Aug. 1990.

Conclusion

1. C.M. Woodhouse, *The Apple of Discord*, Hutchinson, London 1948.

SOURCES CONSULTED

UNPUBLISHED DOCUMENTS

Documents held at the Public Records Office, Kew

Special Operations Executive papers

HS5/868–969: SOE Activities in Yugoslavia.
HS6/13–17: The Clowder Mission.
HS7/266–273: War Diary—Balkans and the Middle East.
HS7/203: SOE History.

Foreign Office papers

FO 371: General Correspondence, Southern European Department.
FO 536: Embassy and Consular Archives Yugoslavia Correspondence.
FO 898: Political Warfare Executive.

War Cabinet papers

CAB 65: War Cabinet Minutes.
CAB 66: War Cabinet Memorandum WP & CP Series.
CAB 67: War Cabinet Memorandum WP(G) Series.
CAB 80: War Cabinet, Chiefs of Staff Committee, Memorandum.

Prime Minister's papers

PREM 3: Operational Papers, Files of the Prime Minister's office kept at the War Cabinet offices, dealing with defence and operational subjects.

War Office papers

WO 105: War Diaries, War Office Directorates.
WO 201: Military Headquarters Paper, Middle East Forces.
WO 202: Military Headquarters Paper, Military Missions.
WO 208: Directorate of Military Intelligence.

Documents held at the Foreign and Commonwealth Office, London

Correspondence with SOE Adviser concerning SOE Archives.

Collected papers

Mountbatten Papers: University of Southampton.
Pavlowitch Papers: private collection.
Jasper Rootham, War Diary and documents: Tonbridge School Library.
George Taylor Papers: King's College London.

INTERVIEWS

Pamela Bisdee: liaison officer with the Yugoslav air force, Cairo 1942–3, then SIS Bari 1943–4. West Sussex, September 1986.

Sir William Deakin: first official SOE mission to Tito, head of Yugoslav desk in Cairo/Bari, then BAF Italy. Royal Overseas League, London, 23 September 1988.

Jean Howard: worked at Bletchley Park, writing reports on the situation in occupied Yugoslavia based on intercepted information from Enigma decrypts. London, 14 July 1988.

Archie Jack: liaison officer with Mihailović forces in Serbia, September 1943 to May 1944. Haute-Savoie, June 1988.

Milomir Kolarević: officer in Yugoslav army, on Mihailović's staff throughout the war. London, 21 June 1994.

Mike Lees: liaison officer with Mihailović forces in Serbia, June 1943 to May 1944. Milton Abbas, Dorset, spring 1987.

Tom Mapplebeck: assistant air attaché in Belgrade 1941, associate of coup-makers. London, 22 September 1988.

Arthur Marlow: W/T operator with ISLD missions to Partisans in Slovenia 1944. Eastbourne, 14 July 1992.

Brian Parker: seconded to SOE from the Commandos, worked with the Partisans on the Adriatic islands and Montenegrin coast, later Greece and Corfu 1943–4. Poole, 21 October 1986.

Jasper Rootham: liaison officer with Mihailović forces in eastern Serbia. Wimborne, Dorset, 2 June 1988.

Ishan Toptani: Albanian guerrilla leader, close to SOE agents there, including Amery. New Forest, 16 January 1988.

Nigel Watson: ISLD, with Partisan forces in Slovenia 1944. Eastbourne, 14 July 1992.

CORRESPONDENCE

Mrs Jean Howard.

Archie Jack.

S. Johnson, SOE W/T operator with 'Brasenose' mission to Macedonian partisans.

Mike Lees.

Nicola Pasić: a member of a group of student Democrats at Mihailović's HQ.

TAPE RECORDINGS

Imperial War Museum, Department of Sound Archives.

Basil Davidson: 10505/3.

Eric Greenwood: 11374/4.

Archie Jack: 10640/4.

Mike Lees: 11085/8.

James Patch: 9961/5.

PUBLISHED DOCUMENTS

Clissold, Stephen, ed., *Yugoslavia and the Soviet Union, 1939–1973*, Royal Institute of International Affairs/Oxford University Press 1975.

Jacobson, H.A., and A.L. Smith, *World War II: Policy and Strategy, Selected Documents*, Santa Barbara & Oxford, 1979.

SECONDARY SOURCES

Aarons, M., and J. Loftus, *Ratlines: How the Vatican's Nazi Network betrayed Western Intelligence to the Soviets*, William Heinemann, London 1991.

Amery, Julian, *Approach March: A Venture in Autobiography*, Hutchinson, London 1973.

Andrew, Christopher, *Secret Service: The Making of the Intelligence Community*, William Heinemann, London 1985.

Auty, Phyllis, and Richard Clogg, eds, *British Policy towards Wartime Resistance in Yugoslavia and Greece*, Macmillan, London 1975.

Barker, Elizabeth, *British Policy in South-Eastern Europe in World War II*, Macmillan, London 1976.

Barker, T.M., *Social Revolutionaries and Secret Agents: The Carinthian Slovene Partisans and Britain's Special Operations Executive*, Columbia University Press, New York 1990.

Beavor, J.G., *SOE: Recollections and Reflections*, The Bodley Head, London 1981.

Beloff, Nora, *Tito's Flawed Legacy*, Victor Gollancz, London 1985.

Bennett, Ralph, *ULTRA and Mediterranean Strategy, 1941–1945*, Hamish Hamilton, London 1989.

Bethell, Nicholas, *The Great Betrayal*, Hodder & Stoughton, London 1984.

Butler, Ewan, *Amateur Agent*, Harrap, London 1963.

Calvocoressi, Peter, *Top Secret ULTRA*, Cassell, London 1980.

The Memoirs of Lord Chandos, The Bodley Head, London 1962.

Churchill, Winston S., *The Second World War*, 6 vols, Cassell, London 1948–54.

Ciano, Galeazzo *Ciano's Diary, 1939–1943*, Heinemann, London 1947.

Clissold, Stephen, *Whirlwind: an Account of Marshal Tito's Rise to Power*, Cresset Press, London 1959.

Clive, Nigel, *A Greek Experience, 1943–1948*, Michael Russell, Salisbury 1985.

Cooper, Artemis, *Cairo in the War, 1939–1945*, Hamish Hamilton, London 1989.

Costello, John, *Mask of Treachery*, William Morrow, New York 1988.

Davidson, Basil, *Partisan Picture*, Bedford Books, London 1946.

———, *Special Operations Europe*, Victor Gollancz, London 1980.

Dedijer, Vladimir, *With Tito through the War: Partisan Diary, 1941–1945*, Hamilton, London 1951.

Deroc, Milan, *British Special Operations Explored: Yugoslavia in Turmoil, 1941–1945, and the British Response*, Columbia University Press, New York 1988.

Dilks, David, ed., *The Diaries of Sir Alexander Cadogan*, Cassell, London 1971.

Djilas, Aleksa, *The Contested Country: Yugoslav Unity and Communist Revolution 1919–1953*, Harvard University Press, Cambridge, MA 1991.

Djilas, Milovan, *Conversations with Stalin*, Penguin Books, London 1963.

———, *Wartime*, Secker & Warburg, London 1977.

Djordjević, Dmitrije, *Scars and Memories*, Columbia University Press, New York 1997.

Dodds-Parker, D., *Setting Europe Ablaze: Some Accounts of Ungentlemanly Warfare*, Springwood Books, London 1983.

Douglas, Roy, *From War to Cold War, 1942–1948*, Macmillan, London 1981.

Feis, Herbert, *Churchill, Roosevelt and Stalin: The War They Fought and the Peace They Sought*, Princeton University Press, 1957.

Felmam, Richard I., *Mihailovic and I*, Neven Publishing, Milwaukee 1979.

Foot, M.R.D., *SOE 1940–1946*, BBC, London 1984.

Gilbert, Martin, *Road to Victory: Winston S. Churchill, 1941–1945*, Heinemann, London 1979.

Glen, Alexander, *Footholds against a Whirlwind*, Hutchinson, London 1975.

Hamilton-Hill, Donald, *SOE Assignment*, William Kimber, London 1973.

Harris-Smith, R., *OSS: The Secret History of America's First CIA*, University of California Press, Berkeley, 1972.

Hertzstein, R.E., *Waldheim: The Missing Years*, Grafton Books, London, 1988.

Hinsley, F.H., *et al., British Intelligence in the Second world War*, vol. III, HMSO, London 1984, 1988.

Hoptner, J.B., *Yugoslavia in Crisis 1934–1941*, Columbia University Press, New York 1962.

Howarth, P., *Undercover: The Men and Women of SOE*, Routledge & Kegan Paul, London 1980.

Howard, M, *The Mediterranean Strategy in the Second World War*, Weidenfeld & Nicolson, London 1968.

Ivanović, Vane, *LX: Memoirs of a Yugoslav*, Weidenfeld & Nicolson, London 1977.

Jebb, Gladwyn, *The Memoirs of Lord Gladwyn*, Weidenfeld & Nicolson, London 1972.

Jones, William, *Twelve Months with Tito's Partisans*, Bedford Books, London 1946.

Jukić, Ilija, *The Fall of Yugoslavia*, Harcourt Brace Jovanovich, New York 1974.

Karchmar, L., *Draza Mihailovic and the Rise of the Chetnik Movement, 1941–43*, Garland, New York 1987.

Kardelj, Eduard, *Reminiscences: The Struggle for Recognition and Independence: The New Yugoslavia, 1944–1957*, Blond & Briggs, London 1982.

Kemp, Peter, *No Colours or Crest*, Cassell, London 1958.

Lawrence, Christie, *Irregular Adventure*, Faber & Faber, London 1957.

Lee, Arthur S. Gould, *Special Duties*, Sampson, Low, Marston & Co, London 1947.

Lees, Michael, *Special Operation Executed*, William Kimber, London 1986.

———, *The Rape of Serbia: The British Role in Tito's Grab for Power*, Harcourt Brace Jovanovich, New York 1990.

Lewis, Laurence, *Echoes of Resistance: British Involvement with the Italian Partisans*, D.J. Costello, Tunbridge Wells 1985.

Lindsay, Franklin, *Beacons in the Night: With OSS and Tito's Partisans in Wartime Yugoslavia*, Stanford University Press, 1993.

McConville., Michael, *A Small War in the Balkans: British Involvement in Wartime Yugoslavia, 1941–45*, Macmillan, London 1986.

MacLaren, Roy, *Canadians Behind Enemy Lines*, University of Brtish Columbia Press, Vancouver, 1981.

Maclean, Fitzroy, *Eastern Approaches*, Cape, London 1946.

————, *Disputed Barricade*, Cape, London 1957.

Macmillan, Harold, *War Diaries: The Mediterranean 1943–1945*, Macmillan, London 1984.

Manderstam, L.H., with Roy Heron, *From the Red Army to SOE*, Harcourt Brace Jovanovich, New York 1985.

Martin, David, *The Web of Disinformation: Churchill's Yugoslav Blunder*, Harcourt Brace Jovanovich, New York 1990.

Maskeleyne, Jasper, *Magic, Top Secret*, Stanley Paul, London 1952.

Novak, B.C., *Trieste 1941–1945: The Ethnic, Political and Ideological struggle*, University of Chicago Press, 1970.

Pavlowitch, Stevan K., *Unconventional Perceptions of Yugoslavia 1940–1945*, Columbia University Press, New York 1985.

————, *The Improbable Survivor: Yugoslavia and its Problems 1918–1988*, Hurst, London 1988.

————, *Tito, Yugoslavia's Great Dictator: A Reassessment*, Hurst, London 1992.

————, *A History of the Balkans*, Longman, Harlow 1999.

————, *Serbia: the History behind the Name*, Hurst, London 2002.

Philby, Kim, *My Silent War*, MacGibbon & Kee, London 1968.

Pimlott, Ben, *Hugh Dalton*, Cape, London 1985.

————, ed., *The Second World War Diary of Hugh Dalton, 1940–45*, Cape, London 1986.

Popović, Koča, *Beleske uz Ratovanje* (Notes During Warfare), BIGZ, Belgrade 1988.

Porter, Ivor, *Operation Autonomous*, Chatto & Windus, London 1989.

Rayner, Louisa, *Women in a Village: an Englishwoman's experiences and impressions of life in Yugoslavia under German occupation*, Heinemann, London 1957.

Ranfurly, Countess of, *To War with Whitaker*, Heinemann, London 1994.

Rendel, Sir George, *The Sword and the Olive*, John Murray, London 1957.

Richardson, General Sir Charles, *Flashback: A Soldier's Story*, William Kimber, London 1985.

Ridley, Jasper, *Tito*, Constable, London 1994.

Roberts, Walter M, *Tito, Mihailović and the Allies, 1941–1945*, Rutgers University Press, New Bruuswick, NJ, 1973.

Rogers, Lindsay, *Guerrilla Surgeon*, Collins, London 1957.

Rootham, Jasper, *Miss Fire: the Chronicle of a British Mission to Mihailović*, Chatto & Windus, London 1946.

Seitz, A.B., *Mihailović—Hoax or Hero?*, Leigh House, Columbus, OH 1953.

Shaver-Clemens, Diane, *Yalta*, Oxford University Press, 1970.

Smiley, David, *Albanian Assignement*, Chatto & Windus, London 1984.

St George Saunders, Hilary, *The Green Beret*, Michael Joseph, London 1949.

St John, Robert, *From the Land of Silent People*, Harrap, London 1942.

Stafford, David, *Britain and European Resistance 1940–1945*, Macmillan, London 1980.

———, *Camp X: SOE and the American Connection*, Viking, London 1987.

Stenton, Michael, *Radio London and Resistance in Occupied Europe*, Oxford University Press, 200.

Swain, Geoffrey, 'Tito and the Twilight of the Comintern' in T. Rees and A. Thorpe, eds, *International Communism and the Communist International*, Manchester University Press, 1998.

Sweet-Escott, Bickham, *Baker Street Irregular*, Methuen, London 1965.

Tolstoy, Nicolai, *The Minister and the Massacres*, Century Hutchinson, London 1986.

Trew, Simon, *Britain, Mihailović and the Chetniks, 1941–42*, Macmillan, London 1998.

Waugh, Evelyn, *The Diaries of Evelyn Waugh*, Weidenfeld & Nicolson, London 1976.

Wheeler, Mark C., *Britain and the War for Yugoslavia 1940–43*, Colombia University Press, New York 1980.

———, 'The British, King Peter and the path to Tito's cave' in *Diplomacy and Intelligence during the Second World War: Essays in honour of F.H. Hinsley*, Cambridge University Press 1985.

———, 'Pariahs to Partisans to power: the Communist Party of Yugoslavia' in *Resistance and Revolution in Mediterranean Europe*, ed. Tony Judt, Routledge, London and New York 1989.

Wilkinson, Peter & Bright Astley, Joan, *Gubbins and SOE*, Leo Cooper, London 1993.

Wilkinson, Peter, *Foreign Fields: the story of an SOE Operative*, I.B. Tauris, London 1997.

Woodhouse, C.M., *Apple of Discord*, Hutchinson, London 1948.

Woodward, Sir Llewellyn, *British Foreign Policy in the Second World War*, HMSO London 1970–6.

Wright, Peter, *Spycatcher*, Heinemann, Richmond (Aus.) 1987.

ARTICLES AND REVIEW ARTICLES

Barker, Elizabeth, 'Tito and the British', review of *Slboda ili smrt* by Radoje and Zivan Knežević; *Vlada na Bespucu* by Veselin Djuretić; *Tito-Churchill strogo tajno* by Dušan Biber; *Secanja* by Vladimir Velebit; *Vlada Ivana Subasica* by Dragovan Sepić in the *Times Literary Supplement*, 10 August 1984.

Bosnitch, Sava, review of *Martovski Pregovori 1943* by Mišo Leković, in *South Slav Journal* vol. 11/no. 2–3 (40–41), summer/autumn 1988.

Kay, Anne, 'British Newspaper Reporting on the Yugoslav Resistance, 1941–1945', *Storia della Relazioni Internationali*, anno VI, 190/2.

Leković, Mišo, 'Boravak Britanske Vojne Misije na Oslobdjenoj Tritoriji Crne Gora I Jouistocne Bosne' (The Visit of the British Military Mission to the Liberated Territory of Montenegro and S. Bosnia), *Istorijski Zapisi*, XXVIII/1–2, 1971.

Leković, Mišo, 'Cinjenice o misiji majora Terenza Atertona' (The facts of the mission of Major Terence Atherton), serialized in *Politica*, May–June 1986.

Milivojević, M., 'The Yugoslav People's Army: the Political Dimension', *Bradford Studies on Yugoslavia*, 13, University of Bradford 1988.

Muller, Klaus-Jürgen, 'A German Perspective on Allied Deception Operations in the Second World War' in a special issue of *Intelligence and National Security*, 2/3 1987.

Pavlowitch, Stevan K., 'London-Moscow through the fog of Yugoslavia's wartime drama: Djuretić's controversial history', *Storia delle Relazioni Internazionali*, III/2 1987.

Simić-Stevens, Alexander, 'Pathfinder Fungus', serialized in *Journal of the British-Yugoslav Society* summer/winter 1984 and spring 1985.

Stafford, David, 'SOE and British involvement in the Belgrade coup d'état of March 1941', *Slavic Review*, XXXVI/3, 1997.

UNPUBLISHED THESES AND PAPERS

Deroc, Milan, 'The Serbian Uprisings of 1941 and the British Response', PhD, University of New England, 1985.

London, Louise, 'Brigadier Maclean's screening mission to Austria', paper presented at Queen Mary College, London, December 1988.

Stafford, David, 'SOE and British Strategy in World War Two', paper presented to the Fourth USWAC International Conference on Intelligence and Strategy, 9–11 May 1989.

Papers Presented to the British National Committee for the History of the Second World War, Anglo-Yugoslav Colloquium, 13–15 December 1982 at the Imperial War Museum, London:

Barker, Elizabeth, 'Yugoslav-Bulgarian relations through British eyes'.

Deakin, Sir William, 'The British and the Italian Surrender'.

Haslam, E.B., 'British Aid and Supplies to the National Army of Liberation, January 1944 to March 1945'.

Kljaković, Vojmir, 'Tito's Talks in Italy and Moscow'.

Velebit, Vladimir, 'The First Military Mission of the National Liberation Army to the British High Command'.

TRANSCRIPTS OF BROADCAST PROGRAMMES

'The Sword and the Shield', BBC, 4 September 1984
'Tito', interviews with Charles Davis, USAF; Richard Felman, USAF; Milton Friend, USAF; Nick Lalich, OSS; David Osborne, USAF; Eli Popovitch, OSS; Zvonimir Vucković, Mihailović forces; Merrill Walker, USAF. BBC Timewatch, 26 February and 4 March 1992.

INDEX

A Force, 233
Airey, Colonel Terence, 52
Albania: 21–2, 25, 30, 37, 40
 as part of SOE Balkan network, 23,
  92
 resistance forces in, 111
Aldington-Tolstoy libel case, 241
Alexander, King of Yugoslavia, 18–19
Alexander, General H.R.L.G., 135,
  147, 236
Alexandria, 199
Allied Advisory Council for Italy, 220
Allied bombing of Yugoslavia, 221,
  230–1
Americans, see United States of
  America
Amery, Julian, 24–5, 49, 53–4, 56–7,
  59
Amery, L.S. ('Leo'), 24–5, 53
Anvil, 236
Anzio, 219
Applebee, Leonard, 11
Armstrong, Brigadier Charles: 167
 and American liaison officers, 179
 Armstrong-Bailey report, 185
 and communications, 194, 195–6,
  249
 head of mission to Mihailović HQ,
  171, 176, 179–80, 211, 212
 and Mihailović: 180–1
  possibility of replacing, 205
  order to withdraw, 204–5
 and SOE Cairo, 188, 197–8, 249
 and 'test operations', 197–8
 and Yugoslav Home Army, 179–80
Atherton, Major Terence, 65–9
Attlee, Clement, 7, 103

Auchinleck, General Sir Claude, 52
Austria: 19
 as part of SOE and SIS network, 23,
  100
 a FO attitude to, 123
 German surrender in, 239, 241
 Partisan links with, 117, 235
 resistance, 235–6
 Slovene minority in, 234
 SOE Clowder mission to, 165, 234–
  6, 241
 Tito's ambitions in, 233–4
Austrian SOE agents, 235
Anti-Fascist Council for the National
  Liberation of Yugoslavia (AVNOJ),
  99, 170, 187, 199, 205, 210, 223,
  224, 226, 239

Ba, Congress of, 205, 226, 231
Bačević, 159–60, 203, 212
Bader, General, 194
Badoglio, Marshal Pietro, 173
Bailey, S.W. (Bill): 3, 23, 25–6, 47, 49,
  53, 54–5, 68, 80, 129
 advice on policy in Yugoslavia,
  101–2, 104, 107–8, 114, 117,
  119–121, 124, 184–5, 205–6, 209,
  210
 and communications, 185, 194
 and Churchill, 228
 as 'FO emissary', 91, 145
 and FO, 207
 mission to Mihailović's HQ: 91–3,
  96, 139, 141, 147, 152, 215
 supports Hudson's assessment, 99
 and loss of SOE codes, 156–7